*Tendencies
and Tensions
of the
Information Age*

Jorge Reina Schement and Terry Curtis

Tendencies and Tensions of the Information Age

The
Production and Distribution
of Information
in the United States

Transaction Publishers
New Brunswick (U.S.A.) and London (U.K.)

Library of Congress Catalog Number: 94-4440
ISBN: 1-56000-166-6 (cloth)
Printed in the United States of America

Library of Congress Cataloging-in-Publication Data

Schement, Jorge Reina.
    Tendencies and tensions of the information age :   the production and distribution of information in the United States / Jorge Reina Schement and Terry Curtis.
      p. cm.
    Includes bibliographical references and index.
    ISBN 1-56000-166-6 (cloth)
    1. Computers and civilization.   2. Information society—United States. 3. Computers—Social aspects—United States.   I. Curtis, Terry.   II. Title.
QA76.9.C66S32   1994
338.4'7001'0973—dc20   94-4440
                                                                                CIP

Contents

Preface

The project resulting in this book was already underway for Schement when the authors met in the fall of 1983 at the Annenberg School for Communications at the University of Southern California, where Schement was on the faculty and Curtis was taking a sabbatical leave. Both of us were new to the concept of the information society and both of us were intrigued by its high visibility and indistinct content as an academic concern. Our long discussions on the social manifestations of the production and consumption of information soon became planning sessions. Early exchanges with Herb Dordick led to the main question. "Does the information society take us beyond industrial society, or is it an extension of industrial society?" Leah Lievrouw, then a graduate student, became a valued collaborator on the idea of information work. Jay Blumler, visiting from the University of Leeds, suggested that the ideology of industrialization has a connection to the information society. He hypothesized how intuition might have given way to reason as the basis for a new attitude toward information, and how this change might underlay the production and distribution of information in the marketplace. Elihu Katz filled important gaps in our thinking regarding media environments and the nature of leisure. Daniél Dayán proposed that the idea of information demonstrates both macro and micro manifestations. At various times, Aimee Dorr, Heather Hudson, Félix F. Gutiérrez, and Everett Rogers, were drawn into running dialogues that have continued to the present. By 1987, our own dialogues had progressed to the point that our interpretations were no longer distinct, so we merged our papers into a book project.

That fall, the focus of the book changed radically upon Schement's joining the faculty of the School of Communication, Information and Library Studies (SCILS) at Rutgers University. At SCILS, conversations with Brent Ruben, David Carr, Nicholas Belkin, Carl Botan, Richard Hixson, Ron Rice, Montague Kern, Michelle Dillon, Hartmut Mokros, and Leah Lievrouw, having joined the faculty at Rutgers upon graduation, forced reconsideration of our ideas on the social uses of information. This led to the recognition of the social and cultural power of the "idea of information," and brought us into the debate on how to relate information, as a phenomenon, to communication, as a process.

Many students involved in communications studies also assisted in our research. They deserve special mention because they spent hours in library archives for scant compensation. Joan Parker, Cynthia J. Shelton, Dong Jeong,

Inhee Lee, Matthew Portella, Beth Willett, Amy Caldwell, Jeff Pierson, and Dan Stout helped us with their good humor and great ability.

In commencing this project, we chose to view our subject from a macro perspective. That is, by taking on the vast sweep of the information society, we accepted as necessary the analysis of large scale phenomena, such as the idea of information, interconnectedness, and the information work force. Furthermore, our choice of scope meant that the project would also be a work of synthesis, since our questions reached beyond any single study or group of studies. In fact, soon after we began, we discovered extensive research beyond our own fields of communication and information studies. We, therefore, formulated the tendencies and tensions by bringing together findings from across many disciplines. We report our own original research alongside the analysis of scholars ranging from classical studies and etymology to labor sociology and macroeconomics. Though we have relied on the work of many scholars, we alone are responsible for the tendencies and tensions, the conclusions, and the theory.

Finally, we both wish to thank our families for their contributions to this project and their tolerance of its demands. Anne understood and indulged Jorge as he spent hours staring out the window, supported him in innumerable ways, and was an ever-gracious hostess to a house guest whose visits were too often the occasion of her isolation while we worked. Elisa asked questions and demanded answers of simple clarity, while Daniel was born during the project and added flavor to our work. Christian, Elly, and Amy patiently surrendered their father's time and attention to "the book" and the computer in which it resided.

Introduction

To anyone old enough to remember manual typewriters and colorless tele-vision pictures, it should be apparent that a wave of changes have overtaken the experience of daily life in America. Cable television, satellite dishes, vid-eocassette players, compact discs, radar detectors, automatic teller machines, answering machines, copy machines, fax machines, multi use telephones, and personal computers populate the topography of nearly every American's fa-miliar terrain.

Beyond the domain of the technological, the majority of Americans work in occupations where they manipulate information as the main activity of their work. In their homes, they create electronic environments where they con-sume information as a major source of leisure. In the news, they routinely encounter stories attesting to the fact that the U. S. economy now exchanges information as its primary commodity. The narrators—journalists and social scientists—trumpet the startling arrival of an information society eclipsing the one engendered by the industrial revolution. Not surprisingly, the momen-tum of this interpretation has captured the popular imagination as the dawn of a new era. But the popular image contains distortions.

In this book, we take issue with the conventional view and present an analysis whose main theme is that the information society emerged gradually through-out the 20th century. We contend that the national orientation to the produc-tion and consumption of information which many Americans observe today stems directly from the organizing principles of industrialization, and the re-alities of capitalism, not from a revolution set loose by the invention of the computer or any other technology. At first glance the change appears to signal the final extinction of the era of coal and steel; however, the new social out-line is actually a synthesis of traditional and new—the dialectic between steel and silicon, factory work and office work, railroads and computer networks, whistle stop campaigns and sound bites.

If one is to penetrate the mask of the information society, one must first contend with the idea of information. From the time of the Enlightenment, Europeans and Americans began to think of information as though it were a thing, doing with it what they did with things—for example, passing laws to prevent information theft and constructing systems to deposit or retrieve in-formation. In the 20th century, Americans led the way toward articulating a vocabulary speaking of information as though it were a material thing. Their doing so signals the emergence of a cultural perspective whereby information

1

is thought of as the common essence of concepts as diverse as a name, an equation, or an essay.

The Idea of Information

In the 20th century, we take it for granted that libraries, clocks, spying, and plagiarism, all have to do with information. We think in terms of information as an influence on our behavior, and we weigh the advantages of specific information in our competition with others. In fact, information is of such value to us that we buy it, sell it, and enact laws to punish its theft. We are so secure in our attitude that we expect others to share the same assumptions. Furthermore, though information exists solely as the symbolic product of our minds, we easily translate it into the material world. So much so that we have reorganized our economy around an idea of information, an idea which guides many of our public interactions. But it was not always so.

In this book, we propose that the idea of information forms the conceptual foundation for the information society. By that we mean a perspective in which information is conceived of as thing-like. As a result, messages are thought to contain more or less "information." Marketplaces exist for the buying and selling of "information." Devices are developed for the storage and retrieval of information. Laws are passed to prevent theft of information. Devices exist for the purpose of moving information geographically. Moreover, and equally important, the thingness of information allows individuals to see diverse experiences, such as a name, a poem, a table of numbers, a novel and a picture, as possessing a common essential feature termed "information." As people endow "information" with the characteristics of a thing (or think of it as embodying material characteristics) they facilitate its manipulation in the world of things e.g., in the marketplace. This is not to say that the idea of information is the only way to think about the products of our brains, nor the most desirable. Nevertheless, the idea of information is understood as concrete by most Americans and Europeans. And, its observable presence serves as an identifying badge of the information society.

Interest in information, however, extends beyond its utility as a virtual material object. For example, in the sciences, information began to show up as a concept in the middle of the 20th century. In 1949, Claude Shannon sought to explain the transmission of a message from one point to another in his mathematical theory of communication, where the measure of information is the logarithmic function which expresses the choice of one message from the set of all possible messages. Shannon's theory set the basis for theories of signal transmission in engineering.[1] Norbert Wiener, another theorist of the 1940s, visualized information as part of the process of a system's adjustment to the outer world. He suggested that, in any system, information encounters change, and hypothesized that a system decays when it can no longer process information from the environment or communicate it within the system.[2] In the early 1950s, one of the founders of information science, Robert M. Hayes, saw a hierarchical connection between information and data, and suggested that information resulted from processed data.[3] Shannon, Wiener, Hayes, and others viewed information as a general concept applicable to all situations, though their definitions did not always harmonize.[4]

Since the 1940s, researchers have joined in the study of the nature of information and produced a literature that sprawls in its lack of consensus. Economists like John Hirshleifer and Donald Lamberton have defined information as consisting of those events which reduce uncertainty in making a decision, while another economist, Fritz Machlup, argued against limiting information to decision making. He proposed that information is both the telling of something and the something that is told. Note that Machlup's view of information does not distinguish it from communication.[5] Information scientists Nicholas Belkin and S. E. Robertson de-emphasized the reduction of uncertainty and proposed that information functions as, "...that which is capable of transforming structures."[6] Still others, like Brenda Dervin in communication studies, have objected to the treatment of information as though it were a phenomenon occurring independently in the natural world. Information, she asserts, is produced by humans and to a degree exists subjectively, as part of the individual's frame of reference.[7]

As more social scientists recognize the importance of information to their theories, definitions and descriptions have proliferated—the majority focusing on the culturally universal, or commodity, properties of information.[8] The resulting literatures cross the boundaries of communication, computer science, economics, information science, sociology, and psychology.[9] Consequently, certain interpretations dominate some social sciences. In economics, for example, information continues to be thought of as the reduction of uncertainty, so that no consensus has yet emerged. Among the "hard" sciences, unanimity is equally elusive. Cellular biologists describe DNA as a "library" containing information,[10] while a few physicists contend that the fundamental elements of the universe consist of binary bits of information.[11]

It appears that the idea of information—and communication—contains utility as a concept for a broad spectrum of researchers. But, though information fascinates many social, biological, and physical scientists, no interdisciplinary agreement on basic concepts seems likely, and no unified theory appears imminent. Furthermore, although, the academic focus reflects the larger society's consciousness of information, few of these theoretical descriptions formulate information as a thing per se.

Our concern in this book is with the ascendance of a concept which we term the idea of information, and with the powerful role played by the idea of information in the emergence of the information society. Therefore, we do not address the validity of the various definitions of information that currently circulate in many fields.[12] Moreover, we do not imply that humans conceive of information as a thing to the exclusion of other formulations. Humans obviously process information cognitively, whether or not thing-like characteristics are ascribed. We argue instead that the idea of information—the social attitude that considers information an abstract essence and treats it as a thing—currently operates as a key term for understanding social change, so much so that it lends itself to the characterization of the times as an information age or information society.

The Idea of Information in the 17th and 18th Centuries

From the time of the Renaissance and the Protestant Reformation, there began a movement which regarded information as a thing, so that by the peak of the Enlightenment new values, influenced by the emerging idea of information, reshaped intellectual life.[13] Europe of the 18th century represented a cosmopolitan society for the dominant classes and those attached to them. Its participants lived interconnected by books and letters, so that an educated person could aspire to participate in the whole of human knowledge. In this atmosphere, reading took on new meaning and books escaped the confines of the medieval *armarium*. Literacy led to a literary appetite—four-thousand subscribers signed up for the first edition of the *Encyclopédie*, while Voltaire's *Candide* passed through eight editions in 1759 alone.[14] By the eve of the 18th century, the medieval conception of the universe as an organic unity according to the great chain of being had given way to a new idea in which a mechanistic universe was imagined as a clock, itself an information device and symbol of rationalism.[15] The emphasis in the 17th and 18th centuries on the recording of thought and observation, on the collection of information in dictionaries and encyclopedias, and on the new libraries that followed printing, established the values that led to the idea of information.[16] For the first time in history, one finds numerous examples of information treated as a thing and of the proliferation of information processing behaviors similar to our own.

Dictionaries, encyclopedias, bureaucratic files, and printing may seem unremarkable to the 20th century, but to the world of the Enlightenment they represented radical departures from what had gone before. Each illustrates an application of the idea of information as it was becoming common in the 17th and 18th centuries.

Alphabetization in wordbooks, for example, reestablished the arbitrary sequencing of words. It appears that printers initiated the popularization of alphabetization when they exploited the advantage of the alphabet as a fixed series, in order to increase the speed of arranging type.[17] In turn, alphabetization heightened sensitivity to the arbitrary nature of words as symbols and drew attention to them as things. For the first time, and in the form that is recognized today, dictionaries presented words completely independently of each other and divorced from their organic relationship to the sentence. While the word "dictionary" appeared in English and in French during the 16th century as a name for wordbooks—not yet modern dictionaries—each word contained therein appeared alone, to be understood individually, and reflecting its new status as a thing.[18]

The Académie of France set off on its first true dictionary project in 1635, with the intent to regulate the French language, and finally brought it to a finish fifty-nine argumentative years later. Across the Channel, the English also sought to "fix" their language, but created no academy comparable to that of France. Instead, guided by the spirit of capitalism, a group of London booksellers approached Samuel Johnson with the idea of producing a national dictionary. Johnson replied with a *Plan for a Dictionary of the English Language*. His dictionary appeared in 1755, eight years after the proposal.[19] Moreover, like the French academicians, Johnson strove to freeze the language, in order to regulate it, as he explained.

> I have, ... attempted a dictionary of the English language, which, while it was employed in the cultivation of every species of literature, has itself been hitherto neglected, suffered to spread, under the direction of chance, into wild exuberance, resigned to the tyranny of time and fashion, and exposed to the corruptions of ignorance, and caprices of innovation.[20]

That English, like any other language, is a dynamic growing network of dialects, usages, and inventions, posed no obstruction to the forces of regulation. By attempting to create a fixed English, Johnson sought to wrest the language from its common folk roots. In fact, his goal harmonized with those of his patrons, who sensed demand for a dictionary reflecting the notion held by the upper and middle classes—but especially among the middle classes—that they spoke "proper English." For at a time when some Englishmen were forging identities as a new and coherent middle class, the dictionary allowed them to use language as a tool for distinguishing themselves from the lower classes, a utility which continues to the present, as Tom McArthur notes of all standard English dictionaries.

> What we are talking about, ... are artifacts of civilization designed in the seventeenth and eighteenth centuries through the slow consensus of the dominant classes for the purpose of inheriting Neo Latin.[21]

That the fixed sequence of the alphabet was taking hold, can be further deduced from the following entry in Johnson's dictionary.

> abeceda' rian. He that teaches or learns the alphabet, or first rudiments of literature.[22]

Indeed, alphabetization served more than one purpose, for Johnson and his milieu were evolving a view of words as things, with consequences for behavior in the material world. For example, during the second half of the 17th century, intellectuals accepted the notion that words could be stolen like any physical possession, and adapted the word "plagiary"(from the Latin for kidnapper or abductor) to describe this novel act of theft.[23] Consequently, in 1710, Britain passed the Statute of Anne of April 10, its first copyright act.[24] Therefore, by fully adopting this new paradigm, the dictionary provided the means for claiming ownership of the language, thus removing words from their social context and arraying them as though they represented objects to be studied in a perfect form, each unconnected from the next. The new middle class then sought to formalize the language they spoke, thereby establishing Standard English and *le bon français*—the versions accepted today—as proper. As a result, the cultural needs of the emerging class structure of the 18th century converged with the new idea that information could be treated as a thing.

The invention of printing constitutes the single most important turn on the road from oral culture to the idea of information. In the first hundred years after Gutenberg printed the 42-line Mazarin Bible, the book left the confines of the monastery and became a thing to be traded and individually possessed.[25] Whereas, manuscripts copied by scribes were necessarily scarce, printed documents became plentiful by comparison. Moreover, unlike the corruption of texts resulting from generations of copyists, printed documents were identical in their accuracy as well as in their mistakes. So, for the first time ever, readers could view identical images all across Europe. Thus, printing changed the rules governing the acquisition of knowledge and set in motion a true revolution in communication.[26]

When printing combined with mass production, books became simple commodities available to large numbers of individuals whose only previous contact had been to see them or to hear them read. With multiple copies available for comparison, readers no longer accepted interpretations by the authorities. The new polyglot bibles printed after 1522 exposed variations in text, causing readers to wonder as to which represented the true Word of God. Consequently, the reconciliation of linguistic uncertainties became a task for scholars who enthusiastically compared and judged for themselves, challenging the authority of the Church in the process. Furthermore, readers, who were no longer channeled by doctrine, sought books out of personal interest, so that, in the 17th century, the titles in a home library reflected personal choice and a new freedom. For the first time, literate men and women read as individuals, according to their own desires.[27]

Print led the way to a new organization of information, in which print shops acted as catalysts by standardizing: title pages; section breaks; running heads; punctuation marks; indexes; footnotes; page numbering; and, spelling.[28] But perhaps more importantly, standardization within the print shop reached out and altered the way in which every reader processed information. For one thing, the growing abundance of printed works led to a decrease in reliance on memory. For though the invention of writing created the potential for transcending human memory, the scarcity of hand-copied books meant that the transmission of knowledge still relied on memory right up to and beyond the invention of the printing press. However, with the diffusion of printed documents, mnemonics became unnecessary, and the fragile mental structure of rhymes and other memory aids gave way.[29] Information could now be retrieved from among one's books, which were stored on the shelf like any other material thing. Concurrently, new forms for presenting information appeared, such as the essay and the scientific paper. In the end analysis, printed works, such as Diderot's *Encyclopédie* and Johnson's dictionary, overwhelmed handwritten manuscripts by offering information in a portable, condensed, and versatile package. Perhaps unwieldy by present standards, printed books could be treated as things for the convenience of the user, rather than as icons to be approached with reverence. Thus, the shift from script to print increased the number of available information packages, which, in turn, opened the way for the exchange of many distinct information commodities in new marketplaces, and, ultimately, shaped a new attitude toward information.

Considering the information in a book to be distinct from the book itself is a behavior most modern individuals take for granted. Indeed, the same can be said for the idea that individual humans are the source of knowledge, or that a scientist must first rely on his or her own reason. These three information processing behaviors are so deeply embedded in the modern psyche as to be transparent. But to thoughtful individuals of the 17th and 18th centuries, these were radical ideas to be approached with caution. The behavior of reading, for example, evolved a new form in the course of the 18th century, as a result of the diffusion of printed books.[30] Members of the Republic of Letters[31] stayed in touch through a network of journals and publications which fostered the concepts of being up-to-date, in the know, and informed.[32] In fact, it is the modern tone of this attitude that one is isolated not by geography but by a lack of information, which places the 18th century philosophes closer to the information society than to the monastery.

When manuscripts were hand-copied, and before printed books were easily available, a climate of scarcity prevailed. Under such circumstances, books were read intensively. Readers consumed them repeatedly, meditating on them, and digesting them alone or in company.[33] Even as late as the beginning of the 18th century, readers seem to have approached books as a totality, emphasizing binding, paper, and typeface, as well as text. In turn, book sellers fretted over whether the reading public would find a particular paper quality worthy of the book's subject. Until the advent of mass production and distribution at the end of the 18th century, each leaf of a book was printed separately by artisan printers who set type by hand and then impressed the plate onto paper that was hand-produced sheet by sheet.[34] In fact, physical continuity existed with the world of manuscripts, for like the volumes locked in the *armarium*, each printed book possessed its own character, and the reader treated each copy as an individual.[35]

However, toward the end of the 18th century, a climate of abundance appeared. More titles and larger print runs meant greater circulation of printed works, so that individuals could read a wider range of subjects in more forms: from fiction to politics; from pamphlets to books. Literate individuals began to read extensively, finishing one publication while reaching for another.[36] Readers were moving away from reverence for a cherished tome and toward a utilitarian appraisal of the book as a package containing sought-after information. Moreover, with the new reading behavior, all books with the same content were recognized as containing information of the same value no matter the quality of the paper or binding. We recognize this attitude toward reading because it is our own. Recognition of the value of information independently of its package proved fundamental to the idea of information. Thus, by severing the message from its package, the new way of reading finally broke away completely from oral culture and its vestige in the handwritten manuscript.[37]

As part of the rise of modernity, the philosophy of empiricism and the scientific method also reinforced the tendency to think in discrete parts by breaking the act of inquiry into building blocks. At the same time, the institutionalization of the scientific paper served to proclaim the scientist's ownership of new findings and so also to treat information as property. These movements emerged as a radical departure from the climate in which Aquinas wrote the *Summa*.[38] The difference lay in the emphasis the new scientists thrust upon the act of acquiring data. From 1600 to 1800, the period of the scientific revolution, investigators increasingly probed nature through observation and experimentation, while excluding explanations that depended upon spirits or magic. They differentiated testable theories from speculations without support; and, yet, like their medieval counterparts, they sought to place all of the facts within a logical structure.

Thus, the new scientific method emphasized the components of the discipline of investigation so as to maximize rigor and minimize subjective bias. The method dictated that each step of the way—from research question, to hypothesis, to operationalization, to experiment, to analysis, to interpretation, to theory—be treated as a distinct activity. In addition, the newly developing practice of science placed a premium on communication, so that scientific reports came to emphasize, as they still do, the presentation of findings which might be of use to other scientists. Consequently, publications like the *Journal des Sçavans*, *Philosophical Transactions, Mémoires, Miscellanea*, and *Acta Eruditorum*, founded by Leibnitz, illustrate the early importance attached to communication by scientists. For example, *Philosophical Transactions,* founded by the Royal Society, pioneered a new form of presentation, in fact an entirely new genre, which evolved into the scientific paper.[39] Following the lead of *Philosophical Transactions*, other scientific journals allowed published findings to serve as claims to intellectual property by placing the claim in print. However, unlike physical property where the claim symbolized the possession—with intellectual property the published claim was itself the property. Therefore, for scientists seeking news of distant advances, the scientific paper took on objective status. Its existence communicated a finding to members of the community, and proclaimed ownership of the idea for the author.

Thus, as it came to be defined in the 17th and 18th centuries, the practice of modern science converged with the rise of individual ownership of ideas to reinforce the acceptance of information as a commodity. The discreteness of the components of the scientific method, along with the emphasis on communication of findings, encouraged new visualizations of information.

From the Enlightenment to the Information Society

Beginning in the 17th and 18th centuries, modern designs for presenting information, such as dictionaries and encyclopedias, were invented and distributed. At the same time, modern approaches to thinking and reading were taking shape. By the middle of the 19th century, the tendency to treat information as if it were a physical object was well entrenched. In the 20th century, these attitudes converged, so that we recognize them as our cultural view, and take them together as the idea of information.

Still, it might be pointed out that 18th century philosophes did not recognize the introduction of the modern dictionary as part of a new attitude toward information, nor did they separate the information in a book from the book itself with much self-consciousness. If so, then how can any linkage of the Enlightenment to the emergence of the Information Age constitute a valid judgment? However, to argue that the idea of information cannot have roots in the Enlightenment because information has only recently gained attention presupposes that names and designations directly accompany actions. More often the opposite occurs. Men and women exchanged information as a commodity before anyone coined the phrase information market. Individuals set out to manipulate, store, retrieve, and sell information without a formalized definition of their actions, simply because their actions made sense implicitly. Others, such as Diderot and William Smellie, the first editor of the *Encyclopedia Britannica*, arranged knowledge according to an arbitrary alphabetic sequence without recognizing that they were imposing upon ideas the qualities of independent things.[40] In the book trade, publishers did not see themselves as members of an information industry. Instead, they explored the potential for profit by producing and selling books. Book buyers who sought information did not, for the most part, think of it as information. Nor did legislators articulate the equation of information with a physical object when they passed laws to prevent plagiarism. Instead, actions preceded words. The diffusion of the idea of information occurred because it was intuitively understood, transparent, and facilitative of daily life. In each instance the parties explored the limits of information for their particular uses.

The tendencies we observe as typical of the information society—growing numbers of information workers, increased interconnectedness, high personal consumption of information, and the proliferation of information technologies—represent responses to demand for information.[41] Indeed, the hallmark of the information society in the United States is its reliance on information as an item of value and economic exchange. Yet, as with the idea of information, the information economy grew more like a mosaic, the patterns emerging slowly.[42] In more recent years, as the idea of information achieved acceptance, this new consciousness has accelerated the restructuring of society to explicitly promote the production and consumption of information.

Having begun, in this Introduction, with the complex cultural attitude that sees and treats information as a thing, the chapters that follow explore the emerging tendencies of the information society and inquire into the inevitable tensions.

Chapter one addresses theories in competition. Contending explanations of the relationship between industrial society and the information society are analyzed. We begin by examining the work of three scholars whose interpretations led to the characterization of American society as organized around the production and consumption of information. Fritz Machlup analyzed the contribution of information activities to the 1958 U.S. Gross National Product and introduced the notion of a knowledge economy.[43] Daniel Bell focused on the post World War II growth of a large service sector and saw the emergence of "Post-Industrial Society."[44] Following closely in the footsteps of Machlup, Marc Porat described the full extent of the information economy and suggested the existence of an information society.[45] It is a measure of his success that, since his research in the mid 1970s, the information society has provoked both the scholarly and the popular imagination.

The notion of the "information economy" encouraged economists to consider the many forms in which information can be exchanged in the marketplace. Likewise, the related idea of information work led sociologists to reconsider the changes taking place in productive life. Opening this conceptual territory created fertile ground for a great deal of fruitful speculating and theorizing. Yet any comprehensive explanation of the information society must first resolve whether the emergence of the information society constitutes a revolution comparable to and superseding the industrial revolution, or a further evolution of industrial capitalism. We review the discussions that have developed over the last fifteen years and the competing visions that have coalesced, in order to place the information society within an historical context.

Chapter two focuses on one of the principal social phenomena of the information society—our increasing interconnectedness at every level. At the micro level, individuals experience numerous personal interactions in their daily lives but can also stay in touch at nearly any distance. Yet, unlike earlier generations, the tendency to depend on information technologies for conducting daily activities leads to many more casual relationships. Americans of the 1990s experience a far greater ratio of secondary to primary relationships. At the middle level, where groups and organizations predominate, increased interconnectedness shows itself in the greatly enhanced movement of information among institutions, e.g., banks, credit card companies, stock brokerage houses and diminished differences among them, as institutions from the industrial era transform themselves into new—and increasingly similar—configurations in the pursuit of profit. At the macro level, increased interconnectedness through communication technologies allows for the integration of organizations on a global scale, so that companies with headquarters in Atlanta, Georgia, for example, can maintain effective control over operations spread across every continent. Moreover, the distance-communication trade-off enabled by information technologies leads to a macro-interconnectedness among the institutions that drive and attempt to regulate the economies, markets, armies, and even nations of the world. Ever since the telegraph sped the pace of human communication to 186,000 miles per second, a spiral of technological development continues to diminish the obstacles of distance and time, resulting in unprecedented interconnectedness—and consequences—for the earth's inhabitants.

In chapter three, we examine information work, and its transition from the early 20th century where workers sold the labor of their hands in fields and factories, to the late 20th century where workers sell the labor of their brains. Although nearly everyone agrees on the direction and magnitude of this shift, attempting to measure it poses significant problems. We assess successive efforts to determine who is, and who is not, an information worker. In so doing, we present data indicating that the information workforce grew to a large size much earlier in the century than previously thought. Still, understanding the growth of information work demands more than definitions and statistical trends. This chapter also examines the personal experience of information work, ranging from those who manipulate information in elite home offices to those who work in factory-like settings. Finally, we ask whether information work contributes to, or ameliorates, older forms of alienation.

How do people adapt their private lives to the information society? We address this question in chapter four, suggesting that the necessary and conspicuous consumption of information forms an important theme in American culture. Individuals construct their private spheres within media environments organized around telephones, radios, TV sets, video cassette recorders, audio cassette/disc players, and computerized TV games, as well as older media such as newspapers, magazines, and books. We analyze disposable income expended on information goods and services in the first part of this chapter, and further examine the relationship between information work and information leisure. In recent years, for example, information technologies have allowed some individuals to integrate the activities of work and home in ways not possible for industrial workers. For these new "tele-commuters," the distinction between work and leisure is problematic. Nevertheless, most information workers continue to experience the environment of work as distinct from that of the home. For them, media consumed in a leisure context constitute a pervasive activity in the home. The superabundance of messages and channels entering the home, brings with it a daunting variety of content, becoming an important basis for interpreting reality. But it is a highly fragmented reality that the media offer. The amount of information received is high but few connections are offered and the amount processed remains low. Yet the experience of media environments—with highly fragmented information—is a fact of life in the information society. Above all else, the media offer escape and the images with which to construct the American dream.

Chapter five asks, "How should information be distributed?" First, we examine the tension between those who believe in the virtues of distribution through the mechanisms of the market versus those who stand behind distribution through the bureaucratic structures of government. Supporters of private enterprise argue that only the market can guarantee maximum efficiency in the delivery of information. Supporters of publicly shared information respond that government is the only guarantor of equitable distribution to the largest number of citizens. For the time being, those championing the efficiency of the marketplace have the upper hand, but because the stakes are high, the debate is not over. Second, we discuss the tension of integration and fragmentation that characterizes political communication. In the information society political candidates depend heavily on national television and the information technologies of commercial marketing to communicate directly to a largely anonymous electorate—in effect, selling to political marketplaces. In the process, political succession has evolved into a contest demanding large sums of money spent on television sound bites—an arena where TV commercial styles dominate the substance of messages. At the receiving end, individuals experience political messages within a disorienting blizzard of commercial information. Personal strategies necessary to cope with information overload mitigate against concentrated attention to political messages unless the individual is predisposed to seek them out. Moreover, the styles adopted for political commercials make it hard to distinguish between electioneering and marketing. Consequently, the age of maximum information may result in minimum civic discourse. Third, we examine the information society's potential for fairness. The possibility of a new age of national discourse enhanced by a more informed citizenry is challenged by the specter of a nation where individuals devote highly fragmented lives to the pursuit of isolated leisure. As the information age unfolds, the prospect of a community of shared civic values remains unclear, while the growing experience of atomistic lives foreshadows a willingness to condemn others perceived as different. Americans face choices as the information age gathers momentum: they must choose a balance between distribution of information by the market and by government, between political process by advertising and by discourse, between social participation and social isolation. The directions chosen will determine if the information society will be a just society.

In chapter six, we explore the machine icons of the information age. We explore the many meanings ascribed to them, and their importance to the hopes and fears projected on to the information age. Of these, the most common theme is the simple acceptance of information technology as a fact of life. The ease with which the public has adapted to each new device from the phonograph to the fax machine indicates high levels of technological comfort. Yet this very comfort may mask the need to critically examine the place of technology in the information society. Willing acceptance of new technologies has deep roots in American culture because it receives nourishment from an optimistic belief in technological progress. Beyond simple acceptance, some Americans also embrace a second theme that annoints information technology as an ideal to be pursued. Mostly scientists and engineers, they experience the joy of inquiry within institutions committed to the pursuit of further technological development. For them and for technophiles in general, information technologies offer the solutions to unyielding social problems, thereby revealing the Eden within the information age. Believers in this theme are especially vulnerable to an uncritical faith in the determinism of technology— a faith that masks negative consequences and encourages believers to explain away harmful outcomes as unrelated to the uses of technology. The polar opposite of this theme can be found in the fear of information technology as the sword of Damocles. Alongside their optimistic views, Americans also hold to a dark vision of the technological future. Dialectically bound to the bright vision, the dark image invokes a comparable miscomprehension of the tensions within the information society. As uncritical as the technophiles, the technophobes scapegoat technology while ignoring other social forces shaping the information society. But whether -philes or -phobes, all Americans find one other meaning in information technology, i.e., information technology serves as a powerful metaphor for American civilization. For if the locomotive was the arch metaphor of the 19th century, then television and the computer are metaphors that dominate the late 20th century. Public discourses connecting television to the health of American culture, the malaise of youth, and to the problems of electoral democracy, reveal television's power. Metaphors used to describe organizations, the brain, and even the universe, reveal the power of the computer to capture our imagination. It is no surprise that Americans see information technology—whether for good or for evil—as the engine behind the information age. Yet such a view is wrong. Information technology interacts with other social forces in ways that prevent any easily identified flow of causality. Depending on the level of interaction—macro, middle, or micro—technology may shape or be shaped. We end chapter six by discussing the question of technological determinism, and by proposing macro, middle, and micro levels of technological causation.

In chapter seven, we review images of the information society and propose a macro theory. There is a lineage of social theories suggesting information variables going back at least to Walter Lippmann's analysis of the pictures in our heads.[46] But explanations of the development of society in terms of information and communication date roughly from Boorstin's *The Image*, and McLuhan's ideas on media and the global village.[47] Not really systematic analyses, these theories focused on the mass media but also alluded to the tension between integration and fragmentation. A more recent group of theories clusters around Bell's description of post-industrial society.[48] These explanations generally accept Bell's premises and extrapolate his ideas to include the information economy, information technology, and changes in daily life.[49] Furthermore, the school surrounding Bell represents the most widely accepted interpretation of the information society. In this final chapter, we challenge the prevailing view and propose a theory derived from a new organization of the salient clues, as well as a synthesis of the ferment of the last 18 years. We suggest that, in the United States, the tendencies of the information society grew out of the confluence of three powerful social forces—the idea of information, capitalism, and industrialization. They combined to form the information economy and it, in turn, re-configured work, interconnectedness, daily life, and technology.

Notes

1. Shannon, C. E., & Weaver, W. (1949). *The mathematical theory of communication*. Urbana, IL: University of Illinois Press, p. 32.
2. Wiener, N. (1950). *The human use of human beings: Cybernetics and society*. New York: Avon Books (pp. 26-27, 31).
3. Hayes, R. M. (1969). Education in information science. *American Documentation, 20*, 362-365.
4. Some theoretical perspectives introduce a notion of information as central to the intent of the theory, while others implicitly rely on some conceptualization of information. For example, see: Bertalanffy, L. v. (1968). *General system theory*. New York: Braziller. Boulding, K. (1956). *The image*. Ann Arbor, MI: University of Michigan Press. Dewey, J. (1926). *Experience and nature*. New York: Norton. Hoskovsky, A. G., & Massey, R. J. (1968). *Information science: Its end, means, and operations*. New York: ASIS. Machlup, F. (1958). *An economic review of the patent system* No. 15). The Subcommittee on Patents, Trademarks, and Copyrights, of the Committee on the Judiciary, Washington DC: GPO. Mackay, D. M. (1952). The nomenclature of information theory. In H. Von Foerster (Eds.), *Cybernetics: Transactions of the Eighth Congress* New York: Macy Foundation. Mayo, E. (1933). *The human problems of an industrial civilization*. New York: The MacMillan Co. McLuhan, M. (1964). *Understanding media: The extensions*

of man. New York: New American Library. Miller, J. G. (1965). Living systems. *Behavioral Science, 10,* 193-237. Mumford, L. (1934/1962). *Technics and civilization.* New York: Harcourt, Brace, and World. Pierce, J. R. (1961). *Symbols, signals, and noise.* New York: Harper and Row. Price, D. J. d. S. (1963). *Little science big science.* New York: Columbia University Press. Rapoport, A. (1966). What is information? In A. G. Smith (Eds.), *Communication and Culture* (pp. 41-55). New York: Holt, Rinehart and Winston. Ruben, B. D. (1972). General systems theory: An approach to human communication. In R. W. Budd & B. D. Ruben (Eds.), *Approaches to human communication* (pp. 120-144). New York: Spartan. Smith, A. G. (Ed.). (1966). *Communication and culture.* New York: Holt. Wiener, N. (1961). *Cybernetics, or control and communication in the animal and the machine* (2 ed.). Cambridge, MA: MIT Press.

5. Hirshleifer, J. (1973). Economics of information: Where are we in the theory of information? *American Economic Association, 63*(2 (May)), 31-39. Lamberton, D. M. (Ed.). (1971). *Economics of information and knowledge.* Harmondsworth, UK: Penguin. Machlup, F., & Mansfield, U. (Ed.). (1983). *The study of information: Interdisciplinary messages.* New York: John Wiley & Sons.

6. Belkin, N. J., & Robertson, S. E. (1976). Information science and the phenomenon of information. *Journal of the American Society for Information Science,* 27(4), 197-204, p. 198.

7. Dervin, B., Jacobson, T. L., & Nilan, M. S. (1981). Measuring aspects of information-seeking: A test of qualitative/quantitative methodology. In M. Burgoon (Eds.), *Communication Yearbook 6* (pp. 71-87). Beverly Hills, CA: Sage.

8. For additional views in the social sciences, see: Anderson, M. P. (1959). What is communication. *The Journal of Communication, 9*(1), 5.

   Artandi, S. (1973). Information concepts and their utility. *Journal of the American Society for Information Science,* 24(4), 242-245. Ashby, W. R. (1964). *An introduction to cybernetics.* London, UK: Chapman and Hall. Boulding, K. (1984). Foreword: A note on information, knowledge, and production. In M. Jussawalla & H. Ebenfield (Eds.), *Communication and information economics: New perspectives* (pp. vii-ix). Elsevier Science Publishers. Farradane, J. (1976). Towards a true information science. *Information Scientist, 10,* 91-101. Fox, R. W., & Lears, T. J. J. (Ed.). (1983). *The culture of consumption: critical essays in American history, 1880-1980.* New York: Pantheon. Krippendorff, K. (1977). Information systems theory and research. In B. D. Ruben (Ed.), *Communication Yearbook 1* (pp. 149-171). New Brunswick, NJ: Transaction-International Communication Association. Lancaster, F. W., & Gillespie, C. J. (1970). Design and evaluation of information systems. In C. Cuadra (Ed.), *Annual review of information science and technology: Volume 5* (pp. 33-70). Chicago, Il: Encyclopaedia Britannica. Mackay, D. M. (1952). In search of basic symbols. In H. v. Foerster (Ed.), *Cybernetics: Transactions of the Eighth Congress* New York: Macy Foundation. Nitecki, J. Z. (1985). The concept of information-knowledge continuum: Implications for librarianship. *Journal of Library History, 20*(4 (Fall)), 387-407. Otten, K. W. (1975). Information and communication: A conceptual model as framework for the development of theories of information. In A. Debons & W. Cameron (Eds.), *Perspectives in information science* (pp. 127-148). Leyden: Noordhof. Pierce, J. R. (1961). *Symbols, signals, and noise.* New York: Harper and Row. Pratt, A. D. (1977). The information of the image. *Libri,* 27, 204-220. Rapoport, A. (1966). What is information? In A. G. Smith (Eds.), *Communication and Culture* (pp. 41-55). New York: Holt, Rinehart and Winston. Repo, A. J. (1989). The value of information: Approaches in economics, accounting, and management. *Journal of the american society for information science,* 40(2), pp. 68-85. Schroder, H. M.,

Driver, M. J., & Streufert, S. (1967). *Human information processing*. New York: Holt, Rinehart and Winston. Shannon, C. E., & Weaver, W. (1949). *The mathematical theory of communication*. Urbana, IL: University of Illinois Press. Yovitz, M. C. (1975). A theoretical framework for the development of information science. In *Problems of information science* Moscow, USSR: VINITI.

9. We do not present a comprehensive history of the idea of information. Neither a comprehensive history, nor a unified theory, currently exists, though both are sorely needed.

10. Dawkins, R. (1976). *The selfish gene*. New York: Oxford University Press. Machlup, F., & Mansfield, U. (1983). Cultural diversity in studies of information. In F. Machlup & U. Mansfield (Eds.), *The study of information: Interdisciplinary messages* (pp. 3–59). New York: John Wiley & Sons.

11. Fredkin, E., & Toffoli, T. (1982). Conservative logic. *International Journal of Theoretical Physics, 21*(3/4). Wright, R. (1989). *Three scientists and their gods: Looking for meaning in an age of information*. New York: Harper & Row. For other views in the physical sciences, see also: Campbell, J. (1982). *Grammatical man*. New York: Touchstone. Simon, H. A. (1969). *The sciences of the artificial*. Cambridge, MA: MIT Press.

12. See, for example, Artandi, S. (1973). Information concepts and their utility. *Journal of the American Society for Information Science, 24*(4), 242–245. Beniger, J. R. (1988). Information and communication. *Communication Research, 15*(2), 198–218. Borgman, C. L., & Schement, J. R. (1990). Information science and communication research. In J. M. Pemberton & A. E. Prentice (Eds.), *Information science: The interdisciplinary context* (pp. 42–59). New York: Neal-Schuman. Braman, S. (1989). Defining information: An approach for policy makers. *Telecommunications Policy, 13*(3), 233–242. Bruner, J. (1990). *Acts of meaning*. Cambridge, MA: Harvard. Buckland, M. K. (1991). Information as thing. *Journal of the American Society for Information Science, 42*(5), 351–360. Campbell, J. (1982). *Grammatical man*. New York: Touchstone. Chamberlin, B. F., & Singleton, L. A. (1987). The law in an information society. In J. R. Schement & L. Lievrouw (Eds.), *Competing visions, complex realities: Social aspects of the information society* (pp. 121–139). Norwood, NJ: Ablex. Childers, T. (1975). *The information-poor in America*. Metuchen, NJ: The Scarecrow Press. Dawkins, R., & Krebs, J. R. (1984). Animal signals: Information or manipulation? In J. R. Krebs & N. B. Davies (Eds.), *Behavioral Ecology: An evolutionary approach* Sunderland, MA: Sinauer. Farradane, J. (1976). Towards a true information science. *Information Scientist, 10*, 91–101. Fox, C. J. (1983). *Information and misinformation: An investigation of the notions of information, misinformation, informing, and misinforming*. Greenwood Press. Fredkin, E., & Toffoli, T. (1982). Conservative logic. *International Journal of Theoretical Physics, 21*(3/4). Geertz, C. (1983). The way we think: Toward an ethnography of modern thought. In C. Geertz, *Local knowledge* (pp. 147–163). New York: Basic Books. Halloran, J. D. (1985). Information and communication: Information is the answer, but what is the question? In B. D. Ruben (Ed.), *Information and Behavior* (pp. 27–39). New Brunswick, NJ: Transaction. Hirshleifer, J. (1973). Economics of information: Where are we in the theory of information? *American Economic Association, 63*(2 (May)), 31–39. Hixson, R. F. (1985). Whose life is it anyway? Information as property. In B. D. Ruben (Ed.), *Information and behavior: Volume 1* (pp. 76–92). New Brunswick, NJ: Transaction. Kibirige, H. M. (1983). *The information dilemma: A critical analysis of information pricing and the fees controversy*. Westport, CN: Greenwood Press. Lamberton, D. M. (Ed.). (1971). *Economics of information and knowledge*. Harmondsworth, UK: Penguin. Machlup, F., &

Mansfield, U. (1983). Semantic quirks in studies of information. In F. Machlup & U. Mansfield (Eds.), *The study of information: Interdisciplinary messages* (pp. 641–671). New York: John Wiley & Sons. Mackay, D. M. (1952). In search of basic symbols. In H. v. Foerster (Ed.), *Cybernetics: Transactions of the Eighth Congress* New York: Macy Foundation. Otten, K. W. (1975). Information and communication: A conceptual model as framework for the development of theories of information. In A. Debons & W. Cameron (Eds.), *Perspectives in information science* (pp. 127–148). Leyden: Noordhof. Repo, A. J. (1989). The value of information: Approaches in economics, accounting, and management. *Journal of the American society for information science, 40*(2), pp. 68–85. Schiller, H. I. (1983). Information for what kind of society? In J. L. Salvaggio (Ed.). (1989). *Telecommunications: Issues and choices for society* (pp. 24–33). New York: Longman. Schement, J. R. (1993). Communication and information. *Information and Behavior, 4*, pp. 3–33. Sharrock, W. W. (1974). On owning knowledge. In R. Turner (Eds.), *Ethnomethodology: Selected readings* (pp. 45–53). New York: Penguin. Thayer, L. (1988). How does information inform? In B. D. Ruben (Ed.), *Information and Behavior* (pp. 13–26). New Brunswick, NJ: Transaction. Wiener, N. (1950). *The human use of human beings: Cybernetics and society.* New York: Avon Books.

13. As social movements, the Renaissance and the Protestant Reformation profoundly affected the emergence of the idea of information. In this chapter, however, we do not address either movement directly. Undoubtedly, the examples we present were influenced by ideas and behaviors originating in these earlier movements. For readings which examine aspects of the Renaissance and the Protestant Reformation, though not explicitly discussing the idea of information, see Braudel, F. (1979). *Civilization and capitalism 15th–18th century: The wheels of commerce.* New York: Harper & Row. Eisenstein, E. L. (1979). *The printing press as an agent of change: Communications and cultural transformations in early-modern europe.* Cambridge: Cambridge University Press. Hall, A. R. (1954/1962). *The scientific revolution 1500–1800: The formation of the modern scientific attitude.* Boston: Beacon Press. Steinberg, S. H. (1955). *Five hundred years of printing.* Edinburgh, UK: Penguin, especially Eisenstein's analysis of the effects of the invention of printing on both the Renaissance and the Reformation.

14. Hampson, N. (1968). *The enlightenment.* Harmondsworth, Middlesex: Penguin Books, p. 128.

15. Hampson, N., pp. 15–40.

16. Johnson, E. D. (1970). *History of libraries in the western world.* Metuchen, NJ: Scarecrow Press, p. 163.

17. Eisenstein, E. L. (1979). *The printing press as an agent of change: Communications and cultural transformations in early-modern europe.* Cambridge: Cambridge University Press, pp. 95–106. McArthur, T. (1986). *Worlds of reference: Lexicography, learning and language from the clay tablet to the computer.* Cambridge, UK: Cambridge University Press, p. 77.

18. 1538, Thomas Elyot, alphabetic wordbook, *Dictionary* of Latin and English.

19. McArthur, T. (1986). *Worlds of reference: Lexicography, learning and language from the clay tablet to the computer.* Cambridge, UK: Cambridge University Press (pp. 94–97).

20. From the introduction to Samuel Johnson's dictionary. McAdam, E. L. J., & Milne, G. (1963). *Johnson's dictionary.* New York: Pantheon, p. 3.

21. McArthur, T. (1986). *Worlds of reference: Lexicography, learning and language from the clay tablet to the computer.* Cambridge, UK: Cambridge University Press, p. 98.

22. McAdam, E. L. J., & Milne, G. (1963). *Johnson's dictionary*. New York: Pantheon, p. 33.

23. Mallon, T. (1989). *Stolen words: Forays into the origins and ravages of plagiarism*. New York: Ticknor & Fields.

24. (1975). Copyright law. In *Encyclopedia britannica* (pp. 153). Chicago: William Benton, V. 5, p. 153.

25. Though the most obvious illustration of the idea of information is the printed book, we have focused on other examples of the idea of information, because the social and economic history of books is better known. Analyses of the development of books can be found in: Darnton, R. (1979). *The business of enlightenment: A publishing history of the Encyclopédie 1775–1800*. Cambridge MA: The Belknap Press of Harvard University Press. Eisenstein, E. L. (1979). *The printing press as an agent of change: Communications and cultural transformations in early-modern europe*. Cambridge: Cambridge University Press. Febvre, L., & Martin, H.-J. (1976). *The coming of the book: The impact of printing 1450–1800* (Gerard, David, Trans.). London, UK: N.L.B. Putnam, G. H. (1896/1962). *Books and their makers during the middle ages*. New York: Hillary House Publishers.

26. Eisenstein, E. L. (1986). Print culture and enlightenment thought. In Hanes foundation for the study of the origin and development of the book. Hanes foundation. Rare book collection/University library. University of North Carolina at Chapel Hill: The Sixth Hanes lecture, pp. 51–53.

27. Darnton, R. (1984). *The great cat massacre and other episodes in French cultural history*. New York: Vintage Books, pp. 215–228. Eisenstein, E. L. (1986). Print culture and enlightenment thought. In Hanes foundation for the study of the origin and development of the book. Hanes foundation. Rare book collection/University library. University of North Carolina at Chapel Hill: The Sixth Hanes lecture, pp. 131–134, 148–152, 224, 331–334. McArthur, T. (1986). *Worlds of reference: Lexicography, learning and language from the clay tablet to the computer*. Cambridge, UK: Cambridge University Press (pp. 70–72).

28. Eisenstein, E. L. (1986). Print culture and enlightenment thought. In Hanes foundation for the study of the origin and development of the book. Hanes foundation. Rare book collection/University library. University of North Carolina at Chapel Hill: The Sixth Hanes lecture, pp. 104–107.

29. Eisenstein, E. L. (1986). pp. 65–67.

30. Admittedly, it is immensely difficult to recreate an activity, like reading, that leaves no trace. Numerous histories of books exist because books are thing-like examples of information. Similarly there are excellent histories of printing because printing is an institutionalized activity which leaves behind traces in the forms of records. But reading can be accessed only through the written references to it left behind in individual correspondences. See: Darnton, R. (1979). *The business of enlightenment: A publishing history of the Encyclopédie 1775–1800*. Cambridge MA: The Belknap Press of Harvard University Press. Deetz, J. (1977). *In small things forgotten: The archeology of early American life*. New York: Anchor Press. Suleiman, S. R., & Crosman, I. (Eds.). (1980). *The reader in the text: Essays on audience and interpretation*. Princeton, NJ: Princeton.

31. A popular 18th century description of intellectual Europe drawn from Pierre Bayle's journal, *Nouvelles de la République des lettres*, repeated in the English-language journal, *Present State of the Republick of Letters*.

32. Eisenstein, E. L. (1986) p. 8.

33. Darnton, R. (1984). *The great cat massacre and other episodes in french cultural history*. New York: Vintage Books, p. 249.

34. Steinberg, S. H. (1955). *Five hundred years of printing*. Edinburgh, UK: Penguin (pp. 188-198).

35. Darnton, R. (1984) p. 223.

36. Darnton, R. (1984) p. 249.

37. Darnton, R. (1984) (pp. 215-251).

38. The scarcity of manuscripts and the pursuit of knowledge for the greater glory of God encouraged summations. Thomas Aquinas completed the *Summa Theologica* in 1273. The organization of his work and those of other medieval thinkers like Vincent de Beauvais set them apart from the encyclopedias that followed 500 years later. The Summa, for example, was organized thematically into three divisions: theology; the human race; the Incarnate Word. Aquinas, T. (1265-1273/ 1912-1936). *The summa theologica* (Shapcote, L., Trans.). London: Burns, Oates.

39. Hall, A. R. (1954/1962). *The scientific revolution 1500-1800: The formation of the modern scientific attitude*. Boston: Beacon Press (pp. 203-204).

40. In Edinburgh, Scotland, a "Society of Gentlemen" sponsored Andrew Bell, Collin Macfarquhar, and William Smellie to carry out a project similar to Diderot's. Their product, published in three volumes between 1768 and 1771, they titled *Encyclopedia Britannica, or a Dictionary of Arts and Sciences, compiled upon a New Plan*. Smellie, the editor, adhered to an alphabetic sequence, juxtaposing one-line entries next to entries of 100 pages, and, though it lacked the political explosiveness of its French counterpart, the Britannica has maintained this form to the present day.

41. Schement, J. R., & Lievrouw, L. A. (Eds.). (1988). *Competing visions, complex realities: Social aspects of the information society*. Norwood, NJ: Ablex.

42. Schement, J. R. (1989). The origins of the information society in the United States: Competing visions. In J. Salvaggio (Ed.). (1989). *The information society* (pp. 29-50). New York: Lawrence Erlbaum.

43. Machlup, F. (1962). *The production and distribution of knowledge in the United States*. Princeton, NJ: Princeton University Press.

44. Bell, D. (1976). *The coming of post-industrial society*. New York: Basic Books.

45. Porat, M. U. (1977). *The information economy: Definition and measurement*. No. OT Special Publication 77-12 (1)). Washington DC: Department of Commerce/Office of Telecommunications.

46. Lippmann, W. (1921). *Public opinion*. New York: Free Press.

47. Boorstin, D. J. (1961). *The image: A guide to pseudo-events in America*. New York: Atheneum. McLuhan, M. (1962). *The Gutenberg Galaxy: The making of typographic man*. New York: New American Library. McLuhan, M. (1964). *Understanding media: The extensions of man*. New York: New American Library.

48. Bell, D. (1976). *The coming of post-industrial society*. New York: Basic Books. Bell, D. (1981). The social framework of the information society. In T. Forestor (Ed.), *The microelectronics revolution* (pp. 500-549). Cambridge, MA: MIT Press.

49. Baer, W. (1978). Telecommunications technology in the 1980s. In G. O. Robinson (Eds.), *Communications for tomorrow: Policy perspectives for the 1980s* (pp. 61-123). New York: Praeger. Dertouzos, M. L., & Moses, J. (Eds.). (1979). *The computer age*. Cambridge, MA: MIT Press. Dizard, W. P. J. (1982). *The coming information age: An overview of technology, economics, and politics*. New York: Longman. Dordick, H. S. (1987). The emerging information societies. In J. R. Schement & L. Lievrouw (Eds.), *Competing visions, complex realities: Social aspects of the information society* (pp. 13-22). Norwood, NJ: Ablex. Dordick, H. S., & Georgette, W. (1993). *The information society: A retrospective view*. Newbury Park, CA: Sage. Edelstein, A. S., Bowes, J. E., & Harsel, S. M. (1978). *Informa-*

tion societies: Comparing the japanese and american experiences. Seattle, WA: University of Washington. Katz, R. L. (1988). *The information society.* New York: Praeger. Martin, J. (1981). *Telematic society: A challenge for tomorrow.* New York: Prentice-Hall. Masuda, Y. (1981). *The information society as post-industrial society.* Bethesda, MD: World Future Society. Ochai, A. (1984). The emerging information society. *International Library Review, 16*(4), 367–372. Pelton, N. J. (1983). Life in the information society. In J. L. Salvaggio (Ed.). (1989), *Telecommunications: Issues and choices for society* New York: Longman. Porat, M. U. (1977). *The information economy: Definition and measurement.* No. OT Special Publication 77-12 (1)). Washington DC: Department of Commerce/Office of Telecommunications. Toffler, A. (1980). *The third wave.* New York: William Morrow. Williams, F. (1982). *The communications revolution.* Beverly Hills, CA: Sage.

1

The New Industrial Society

Behind the Thomson and Homestead and Keystone plants were the famous Lucy and Carrie furnaces for making pig iron; and behind them was the enormous Henry Clay Frick Coke Company with its 40,000 acres of coal land, its 2,688 railway cars, and its 13,252 coking ovens; and behind this, in turn, were 244 miles of railways (organized into three main companies) to ship materials to and from the coking ovens; and then at a still more distant remove were a shipping company and a dock company with a fleet of Great Lakes ore-carrying steamers; and then at the very point of origin of the steel-making process, was the Oliver Mining Company with its great mines in Michigan and Wisconsin.—Robert Heilbroner[1]

World satellite systems now make distance and time irrelevant. We witness and react to crises simultaneously with their happening. Networks of telephones, telex, radio, and television have exponentially increased the *density* of human contact. More people can be in touch with one another during any single day in the new communications environment than many did in a lifetime in the 14th century. The convergence of telecommunications and computing technologies distribute information automation to the limits of the world's communication networks. We are well past the point of having the capability to transform most of human knowledge into electronic form for access at any point on the earth's surface.—Frederick Williams[2]

Heilbronner's panorama evokes a familiar image of industrial America because it links America's present to its past. The second image has gained familiarity more recently and associates the present with the future. It portrays America as an information society. The idea that a society can organize itself around the production and consumption of information comes from the theories of two social scientists and the reinterpretations of a third. Fritz Machlup, an economist, first introduced the theory of a knowledge economy from his analysis of the contribution of information activities to the 1958 U.S. Gross National Product.[3] Daniel Bell, a sociologist, identified the decline of the industrial sector and the expansion of the service sector as leading indicators of the advance of "post-industrial society."[4] While a doctoral student in communication studies, Marc Porat described a new information sector within the 1967 U.S. economy by breaking down the traditional sectors of agriculture, industry, and service.[5] As a result, he found the information sector to be the largest of the four, and on that basis declared the U.S. an information economy. More than anyone else, Porat contributed to the popularization of the idea of an information society built on an information economy.

The information society is a powerful idea precisely because it provokes the imagination. To Americans concerned about the direction of their society, it proposes an exotic but increasingly familiar future. To economists, sociologists, communications researchers, and information scientists, it provides a framework for interpreting patterns of culture and behavior. The notion of an information economy, for example, encouraged economists to consider information as a good exchanged in the marketplace, and to ponder its contribution to the GNP. Likewise, the growing importance of information work led sociologists and communications researchers to reconsider the roles of information technologies in everyday life. Across the social sciences, the idea of an information society opened conceptual territory and sparked a great deal of fruitful speculation and theorizing.

But if recognition of the existence of the information society has lately spread across the social sciences, pieces to the puzzle have been lying around much longer. Shortly after the end of World War II, social observers began noting the importance of various informational activities. Derek J. de Solla Price surveyed the growth of "big science" in the 1950s and discovered that the size of scientific literatures doubled every 10 to 15 years.[6] At the end of his administration, president Eisenhower recognized the economy's increased dependence on the products of scientific research and warned the nation against the alliance of science with industry and the military.[7] Already in the '50s, a few social scientists found evidence of the commercial exchange of information and of the presence of information work, and suggested the importance of these activities. Machlup thought so in 1962, when he noted of the 1958 U.S. economy,

> As an economy develops and as a society becomes more complex, efficient organization of production, trade, and government seems to require an increasing degree of division of labor between knowledge production and physical production. A quite remarkable increase in the division of labor between 'brain work' and largely physical performance has occurred in all sectors of our economic and social organization.[8]

To others, these emerging patterns implied new social relations. From his observations of changes in the workforce, Bell suggested that the post-war growth of informational activities offered conclusive evidence that industrial society was giving way to a "post-industrial" society. The growth of the information economy, the increase in numbers of information workers, the drop in numbers of factory workers, and the proliferation of computer based technologies led numerous social scientists to infer the passing of the industrial era and to describe the information society as post-industrial. Feeling the momentum, scholars who support a post-industrial interpretation have at times seemed ready to close the book on industrial society.[9] But they would be hasty.

Attractive though the evidence might be, it leaves important questions unanswered. What gave rise to an information society? Has the industrial framework of society given way to some other form of social organization? If so, what are the characteristics of this post-industrial form? Can an information society also be industrial? If the information society is post-industrial, as claimed by Bell[10] and others, then is it also post-capitalist? The answers to these questions are important because a theory of the information society must account for the historical forces that generated the tendencies and tensions of the information society. A theory that cannot answer these questions is a theory out of time, since it cannot place the information society in a historical context. Thus, if we fail to resolve the question of origins, we lack the historical perspective necessary to build a theory that accounts for the pervasiveness and diversity of information and communication patterns in modern society.

A logical resolution to the question of origins depends on the following premises:

1. Since capitalism played an indispensable role in the kindling of the industrial revolution, capitalism's role in the ascent of the information society must be explained as well.

2. If the information society is to be considered a post-industrial society, then it must be shown that the primary social forces driving industrial society—that is, the framework within which change occurs—have given way to a different set of social forces.

To argue, for example, that the expansion of the information workforce constitutes sufficient evidence for the passing of industrial society is to assume that the growth of information work results from a different set of social forces than those that formed the industrial workforce. If there are new social forces whose existence has prompted the growth of information work, or the information economy, or changes in private media environments, then there is indeed a basis for proposing that the information society is post-industrial. On the other hand, evidence for the continuing influence of industrial capitalism would indicate a strong connection between industrial work and the information work. Therefore, in order to understand the origins of the information society, its relationship to industrial society must be clarified.

Contending Views on the Origins of the Information Society

Breaking with the past is a popular image in the literature that explores changes in the 20th century. By choosing *The Age of Discontinuity* as his title, Peter Drucker took change as his basic premise.[11] Daniel Bell resolved the question of continuity by forecasting *The Coming of Post-Industrial Society*.[12] Fred Williams chose the disjunctive phrase communications revolution, and others have similarly described recent changes in society.[13] Wilson Dizard paid homage to Bell's *The Coming of Post-Industrial Society*, by titling his book, *The Coming Information Age*, and by identifying a new stage of socio-economic development.

> The resources are so pervasive and influential that it is now becoming clear the United States is moving into a new era—the information age. Ours is the first nation to complete the three-stage shift from an agricultural society to an industrial one and to a society whose new patterns are only now emerging.[14]

At its briefest, this is the gist of the post-industrial position. The prevalence of information related activities seems to prove that a revolutionary social change has taken place. In *The Coming of Post-Industrial Society*, Bell identified 11 transformations occurring in the 1950s and '60s, and proposed that their interplay was reweaving the American social fabric into a post-industrial society.[15]

The shape of the new society: 1) *The centrality of theoretical knowledge—* will become the primary source for inventions, as big science institutionalized the process of innovation; 2) *The creation of a new intellectual technology—* experts can now exploit computers to make use of mathematical techniques to construct algorithms, models, and simulations, for the purpose of engineering more efficient and rational solutions to economic, material, and even social problems; 3) *The spread of a knowledge class*—will emerge from the ranks of the rapidly growing technical and professional workforce; 4) *The change from goods to services*—by 1970, the U.S. had evolved into an economy where 6.5 out of every 10 workers were engaged in the provision of services; 5) *A change in the character of work*—in post-industrial society, work will primarily be a game against people, human behavior, and facing completely new and unparalleled circumstances; 6) *The role of women*—in post-industrial society the nature of service work will expand their employment opportunities, providing women with the basis for economic independence; 7) *Science as imago*—the practice of science will become more bureaucratized and tied to the payoffs derived from its applications; 8) *Situses as political units.*—political and social conflicts of the future will arise amidst the new social groupings created from within the service sector, possibly even preventing class formation among the new technocrats; 9) *Meritocracy*—a more efficient and rational society will reward education and skill at the expense of inheritance and property; 10) *The end of scarcity*[?] [his punctuation]—post-industrial society will place new scarcities of information and time alongside the old scarcities of material resources, causing even more complex problems of efficient allocation; 11) *The economics of information*—there will be a growing need for cooperative strategies to insure the optimal distribution of knowledge in society.

Bell's extrapolations helped establish the idea that a new information society has replaced industrial society. Although he initially resisted the idea of an information society, by the early '80s he had adopted the concept.[16] According to this view, the *rate* of technological and social change has increased to the point where a genuine discontinuity has occurred. Conse-

quently, the U.S., as the second industrial nation, becomes the first information society.

To arrive at their version of the information society, post-industrialists depend on five basic assumptions. The first principle holds that industrial society, and its forms of social organization are believed to have largely passed;
proponents describe new products, industries, and social classes. Secondly,
the sheer volume of information-related activities seems to validate the idea
of a post-industrial information society, though not all scholars pay equal attention to all information-related activities; nevertheless, they have amassed
much empirical evidence to document the existence of these activities. In a
third assumption, post-industrial interpretations assume sequential development, where all the world's nations presumably travel a single evolutionary
path, from hunting and gathering to informational; and, in so doing, the post-
industrial view draws a parallel with evolutionary social theories, such as Walt
Rostow's stages of economic growth.[17] From this perspective, we may imagine a post-industrial information society as the most advanced stage of economic growth, or as Nora and Minc exult, the ultimate civilization.[18] Fourth,
only Bell reviews the period of industrialization, and his critics have accused
him of being a selective historian.[19] The rest of the post-industrial literature
accepts his proposition that great discontinuities result from periods of high
rates of change, concluding, like Dizard, that rapid changes in information
retrieval and distribution mean fundamental societal transformations. As a
result, Bell's followers focus on the future—his book is subtitled, "A Venture
in Social Forecasting"—while neglecting the influence of the past. Fifth, none
of these writers acknowledge an effect on capitalism from the withering away
of industrialism. They assume that post-industrial society replaces the industrial era while capitalism remains undisturbed. Bell alone foresaw a new capitalist society where technocratic efficiency would dominate policy and
economics, though Michael Harrington has pointed out that any society where
social goals supersede the economic function is also post-capitalist.[20] But Bell
wavers, while other authors seem to treat capitalism as mere background noise
to the information revolution.[21]

Considerable research on the production, distribution, and use of information has followed Bell's initial premise. What we know of the specific patterns comes mostly from researchers who built on the post-industrial theme.
But they have not substantially added to Bell's theory, so that his original
interpretation remains the dominant context for thinking about information
and society—though not without critics.

Herbert I. Schiller first criticized the post-industrial view in *Who Knows:
Information in the Age of the Fortune 500.*[22] In the first pages, he rejects any
attribution of uniqueness to the patterns of change identified by Bell, especially those changes involving information technology and work.[23] He further
charges that the entire information society idea can be understood within the

framework of the processes that have characterized American capitalism. He documents the motivating role played by capitalist values in the transfer of information from the public sector to the private sector. Resulting privatization of information, he maintains, leads to a greater concentration of ownership among large American corporations, developing along the same lines experienced in non-informational industries. Moreover, this trend does not result from the computer revolution. Instead, the information society operates within the "long prevailing imperatives of a market economy."[24]

In his analysis of teletext, Vincent Mosco continues Schiller's argument and points out that the characteristics associated with a post-industrial information society permit increased control of the labor process, a relationship closely associated with the evolution of capitalism. He criticizes enthusiasts for selling "tinny visions of utopia" while ignoring the negative consequences of capitalist development.[25] Like Schiller, he concludes that much of what goes under the rubric of the information society can be explained as part of the progress of capitalism. Sarah Douglas and Thomas Guback, in their review of the same literature, question one of its basic assumptions, the idea that information society is revolutionary.[26] They argue that the term "revolution" is poorly understood in the literature where it often appears as a buzz word. They find no evidence that historically significant social relationships, such as the class struggle, have disappeared. In addition, they challenged the claim that information may replace capital as a primary resource. Douglas and Guback further criticize information economists for focusing on information as output, rather than as part of the social process, thereby confusing imaginary revolutionary change with the effects of capitalism. Like Schiller and Mosco, they explain all information activities as resulting from the forces of capitalism, implying that the idea of an informationally oriented society lacks validity.

In Eileen Meehan's "Towards a Third Vision of an Information Society," she presents a less extreme perspective, criticizing both optimistic and pessimistic visions of the information society. She criticizes those who predict a computerized utopia of electronic cottages as well as those who envision an Orwellian dystopia of masses of information poor watched over by Big Brother. Meehan disagrees with the excessive negativism of Schiller and Mosco, but she accepts their view of unmodified capitalism. She, therefore, predicts that life in a future information society will be just as boring and tedious as it is now, "an ordinary dystopia of material relationships driven by the momentum of traditional capitalist values."[27]

Bell's theory of post-industrial society (and his implicit assumptions) constitutes the foundation for most studies that focus on the information society. In the meantime, his critics have laid out the territory of the debate by introducing competing visions. As each side's strengths provide the basis for verifying the existence of an information oriented society, their weaknesses point to the need for a synthesis.

Writers who adopt Bell's point of view show little concern for proposing a fundamental social shift so soon after the previous one. The industrial revolution was in full swing only in the last decades of the 19th century. Yet just a century later, another equally momentous revolution is hypothesized. Aside from the problems created by positing a social model based on ever increasing rates of change, taking this position also requires an overly narrow view of industrial society. In the post-industrial literature, the industrial revolution is usually defined by its earliest technology, e.g., the steam engine. Consequently, inventions of the 20th century (computers, satellites) seem "post-industrial." That is, by arguing that an increase in the *rate* of change constitutes a societal revolution, those who assume the post-industrial position confound change with the context in which it takes place. For a social revolution to occur, the basis for social organization—the very context of change—must shift. For example, the overthrow of the king's government in the American revolution established the basis for a new political framework. Similarly, the invention and diffusion of the alphabet changed the rules of communication and altered human modes of thought. What Bell and others overlook, by holding that a post-industrial revolution emerged from an increase in the rate of change, is that capitalism is a context that encourages certain kinds of change. Entrepreneurs of the industrial revolution pursued profits by encouraging social change. Industrial entrepreneurs sought wealth through the growth of firms, economies of scale in production, increased productivity, deskilled labor, and mechanization, i.e., by concentrating on the processes of industrialization. These same tendencies appear today in the "new" information industries, in virtually all of the same recognizable forms. The logic of the post-industrial point of view, therefore, rests on a tenuous foundation.

If the logic of post-industrialism is weak, then why is its appeal so strong? Post-industrialism is popular because it conforms to our general belief that we live in times of rapid and revolutionary change—that we late 20th century Americans are somehow exempt from the course of history. Certainly academics and professionals, in such fields as information science, computer science, systems analysis, communication, engineering, and management— especially those who have led the way in computer applications—seem willing to assume that technological advances in information retrieval constitute the whole of a fundamental revolution altering the social fabric. The products or outcomes of change have been mistaken for the process or context of change.

Led by Schiller, the critics have introduced questions concerning the processes and effects of capitalism to a literature largely focused on scenarios of the future. By establishing capitalism as a cause of the changes Bell identified, they warn against accepting these changes as the dawn of a new era, and challenge those explanations that see the information society as primarily determined by technological innovations. By demonstrating that capitalism continues to operate within the same framework, they venture an interpretation that stresses continuity and undermines visions of the information society as an era breaking with the past. By applying theories of capitalism such as those of Karl Marx, they connect the information society literature with an older richer literature offering insights into the essence of the tendencies and tensions. By introducing capitalism as a cause of change, Schiller, Mosco, and others address a glaring omission; and, in so doing, they draw attention to changes in the quality of life brought on by the information society, as well as provide a basis for testing the assertions made by supporters of post-industrial theory. They have broadened the scope of analysis by recognizing the role played by capitalism; thus, acknowledging the importance of other social influences like the idea of information. However, they overlook the primary theme, i.e., industrialization giving way to post-industrialization. They explain the role of capitalism in the formation of the information society, but they do not distinguish the influence of industrialization from that of capitalism. To be fair, they may not believe the distinction carries validity. Oscar Gandy is one who argues that it is not possible to distinguish between the impact of industrialization and the constraints of capitalist relations.[28] Yet by focusing solely on the dynamics of capitalism, their critique remains incomplete and does not answer the question we have asked of Bell, "Does industrial society end where the information society begins?"

As they stand, the two positions do not actually oppose each other. Rather, like ships in the night, their directions are skewed. Each addresses what the other ignores. The advocates of post-industrialism hold that new social relations emerge as the old ones of the industrial era fade, while the critics led by Schiller argue that social relations characteristic of capitalism continue to dominate society. To move the discussion beyond these poles, we must clarify how capitalism and industrialism interact, and how they affect the tendencies manifest within the information society.[29]

Capitalism and the Commoditization of Information

All parties to the debate acknowledge the purchase and sale of information as the most visible consequence of an information economy. Proponents of the post-industrial view have pondered the peculiarities of information commodities as compared to material commodities, while critics have expressed alarm at the adaptation of information to the requirements of advanced capitalism. The ease and inexpensiveness with which information can be replicated attracts the profit seeker. Yet that same ease of replication torments the entrepreneur who fails to control the dissemination of her/his property. For information to function as a commodity, it must fit into the order imposed by capitalism—an economic order based on the profit motive, and founded on the right of the individual to own private property. In capitalist societies, many individuals devote considerable energy trying to get rich. Moreover, they do not measure their wealth simply by the extent of their private property, as did feudal barons, but by the capital value, or worth, of that property.[30] These two characteristics, private property and the pursuit of profit, are the driving forces behind the conversion of information into a commodity. Economically speaking, the history of the United States is the story of individuals who sought to exploit for profit the nation's many resources. The intensifying commoditization of information is the most recent part of this story. But the seeds of the information economy were sown early in the nation's history.

In Article I, Section 8, the writers of the Constitution gave the U.S. Congress the power, "To promote the Progress of Science and the useful Arts." Exercising this power in the passage of the first patent law in 1790, the Congress guaranteed inventors exclusive rights to the value of their discoveries.[31] Both documents expressed the beliefs that there is a natural property right to ideas, that society should reward citizens for useful ideas, and that inventors will only refine and put their ideas to work when they know their property right has society's protection.[32] The entire United States now conformed to a trend begun in 1641, when the Massachusetts General Court granted Samuel Winslow the first patent in North America to protect his invention of a new process for making salt.[33] Yet even as they asserted their commitment to the supremacy of individual property, the founders recognized intrinsic contradictions. As followers of Adam Smith, they believed in the evil of monopolies. Nevertheless, they accepted "temporary monopolies" in order to reward inventors for their contributions and to compensate them for their risk and expense.[34] They understood the essential meaning of information as well as its economic value, because they acknowledged complaints that something could not be stolen if the inventor still possessed it, but overruled striking down the patent laws on the basis of this argument.[35]

The copyright statute of 1790 attempted to reconcile two opposing principles: (1) access—the freest possible dissemination of knowledge; versus, (2) protected profit—legal restrictions to secure intellectual property. The framers of the Constitution committed themselves to both views and, by laying a copyright statute alongside the First Amendment, laid the basis for the growth of publishing. Because the First Amendment to the Constitution guaranteed freedom of the press, 19th century newspaper publishers wrote without fear of government censorship. Their views were varied and impassioned, but their principal interest lay in the sale of their newspapers. In 1760, seventeen newspapers existed in the colonies. By 1850, 254 dailies circulated the news to approximately 758,000 readers.[36] The New York Sun, whose masthead declared "It Shines for All," claimed a circulation of 50,000 by 1851. It shared New York, population 515,547,[37] with four other penny dailies and ten six-penny papers.[38] Ultimately, their success in the first half of the 19th century established foundations for the commercial dissemination of information in the 20th.

The profit motive also encouraged the commercial implementation of information technology, though disapproving voices were hardly silent. In an 1844 letter to the U.S. House of Representatives, Samuel F. B. Morse, inventor of the telegraph, expressed his desire to avoid privatization, "For myself, I should prefer that the government should possess the invention, although pecuniary interests of the proprietors induce them to lean towards arrangements with private companies."[39] Accordingly, the government completed a line from Washington to Baltimore in 1844. But the commercial potential was obvious and Congress soon leased the line to the Magnetic Telegraph Company.[40] From then on, the pattern was set. Thirty years later, Alexander Graham Bell sought commercial exploitation from the moment of his earliest tinkering.[41] His machine worked for the first time in 1876 ["Mr. Watson—come here—I want to see you."].[42] In 1877, the Bell Telephone Company issued its first 5,000 shares, with Bell receiving 10. It's not as bad as it appears. Mabel Hubbard received 1,497 shares and she soon married Bell.[43] Similarly, David H. Houston invented the first practical roll film camera, his 1881 Kodak. His partner George Eastman bought most of the patents when he formed the Eastman Dry Plate and Film Company in 1884, and by 1892 the Eastman Kodak Company owned all of the available patents.[44]

Although Eadweard Muybridge did not exploit the commercial potential of his motion picture camera, the Zoopraxiscope, others pursued business possibilities. William Dickson, an assistant to Thomas Edison, perfected the motion picture camera/projector and in 1889 Edison patented the essential components as the Vitascope. However, the profit potential of motion pictures was so obvious that tinkers and inventors jumped in with their copies, improvements, and creations. Dickson himself left Edison to go it alone with his Biograph projector. Soon Edison found himself tangled in a melee of patent litigation for control of the medium's technology and its commercial opportunities. In the 20th century, a persistently receptive American market for information machines has encouraged entrepreneurs to exploit each new invention for its money making potential, so that a stream of inventions, often subsidized by the federal government, spews from corporate research laboratories, each one aimed at securing a market advantage.[45]

Beyond the invention of information devices, the desire for greater profits has also encouraged entrepreneurs to exploit the media's power to urge consumers to buy more goods. The New York Sun might shine for all, but it was only one of many beacons beckoning consumers. In the early 19th century, handbills and posters carried the weight of consumer ads, though the proliferation of the penny press quickly eclipsed them in volume.[46] After the Civil War, factory-made goods began to pour into local markets replacing goods produced by cottage industries.[47] Marketing initiatives centered on advertising to complement innovations in organization and distribution. Capitalizing on the integration of factories and managerial hierarchies, Montgomery Ward utilized an improving postal system to mail a 540-page catalog in 1887.[48] One by one, in each new industry, thousands of small local and regional markets were welded into a national market for consumer goods. Within the new integrated production-distribution structure nationwide advertising campaigns made sense. The National Biscuit Company promoted the Uneeda Biscuit with the first million dollar campaign in 1889, at a time when the U.S. GNP barely topped 12.5 billion.[49] As Michael Schudson explains, "For nationally advertised, branded products that arose in continuous-process production industries after 1880, advertising was one important element in a marketing mix that included direct salesmanship, packaging, and the establishment of hierarchical, national marketing organizations."[50]

When incorporated along with the direct sale of information machines, products, and services, advertising contributed to the formation of the complex and interdependent markets that permeate the American economy. In the 19th century, advertising emerged as the principal source of revenue for the modern mass media, and it encouraged their proliferation in the 20th century. In step with demand for information goods as final products, advertising accelerated the momentum of the information economy, up from 25% of the 1967 GNP to 34% of the 1980 GNP.[51] Moreover, the growth of these markets has also affected the distribution of labor [see chapter 3].

Capitalism provided the incentive to convert information into a commodity. Commoditization, in turn, affects technology and labor. Though it never went unopposed, the tendency to commoditize information was apparent at the birth of the republic; and, by 1889, was clearly a vital part of American business. Yet, capitalism alone does not fully explain the scope of all of the activities associated with the information society. Managerial systems, white collar workers, and bureaucracies have more to do with process than with product. Independent of the goods they contribute to the marketplace, these corporate structures are the result of industrialization.

Industrialization, Management, and the Information Economy

Industrialization is the path that capitalism took in the United States, where entrepreneurs brought capital, labor, and machines together in one place to recreate the industrial system from its English prototype. Aspiring industrialists had to amass and expend enormous amounts of capital, and invent new forms of organization in order to effectively coordinate the elements. Or, as Harry Braverman put it in his influential work, *Labor and Monopoly Capital*, holds that, "Industrial capitalism begins when a significant number of workers is employed by a single capitalist."[52] Workers formerly laboring within the craft system increasingly found themselves at the receiving end of a strict division of labor similar to the one observed by Adam Smith in his famous visit to a British pin factory.[53] Machines were introduced into the work process so extensively that eventually production could not occur without them. Then, with the introduction of machines, individual workers encountered a new relationship. They became one of several elements that might be substituted for each other in the total production process. In fact, the relationship between machines and human labor is so significant that for some sociologists like Anthony Giddens, the transformation of human labor via the application of inanimate sources of energy into productive activity constitutes the essential feature of industrialism.[54] When Francis Cabot Lowell recruited farmers' daughters to work in his textile mill between 1813 and 1817, he introduced industrialism within a social context already committed to an established economic system.[55] That is, the U.S. was already a capitalist society before entrepreneurs began adapting the industrial system to the pursuit of profit. Thus capitalism, which spawned the industrial revolution, was channeled into the forms of organization required by industrialization.

The principal advantage of the industrial system is its ability to exploit the momentum of growth. When factories increase production, the numbers of units produced goes up but the cost per unit goes down. These economies of scale result from higher productive efficiency and offer greater profit margins, as well as competitive advantages in the marketplace.[56] To early capitalists, the allure of growth proved so irresistible that they sought any means available to expand the size of their operations and create larger businesses. Soon, they discovered that the benefits of growth reached beyond the domain of commerce into the arena of politics. President Ulysses S. Grant enjoyed the company of Jay Cooke, Jim Fiske, and Jay Gould, all wealthy directors of large railroad companies. Leland Stanford, a partner in the Southern Pacific Railroad monopoly, later became governor of California and endowed a university with his profits.[57] Larger business organizations wielded more influence with government. Moreover, their political weight could be coupled with their economic advantage to gain and protect large shares of the market.[58]

Sheer size, however, also brought problems. Huge firms that dominated their industries also suffered growing pains. For example, in 1841, the Western Railroad's efforts to run three trains in each direction between Albany and Worcester, thereby maximizing the productivity of the rail line, led to a head-on collision with fatalities. Western's size had outstripped management's ability to control scheduling and communications.[59] Corporate growth created a crisis of control, whose solution was found in the development of a system of supervision.[60] Not surprisingly, railroads, where the crisis first surfaced, contributed the first solutions. At the New York and Erie Railroad, a general superintendent named Daniel C. McCallum pioneered the system that evolved modern administrative management. He recognized that an organization's principal administrator should be the focus of both authority and communication. The key to controlling a complex organization such as a railroad rests in the continuous flow of information from the bottom to the top. He restructured the railroad and stimulated the flow of information through hourly, daily, weekly, and monthly reports on all matter of operations. He received many of these reports by telegraph and condensed them into statistical summaries; and, as part of the reorganization of 1855, he drew what was probably the first organization table.[61] The chart itself is lost, but Alfred Chandler has preserved a description:

> The design of the chart was a tree whose roots represented the president and the board of directors; the branches were the five operating divisions and the service departments, engine repairs, car, bridge, telegraph, printing, and the treasurer's and the secretary's offices; while the leaves indicated the various local ticket, freight, and forwarding agents, subordinate superintendents, train crews, foremen, and so forth.[62]

McCallum's innovation of technique was followed by communication breakthroughs, such as the memo, whereby executives learned to rationalize their own internal communications.[63] These inventions and others became the basis for administrative management and the massive corporate bureaucracies that exist today.

Once adopted, administrative management required two commitments from managers. First, they needed to believe in the superiority of rational decision making over intuitive decision making. They could not allow themselves the excitement of wheeling and dealing in the manner of their predecessors. As McCallum wrote to the president of the New York and Erie, "It is very important, however, that principal officers should be in possession of all the information necessary to enable them to judge correctly as to the industry and efficiency of subordinates of every grade."[64] Henry Varnum Poor, the influential editor of the *American Railroad Journal*, also noted this new attitude, "By the energies and genius of our superintendents, it [railroad management] is approaching the position of an accurate science; not limited to theoretical discussion, but developing reliable formulae for the practical estimates of the engineer."[65] By contrast, Jay Gould wheeled and dealed himself into an enormous railroad empire by manipulating stocks and favors. But his machinations risked the entire enterprise more than once.[66] With the new attitude in mind, his successors eschewed such intuitive behavior in favor of the security of systematic planning and organization. If decisions were to be made systematically, then the decision makers would need to make informed judgments. The new approach demanded more information.

Second, rational decision making could not function without clear and easy access to whatever information managers deemed necessary. Like the New York and Erie, large firms began to sprout staff departments. More personal styles of management became inappropriate as proprietors found themselves unable to attend to every detail or to visit every factory owned by the company. Entrepreneurs who started these growing enterprises often did not have the personalities or skills to run complex organizations. When Alfred P. Sloan came to General Motors in 1918, he noted to his surprise that, "...no one knew how much was being contributed—plus or minus—by each division to the common good of the corporation."[67] Staff departments were the solution. They, and the new middle managers that came with them, introduced new forms of administration and coordination. Sloan stood at the cusp of this transition within General Motors. "Mr. [William C.] Durant had been able to operate the corporation in his own way, as the saying goes, 'by the seat of his pants.' When Sloan took over, he led an administration made up of men with very different ideas about business administration, men who desired a highly rational and objective mode of operation."[68]

Sloan's organization study of GM was the vehicle. He recommended broad changes, among them: 1) Determining the actual functioning of the various departments, not only in relation to one another, but in relation to the central organization; 2) Developing statistics to determine the relation between net return and the invested capital of each operating division; 3) Centralizing the power of all executive functions in the president, as chief executive of the corporation; and, 4) Limiting to the practical minimum, the number of executives reporting directly to the president.[69] The last two, in particular, required building an enormous infrastructure to funnel information from the distant corners of the corporation to the president through a series of progressive summaries. General Motors came to be administered by employees who were not owners but professionals. Similarly, the Gambles, Swifts, Armours, Eastmans, Bordens, Deerings, and McCormicks gradually removed themselves from operational control of the firms they had founded. They owned but no longer managed.[70]

In the end, belief in rational decision making, along with commitment to institutionalize it in an information system, resolved the crisis of control and laid the foundation for the "technostructure" observed in all corporations of the 20th century.[71] Corporations now devote a large proportion of their resources to maintaining their managerial bureaucracies by purchasing information from outside vendors as well as from internal sources. So successfully do managers apply these organizational techniques that they regularly seek to rationalize activities beyond the firm as well. Large corporations try to manage the marketplace itself by influencing prices and encouraging specific demand for their products, as John Kenneth Galbraith notes in *The New Industrial State*:

> Although advertising will be thought the central feature of this management, and is certainly important, much more is involved.... The management of demand consists of devising a sales strategy for a particular product. It also consists in devising a product, around which a sales strategy can be built. Product design, model change, packaging and even performance reflect the need to provide what are called strong selling points. They are thus as much a part of the process of demand management as an advertising campaign.[72]

The language of management refers to this as the "marketing mix." Its successful implementation requires the extension of the information infrastructure beyond the boundaries of the organization and into the affairs of all who come in contact with the market. Thus, corporate managers devise complex price, product, package, and promotion strategies to penetrate the media environments of consumers (For an analysis of media environments, see chapter 4).

Industrialization created the system that operationalized the profit motive within capitalism and transformed American values by introducing new ways to make decisions and accomplish goals. In this century, administrative management has been the dominant paradigm for decision making and has diffused far beyond industrial enterprises, even to interpersonal services like health care and religious organizations. It has become *the* culturally approved way to make decisions in all organized settings, so that even if intuition is the actual basis for making a judgment, the form of administrative management is followed. Information replaced intuition and tradition as the currency for making decisions, first within the corporation and later beyond it. Even though the goals of government are different from those of the corporation, it too has modeled itself along these same lines. McCallum and Sloan, and all of those who contributed to the building of industrial enterprises, instituted a new system of organization in response to the powerful stimulus of capitalism. Administrative management, as one characteristic consequence of the industrial revolution, contributed heavily to the establishment of an information infrastructure and an information economy.

Within the theme of capitalism and the industrial origins of the information society, one book merits special attention. In his influential book, *The Control Revolution*,[73] James Beniger presents the view that the information society emerged from within the industrial revolution.[74] He maintains that changes in the collection, processing and retrieval of information, developing during the last decades of the 19th century, led to increased dependence on formal and programmed decision making and resulted in greater control over organizations and all manner of activities in society. Prior to the industrial revolution material, processing operated at the pace of human motion, industrialization speeded up the pace of material processing so that direct human control became impossible. Starting with the railroads, industries encountered crises of control and each solved their particular dilemma by increased reliance on managerial techniques facilitated by information processing and communication technologies. In Beniger's words, "As the crisis of control spread through the material economy, it inspired a continuing stream of innovations in control technology."[75] The resulting revolution in control allowed increased reliance on programmed decisions, the only possible way to control large scale operations.

For Beniger, control depends on information processing and reciprocal communication, so that advances in these two areas resolved the crisis. Beniger sees these changes constituting so profound a shift in the ways in which humans organize themselves that he perceives the control revolution to be as momentous as the industrial revolution itself. He therefore rejects the notion that the information society emerged out of recent social and technological changes. Instead, the information society emerged out of the control revolution and continues as changes in control penetrate society.

Beniger amasses ample evidence to make the case that the forces set in motion by the industrial revolution required a subsequent control revolution, in order to prevent the new industrial economy from being overwhelmed by its own creations. By identifying the control revolution as a disjunctive shift in the rules for making decisions, he overcomes Bell's faulty definition of a revolution caused only by an increase in the rate of change. His analysis of the crisis and response within the railroads is superb and adds to Chandler's discussion in *The Visible Hand*.[76] In addition, Beniger carefully documents, industry by industry, the growth of administrative management techniques and corporate bureaucracies. However, like Bell, he largely ignores Schiller's critique, so that capitalism is dealt with more as context than cause. Beniger does distinguish between commercial, or mercantile, capitalism and industrial capitalism, and demonstrates how industrial capitalism acted as a precondition for the industrial revolution.[77] Furthermore, he recognizes the role played by capitalism in generating industrial markets for physical products and stimulating technological innovation. "If profit provided the incentive to process matter faster, then steam power provided the means."[78] But he does not consider the role of capitalism in stimulating the growth of information markets. To be fair, when seen from within the framework of his theory of control, economic man seems less important since human behavior is explained by a series of control revolutions embodying culture, bureaucracy, and technology.[79] Actually, Beniger's theory extends far beyond the industrial origins of the information society to encompass all living things, because as he says, "Life itself implies purposive activity and hence control...."[80] This broader theory, a general theory of life from an information perspective, presents interesting conclusions about the prevalence of controlling behaviors in all living things but falls outside the scope of our analysis here.[81] Therefore, his analysis adds to our understanding of industrialization as a cause of the information society, but does not integrate it with an analysis of the dynamics of economic behavior. Capitalism and industrialization appear as distinct non-interactive phenomena. In this regard, he typifies most of the literature.

The Information Society as a Species of Industrial Capitalism

Morse and McCallum traveled along the same lines. Morse took the first unwilling steps toward a technology that would facilitate the sale of information as a major commodity. McCallum laid the foundation for an organizational structure to exploit what Morse had wrought. From the 1850s, the growing demand for information to coordinate the production and distribution of all goods and services complemented the sale of information as a commodity. But if the roots of the information society are embedded in early American capitalism and industrialization, then what evidence exists to support the argument that the information society has grown gradually and continuously throughout the 19th and 20th centuries? After all, those holding to the post-industrial view could easily accept the changes of the 19th century while still claiming great discontinuities in the decades of the 1950s and '60s, the decades when post-industrial society supposedly began. Chapters 2, 3, and 4 provide evidence that the essential tendencies intensified throughout the 20th century. For our purposes here, patents, copyrights, and trademarks typify the uses of information as a commodity and represent gross measures of the exchange of certain kinds of information in the marketplace; similarly, the growth of the information workforce reflects the impetus of administrative management, as well as the labor demands of information markets. Taken together, they illustrate the interplay of capitalism and industrialization in forging the information society.

As the instrument by which Morse and Bell protected their ideas, the buying and selling of patents constitute the oldest information markets in the United States for which we have consistent data. Though patent registrations do not actually represent sales, they do indicate the growth of new ideas with commercial value. Moreover, as a function of population, they also offer a measure of the idea pool in society. Therefore, they present a good measure of the growth of a key resource of the information economy. When examined for rapid growth, the curve for patents issued per 100,000 population does show a dramatic increase, but that increase occurred during the 1850s and '60s, and continued into the 1890s. The discontinuity that might be expected in the decades when post-industrial theorists locate the revolution that engendered the information society does not appear in the data. Instead, the data reflect the disjuncture of the industrial revolution and, by association, the control revolution.

Copyrights and trademarks also represent a turn toward the commoditization of information and the rise of the information economy. In fact, copyright registrations do increase noticeably after 1970, in the years when the information economy became most visible. But the curve hardly demonstrates a disjuncture from the previous decades. The number of trademarks also rose rapidly between 1900 and 1930, the years when large scale consumer markets were established. And, as with copyrights, trademarks display significant growth during the decades associated with the information economy, all three reflecting the growing importance of information as a commodity. Still, industrial era interpretations suffice to explain the growth in each of the curves without having to resort to a break in history.

FIGURE 1-1

Patents, Copyrights, Trademarks, per Units of Population 1790–1990

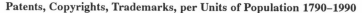

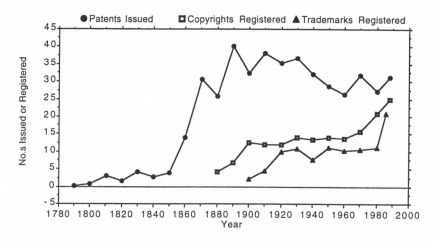

Source: Compiled from, Tables W99, W107, W82, A2 (1975). Historical statistics of the United States, colonial times to 1970 (Bicentennial Ed.). Washington, DC: GPO. Tables 1, 945, 975 (1981). Statistical abstract of the United States: 1981. Washington, DC: U.S. Bureau of the Census. Table 2, 886, 931 (1989). Statistical abstract of the United States: 1990 . Washington, DC: Bureau of the Census.

Note: The curves reflect the following units of population.
Patents Issued per 100,000 Population
Trademarks Registered per 100,000 Population
Copyrights Registered per 1,000 Population

Growth of information workers in the labor force is another good measure, especially since it reflects managerial demands and the sale of information.[82] In chapter 3 we analyze the information workforce extensively. See especially figures 3-9, 3-10, and 3-11, in chapter 3, but a quick review of some findings supports the data for patents, copyrights, and trademarks. Information workers also increased as a percentage of the labor force throughout the century. With the exception of the Great Depression, the numbers and percentage of information workers shows no significant change in slope between 1900 and 1990. Contrary to post-industrial interpretations that focus on the workforce in the 1950s and '60s, this data shows the information workforce becoming the largest of the four work sectors just prior to 1930. Thus, data on the information workforce conforms well to data on patents, copyrights, and trademarks, all indicating the emergence of an information economy in harmony with the industrial economy rather than in schism.[83]

Desire for profits and for rational solutions to problems of production and distribution led to the present configuration of information workers, information technologies, messages and channels. Capitalism *and* industrialism caused the expansion of those activities collectively defined as the information society. Nevertheless, we are just now getting a feel for the actual progression of the information society amidst a tidal wave of questions.

For example, how does information become a public resource and how does information become a commodity? Though aspects of the conversion of information from a public resource into a commodity have been analyzed in specific cases, we know from studying the framing of the Constitution and the development of the telegraph that these are complex phenomena.[84] After all, capitalism, which drives commoditization, acts amidst countervailing forces. Thinking of them as a tension provides greater understanding.

How do information occupations experience industrialization? Evidence presented in chapter 3 indicates that some white-collar work bears striking similarities to factory work. The experience of the current recession indicates that information jobs are susceptible to mechanization and that they differ in levels of susceptibility.[85] But categories for defining information work are still being worked out.

How does the movement toward the information society differ when capitalism is removed from the equation? The box included in this chapter conveys a hint of the differences. Further study of those industrialized societies that did not develop under capitalism will almost certainly provide clues to the relative influence of industrialization in forming information economies, while comparative analyses of the former Soviet Union, the United States, the United Kingdom, Japan, France, and Korea, to name a few, will further our understanding of the variety of interactions between capitalism and industrialization, i.e. of the different paths to the information society.

The key to understanding the information society depends on recognizing elements of both change and continuity. American industry is no longer hog butcher to the world, because it has changed, or more properly, evolved away from its earlier form. Instead, it is now educator, banker, entertainer, and data processor to the world, and for the same reasons as before—because of the profit motive and the industrial character of these activities.

To view the information society as unique or historically unprecedented, reinforces a myth, albeit a powerful one. Because of it, researchers mistook the early forms of industrialization—the smokestacks and the factories—for the entire range of possibilities. Schiller and his colleagues pierced the myth by identifying capitalism as a cause, but did not push their analysis to include industrialization. However, we now see the U.S. producing and distributing information as its primary economic activity precisely because capitalism remains the motivator and industrialism remains the organizing principle. Thus, between the ore cars and smoke stacks of the 19th century, and the satellites and microchips of the 20th century, lie changes that transformed the United States into an information society.

Notes

1. Heilbroner, R. L. (1977). *The economic transformation of America*. New York: Harcourt Brace Jovanovich. p. 95.
2. Williams, F. (1982). *The communications revolution*. Beverly Hills, CA: Sage. p. 230.
3. Machlup, F. (1962). *The production and distribution of knowledge in the United States*. Princeton, NJ: Princeton University Press.
4. Bell, D. (1976). *The coming of post-industrial society*. New York: Basic Books.
5. Porat, M. U. (1977). *The information economy: Definition and measurement*. No. OT Special Publication 77-12 (1). Washington DC: Department of Commerce/Office of Telecommunications.
6. Price, D. J. d. S. (1963). *Little science big science*. New York: Columbia University Press.
7. Eisenhower, D. D. (1960). Farewell Radio and Television Address to the American People, January 17, 1961. In *Public Papers of the Presidents of the United States, Dwight D. Eisenhower, 1960–61* (pp. 1035–40). Washington D.C.
8. Machlup, F. (1962) p. 6.
9. Bell, D. (1981). The social framework of the information society. In T. Forestor (Ed.), *The microelectronics revolution* (pp. 500–549). Cambridge, MA: MIT Press. Crawford, S. (1983). The origin and development of a concept: The information society. *Bulletin of the Medical Library Association, 71*(4), 380–385. Dizard, W. P. J. (1982). *The coming information age: An overview of technology, economics, and politics*. New York: Longman. Ochai, A. (1984). The emerging information society. *International Library Review, 16*(4), 367–372. Williams, F. (1982). *The communications revolution*. Beverly Hills, CA: Sage.
10. Bell, D. (1981).
11. Drucker, P. F. (1969). *The age of discontinuity*. New York: Harper and Row.
12. Bell, D. (1976).
13. Williams, F. (1982). *The communications revolution*. Beverly Hills, CA: Sage. But see also: Forester, T. (Ed.). (1981). *The microelectronics revolution: The complete guide to the new technology and its impact on society*. Cambridge, MA: MIT Press. Nora, S., & Minc, A. (1980). *The computerization of society: A report to the president of France*. Cambridge, MA: MIT Press. Toffler, A. (1980). *The third wave*. New York: William Morrow. In *The Control Revolution*, Beniger lists 75 authors who, between 1950 and 1984, identified major social transformations as the basis for their books. Beniger, J. R. (1986). *The control revolution*. Cambridge, MA: Harvard University Press (pp. 4–5).
14. Dizard, W. P. J. (1982). *The coming information age: An overview of technology, economics, and politics*. New York: Longman, p.12. Dizard's three-stage shift ignores the existence of hunting and gathering societies prior to the invention of agriculture.
15. Bell, D. (1976) pp. xvi–xix.
16. Bell, D. (1981). The social framework of the information society. In T. Forestor (Ed.), *The microelectronics revolution* (pp. 500–549). Cambridge, MA: MIT Press. Bell, D. (1983). Communication technology—For better or worse? In J. L. Salvaggio (Ed.). (1989), *Telecommunications: Issues and choices for society* (pp. 34–50). New York: Longman.
17. Rostow, W. W. (Ed.). (1963). *The economics of take-off into sustained growth*. New York: St. Martin's Press. Rostow, W. W. (1971). *The stages of economic growth* (2nd ed.). Cambridge, UK: Cambridge University Press. Rostow, W. W.

(1978). *The world economy: History & prospect*. Austin, TX: University of Texas Press. In *The world economy*, Rostow rejects the idea of a post-industrial society and holds to his original theory of five stages.

18. Nora, S., & Minc, A. (1978). *L'Informatisation de la societe*. La Documentation Francaise. Nora, S., & Minc, A. (1980). *The computerization of society: A report to the president of France*. Cambridge, MA: MIT Press.

19. Stearns, P. N. (1984). The idea of post-industrial society: Some problems. *Journal of Social History, 17*(Summer), 685-694. Harrington, M. (1977). Post-Industrial society and the welfare state. In L. Estabrook (Ed.), *Libraries in post-industrial society* (pp. 19-29). Phoenix, AZ: Oryx Press.

20. Harrington, M. (1977).

21. Bell, D. (1976) (pp. 51-52, 112).

22. Schiller, H. I. (1981). *Who knows: Information in the age of the Fortune 500*. Norwood, NJ: Ablex (pp. xii-xviii).

23. International criticisms of post-industrialism surfaced even before Bell published his book and have persisted. See, for example, Heilbroner, R. L. (1973). Economic problems of a 'post-industrial' society. *Dissent, 20*(2), 163-176. Julien, P. A., Lamonde, P., & Latouche, D. (1976). Post-Industrial society: Vague and dangerous concept. *Futuribles, 7*, 309-320. Ssewczyk, J. (1970). Totalna aliencja i prymtiywny hedonizm: Kapitalizm ery postindustrialnej [Total alienation and primitive hedonism: The post-industrial era capitalism]. *Studian Filozoficzne, 1*, 171-188. Stearns, P. N. (1984). The idea of post-industrial society: Some problems. *Journal of Social History, 17*(Summer), 685-694.

24. Schiller, H. I. (1981) (pp. 47-78, 12).

25. Mosco, V. (1982). *Push button fantasies*. Norwood, NJ: Ablex (pp. 2, 123-124).

26. Douglas, S., & Guback, T. (1984). Production and technology in the communication/information revolution. *Media, Culture and Society, 6*(July), 233-245.

27. Meehan, E. R. (1984). Towards a third vision of an information society. *Media, Culture and Society, 6*(July), 257-271.

28. Gandy, O. (1988). Book Review. *Journalism Quarterly, 65*(3), 785-787.

29. For shedding light on this debate at an early stage in our thinking, we are indebted to the members of the informal seminar on the information society, conducted from 1984-1986 at the Graduate School of Library and Information Science, UCLA, especially Donald Lamberton, Robert M. Hayes, Hal Borko, Donald O. Case, Christine Borgman, and Cynthia J. Shelton.

30. Baran, P. A., & Sweezy, P. M. (1966). *Monopoly capital*. New York: Monthly Review Press. Hacker, L. M. (1940). *The triumph of American capitalism*. New York: Simon and Schuster. Heilbroner, R. L., & Singer, A. (1984). *The economic transformation of America: 1600 to the present* (2nd ed.). New York: Harcourt Brace Jovanovich. Katz, M. B., Doucet, M. J., & Stern, M. J. (1982). *The social organization of early industrial capitalism*. Cambridge, MA: Harvard University Press.

31. (1981). *The story of the United States patent and trademark office*. Washington DC: Department of Commerce/Patent & Trademark Office, U. S. Government Printing Office, p. 3.

32. Machlup, F. (1958). *An economic review of the patent system* (No. 15). The Subcommittee on Patents, Trademarks, and Copyrights, of the Committee on the Judiciary, Washington DC: GPO, pp. 3, 21.

33. (1981). *The story of the United States patent and trademark office*. Washington DC: Department of Commerce/Patent & Trademark Office, U. S. Government Printing Office, p. v.

34. Machlup, F. (1958) p. 19. But see also Smith, A. (1776/1902). *An inquiry into the nature and causes of the wealth of nations.* New York: American Home Library, volume III, book IV, chapter 7, note 89.
35. Machlup, F. (1958) p. 22.
36. Series R 244-257, (1975). *Historical statistics of the United States, colonial times to 1970* (Bicentennial Ed.). Washington DC: GPO. The figure cited here represents those daily newspapers and periodicals which reported annual receipts of $500 or more. Brown lists 518 newspapers in 1820, but he probably includes those publications reporting receipts of less than $500. Brown, R. D. (1989). *Knowledge is power: The diffusion of information in early America, 1700–1865.* New York: Oxford.
37. The population of New York City as estimated in the 1850 census (1910). *Statistical abstract of the United States.* Washington DC: Bureau of the Census.
38. Schiller, D. (1981). *Objectivity and the news: The public and the rise of commercial journalism.* Philadelphia, PA: University of Pennsylvania Press (pp. 14–17). One should bear in mind that the penny press capitalized on widespread literacy among white men. Probably half could sign their names, a percentage as high as any among European nations. See Brown, R. D. (1989) (pp. 11–12).
39. December 17, 1844, House Executive Doc., No. 24, 28 Cong., 2 session, pp. 1–9.
40. Thompson, R. L. (1947). *Wiring a continent: The history of the telegraph industry in the United States 1832–1866.* Princeton, NJ: Princeton University Press (pp. 26, 27, 34).
41. Brooks, J. (1975). *Telephone: The first hundred years.* New York: Harper & Row, p. 40.
42. Watson, T. A. (1926). *Exploring life: The autobiography of Thomas A. Watson.* New York: D. Appleton (pp. 57–59).
43. Brooks, J. (1975) p. 55.
44. Houston was independently wealthy and did not care to profit from his invention, to Eastman's good fortune. Hammer, M. F. (1940). *History of the Kodak and its continuations: The first folding and panoramic cameras.* Walla Walla, WA: Pioneer Publications (pp. 33–37).
45. Marcus, A. I., & Segal, H. P. (1989). *Technology in America.* New York: Harcourt Brace Jovanovich (pp. 212–214, 176–177)
46. As newspapers changed from the broadsides of the 18th century, the innovation of the newsboy, initially a young white boy or a black man, aided newspaper advertising by appending a personal component to the message. Beniger, J. R. (1986). *The control revolution.* Cambridge, MA: Harvard University Press, p. 130. Brown, R. D. (1989). *Knowledge is power: The diffusion of information in early America, 1700–1865.* New York: Oxford, pp. 129, 261, 284]. Schiller, D. (1981). *Objectivity and the news: The public and the rise of commercial journalism.* Philadelphia, PA: University of Pennsylvania Press.
47. Schudson, M. (1984). *Advertising, the uneasy persuasion: Its dubious impact on American society.* New York: Basic Books, p. 156.
48. Beniger, J. R. (1986). *The control revolution.* Cambridge, MA: Harvard University Press (pp. 285, 330). Chandler, A. D. J. (1977). *The visible hand: The managerial revolution in American business.* Cambridge, MA: Harvard University Press (pp. 209–235).
49. Series F 1-5. (1975). *Historical statistics of the United States, colonial times to 1970* (Bicentennial Ed.). Washington DC: GPO. Beniger, J. R. (1986) p. 344.
50. Schudson, M. (1984) p. 168.
51. "The 'primary information sector' includes those firms which supply the bundle of information goods and services exchanged in a market context" Porat, M. U.

(1977) p. 4. Rubin and Huber rely on Machlup's concept of knowledge production which is very similar to information production and occurs, for economic purposes, within the knowledge industry sector. Rubin, M. R., & Huber, M. T., with Taylor, E.L. (1986). *The knowledge industry in the United States 1960–1980*. Princeton, NJ: Princeton, p. 3. Machlup, F. (1962). *The production and distribution of knowledge in the United States*. Princeton, NJ: Princeton University Press (pp. 44–45).

52. Braverman, H. (1974). *Labor and monopoly capital: The degradation of work in the twentieth century*. New York: Monthly Review Press, p. 59.

53. "To take an example, therefore, from a very trifling manufacture; but one in which the division of labor has been very often taken notice of; the trade of the pin-maker; a workman not educated to this business [which the division of labor has rendered a distinct trade], nor acquainted with the use of the machinery employed in it [to the invention of which the same division of labor has probably given occasion], could scarce, perhaps, with his utmost industry, make one pin in a day, and certainly could not make twenty.... I have seen a small manufactory of this kind where ten men only were employed, and where some of them consequently performed two or three distinct operations. But though they were very poor, and therefore but indifferently accommodated with the necessary machinery, they could, when they exerted themselves, make among them about twelve pounds of pins in a day. There are in a pound upward of four thousand pins of middling size." Smith, A. (1776/1902). *An inquiry into the nature and causes of the wealth of nations*. New York: American Home Library, pp. 44–45. Though Smith recognized the advantages of the division of labor, it was not yet recognizable as the industrial system.

54. Giddens, A. (1973). *The class structure of advanced societies*. New York: Hutchinson, Anchor Press, p. 141.

55. Lowell promised chaperoned dormitories next to his mill, in order to insure the respectability of his workers, most of whom hoped to accumulate dowries. Heilbroner, R. L., & Singer, A. (1984). *The economic transformation of America: 1600 to the present* (2nd ed.). New York: Harcourt Brace Jovanovich, p. 103.

56. Brownlee, W. E. (1974). *Dynamics of ascent: A history of the American economy*. New York: Knopf (pp. 104–105).

57. Josephson, M. (1934). *The robber barons: The great American industrialists 1861–1901*. New York: Harcourt Brace Jovanovich, pp. 80, 347. Stanford set aside a sizable parcel of land adjacent to Palo Alto, California, and named the university after his deceased son, Leland Stanford Junior, the university's official name.

58. Heilbroner, R. L. (1977). *The economic transformation of America*. New York: Harcourt Brace Jovanovich (pp. 102–104).

59. Beniger, J. R. (1986). *The control revolution*. Cambridge, MA: Harvard University Press (pp. 221–225).

60. Heilbroner, R. L. (1977) pp. 72–80.

61. An extensive treatment of McCallum's innovations can be found in Chandler, A. D. J. (1977). *The visible hand: The managerial revolution in american business*. Cambridge, MA: Harvard University Press (pp. 101–121).

62. Interestingly, McCallum's picturesque illustration did not last. Within a few years, the New York and Erie had adopted the abstract form of lines and boxes familiar today. Chandler, A. D. J. (1956). *Henry Varnum Poor: Business editor, analyst, and reformer*. Cambridge, MA: Harvard University Press. Although the McCallum's chart was reproduced in large numbers by Henry Varnum Poor, a search Schement conducted in libraries and antiquarian bookstores during 1985–1986 failed to locate a single surviving copy.

63. Yates, J. (1989). The emergence of the memo as a managerial genre. Academy of Management Review, 2(4), 485–510.
64. McCallum, D. C. (1956). Superintendent's report, March 25, 1856. Annual Report of the New York and Erie Railroad Company for 1855 [p. 39]. In A. D. J. Chandler (Ed.), *Railroads—the nation's first big business: Sources and readings*, p. 104. New York: Harcourt Brace & World.
65. (1855, Sept. 8). [Description of the first organization chart]. *American Railroad Journal, XXVIII*, 568.
66. Heilbroner, R. L. (1977). *The economic transformation of America*. New York: Harcourt Brace Jovanovich (pp. 72–74). O'Connor, R. (1962). *Gould's millions*. New York: Doubleday.
67. Sloan, A. P. J. (1963). *My years with General Motors*. New York: Doubleday, p. 48.
68. Sloan, A. P. J. (1963) p. 52. Durant later lost his fortune in the stock market crash of 1929 and died trying to recoup his lost riches.
69. Sloan, A. P. J. (1963) pp. 50, 53, 54.
70. Chandler, A. D. J. (1977). *The visible hand: The managerial revolution in american business*. Cambridge, MA: Harvard University Press, p. 414.
71. Galbraith, J. K. (1967). *The new industrial state*. New York: The New American Library (pp. 71–82).
72. Galbraith, J. K. (1967) p. 213.
73. Beniger, J. R. (1986). *The control revolution*. Cambridge, MA: Harvard University Press.
74. For another discussion from this point of view see Schement, J. R. (1989). The origins of the information society in the United States: Competing visions. In J. Salvaggio (Ed.). (1989). *The information society* (pp. 29–50). New York: Lawrence Erlbaum.
75. Beniger, J. R. (1986) p. 429.
76. Beniger, J. R. (1986) pp. 227–232. Chandler, A. D. J. (1977) pp. 101–121.
77. Beniger, J. R. (1986) pp. 122, 167, 169, 175.
78. Beniger, J. R. (1986) p. 169.
79. Beniger, J. R. (1986) p. 103, 112.
80. Beniger, J. R. (1986) p. 434.
81. Beniger, J. R. (1986) pp. 32–118.
82. Machlup, F., & Kronwinkler, T. (1975). Workers who produce knowledge: a steady increase, 1900 to 1970. *Weltwirtschaftliches Archiv., 111*(4), 752–759.
83. Although the information economy results from interactions of the forces of capitalism and industrialization, they are virtually inseparable when examining data at this level of abstraction.
84. Bates, B. J. (1990). Information as an economic good: a reevaluation of theoretical approaches. In B. D. Ruben & L. A. Lievrouw (Eds.), *Information and behavior* (pp. 379–394). New Brunswick, NJ: Transaction. Chamberlin, B. F., & Singleton, L. A. (1987). The law in an information society. In J. R. Schement & L. Lievrouw (Eds.). (1988). *Competing visions, complex realities: Social aspects of the information society* (pp. 121–139). Norwood, NJ: Ablex. Hayes, R. M. (Ed.). (1985). *Libraries and the information economy of California: A conference sponsored by the California state library*. Los Angeles, CA: GSLIS/UCLA. Hixson, R. F. (1985). Whose life is it anyway? Information as property. In B. D. Ruben (Ed.), *Information and behavior: Volume 1* (pp. 76–92). New Brunswick, NJ: Transaction. Intner, S. S., & Schement, J. R. (1987). The ethic of free service. *Library Journal* (1 October). Lyon, D. (1988). *The information society: Issues*

and illusions. Cambridge, UK: Polity Press. Mosco, V. (1989). *The pay-per-view society: Computers and communication in the information age.* Norwood, NJ: Ablex. Oettinger, A. G., Bergman, P., & Read, W. (1977). *High and low politics: Information resources for the '80s.* Cambridge, MA: Ballinger. Schiller, H. I. (1981). *Who knows: Information in the age of the Fortune 500.* Norwood, NJ: Ablex. Schiller, H. I. (1983). Information for what kind of society? In J. L. Salvaggio (Ed.). (1989). *Telecommunications: Issues and choices for society* (pp. 24–33). New York: Longman. Schiller, H. I. (1985). Privatizing the public sector: The information connection. In B. D. Ruben (Ed.), *Information and behavior: Volume 1* (pp. 387–405). New Brunswick, NJ: Transaction. Wessel, A. E. (1976). *The social use of information: Ownership and access.* New York: John Wiley & Sons. Williams, F., & Hadden, S. (1992). On the prospects for redefining universal service: From connectivity to content. *Information and Behavior, 4,* 49–63.

85. Downing, H. (1981). Word processors and the oppression of women. In T. Forestor (Eds.), *The microelectronics revolution* (pp. 275–287). Cambridge, MA: MIT Press. Schement, J. R., Curtis, T., & Lievrouw, L. A. (1985). Social factors affecting the success of introducing information technology into the workplace. In *48th annual meeting of the American society for information science*, (pp. 278–283). Knowledge Industry Publications Inc.

2

Interconnectedness

We are in great haste to construct a magnetic telegraph from Maine to Texas; but Maine and Texas, it may be, have nothing important to communicate—Henry David Thoreau[1]

One of Durkheim's insights concerned the role of integrative mechanisms under conditions of growing social heterogeneity. One of the concomitants of a growing division of labor, (differentiation), he argued, is an *increase* in mechanisms to coordinate and solidify the interaction among individuals with increasingly diversified interests.—Neil J. Smelser[2]

Of all the factors giving birth to the dawning of the Information Age, that which appears most personal and most global, is the degree to which everyone—and everything—seem to have become interconnected. Whether one measures personal contacts or the total volume of international telecommunication traffic, the increase*d* frequency of communication events is already striking and continues to accelerate. Even more impressive is the degree to which we have come to depend on these contacts. In fact, this increase in communication volume would be noteworthy even if we were merely flooding the network with small talk, as Thoreau feared would happen. But something much more important is underway. By increasing the flow of information, Americans are attempting to amplify the scale and scope of social organization. Interconnectedness is actually a technology for coping with interdependence.

The phenomenon of interconnectedness can be understood along three dimensions, each providing evidence of the same process underway. At the micro level, individuals experience interconnectedness as a change in the nature of their social relationships. For most people, this means an increase in the number of relationships, but a decrease in their depth. That is, we are in regular—if not frequent—contact with more people, but we don't know many of them very well. At the meso level, businesses and other organizations are developing new information structures and channels of communication, to cope with uncertainty in their environments. The development of social and material technologies—for the gathering and processing of information, as well as for the application of that information to decision-making—generates interconnectedness, and dominates the agenda of the business world. At the macro level, new institutions, and the technologies to support them, are coming into existence in order to accommodate demand for global interconnectedness in response to economic and environmental realities imposed upon all of the planet's inhabitants.

At first glance, the growth of interconnectedness at these three levels has the appearance of events entirely separate and unconnected; were Thoreau alive today he might make a comment similar to the one quoted above. But below the surface, the three phenomena are intertwined. In this chapter, we discuss these changes, their associated perceptions, and underlying causes, in order to describe those flows of information which create and maintain increasingly common, and commonly held, forms of interconnectedness.

Interconnectedness at the Micro Level

Eli Noam, the widely respected director of the Institute for Tele-Information at Columbia University's Business School, tells of his mother chiding him as mothers often do—but with an information age twist. "Eli," she says, "you never write, you never call, you never fax!" Mrs. Noam understands the basic reality of micro interconnectedness. At the level of personal interaction we all experience the information age as a variety of new communication media by which we maintain contact with an ever-growing number of social relationships.

Once, family gatherings were held three or four times a year, on holidays and at anniversaries of various sorts. But for most individuals today, assemblies of kin are rare events, with fewer in attendance, and mostly occasioned by weddings and funerals. With 25% of all households containing a single individual, the personal interdependencies which have tied families together are now virtually impossible for large portions of the population to maintain.[3] Furthermore, the geographic dispersion of most extended families effectively discourages large group meetings. So, to keep in touch with family members, we now rely on frequent electronic contact. In recognition of this fact of life, special marketing programs by telephone companies appeal to this necessity and sell low cost or flat-rate long distance services specifically targeted at people who want to reach family and friends.

For others who seldom see extended family members, the office has become a surrogate family. There, a person can find confidantes, parental figures, hierarchies organized by age, imposed obligations, and power struggles for influence similar to those played out by family members in earlier times. In lives where little is constant, it is one place where, once formed, relationships can be reinforced daily. But as corporations relentlessly thin out their information workforces, even the office appears less permanent. Here, too, there is a tendency to substitute telecommunication interfaces for some of the face-to-face, give-and-take of "family" life.

TABLE 2-1
Indicators of Material Technologies of Information—1929, 1987
[per 1,000 members of the population]

	1929	1987
Telephones[1]	160	650 (1982)
Radio/Audio equipment shipped, domestic[2]	40	260
Phonographs shipped, domestic[2]	6	190
Video equipment shipped, domestic[2]	[na][3]	150
Video/Audio equipment shipped, imported[2]	[na][3]	1,200

Source: Tables R1-12, P231-300, W96-106 (1975). Historical statistics of the United States, colonial times to 1970 (Bicentennial Ed.). Washington DC: GPO. Tables 2, 917, 1353, 1352, (1989). Statistical abstract of the United States: 1990. Washington DC: Bureau of the Census.

[1] Includes company, service, and private. No statistics for numbers of telephones are published in the statistical abstracts after 1982.

[2] What is a phonograph, or a radio? In 1929, only radio receivers, phonographs, and radio-phonograph combinations existed. But in 1987, the range of possible types and combinations were so diverse, that the construction of discrete categories poses an impossible challenge for the researcher. Therefore, the following operational categories apply to this table: radio/audio equipment includes radios, compact systems, headphones, automobile sound systems, and radio-phone combinations; phonographs include amps., compact disc players, speakers, receivers, turntables, tape decks, portable tape equipment, racked systems, and cartridges; video equipment includes color TVs, black and white TVs, videocassette recorders, camcorders, projection TVs, video cameras, videocassette players, and videodisc players.

[3] Not available.

For example, among computer users, electronic bulletin boards and electronic mail support some social functions, by replacing face-to-face settings with electronic text. These faceless communities of communication have led to the formation of special interest groups (SIGs) around such diverse topics as the use of a particular piece of computer hardware, evaluation of software, advice on personal experiences, and even shared emotional support among single parents. Plus, for those whose life is so itinerant or isolated that they lack a spontaneous social group with whom to communicate electronically, there are even commercial services which—for a fee—provide discussion groups on a variety of topics by means of conference calls.

Tables 2-1 and 2-2—"Indicators of Material Technologies of Information 1930-1988"; and, "Indicators of Social Technologies—1930, 1988"—give some feel for the rates of increase in the use of media, along with the vast scale of interconnections. The overall picture which emerges is one of ever increasing density, although with some significant counter trends e.g., illiteracy has gone up, and fewer people read daily newspapers. Yet, though statistical abstractions of this sort attest to the astounding increase in messages transmitted, they do not reflect the unquantifiable texture of life.

TABLE 2-2
Indicators of Social Technologies of Information—1930, 1988
(per 1,000 members of the population, unless otherwise noted)

	1930	1988
Percent Illiterates in the Population[1]	4.3	8.2 1986
Annual volume of mail.	22,000	65,500
Daily circulation, newspapers[2]	320	260
Avg. daily telephone conversations	670	6,900
Advertising expenditures[5]	$2,100	$48,000

Source: Tables H664-668, R172-187, R224-231, R1-12, W96-106, T444-471 (1975). Historical statistics of the United States, colonial times to 1970 (Bicentennial Ed.). Washington DC: GPO. Tables 2, 911, 928, 918, 932 (1989). Statistical abstract of the United States: 1990. Washington, DC: Bureau of the Census. "Illiteracy Rates by State," Harris, S., & Harris, L. (Eds.). (1986). The teacher's almanac 1986-1987, pp. 239-245. New York: Harper.

[1] In 1930, persons 14 years of age or older were considered illiterate if they could not read or write in any language. Information was obtained from direct questions in the census. No comprehensive illiteracy statistics have been published in the statistical abstracts since 1970, when illiteracy was listed as 1.2% [table 234 (1981). Statistical abstract of the United States: 1981. Washington DC: U.S. Bureau of the Census.]. According to the English Language Proficiency Survey published by the Department of Education in 1986, 13% of the nation was considered illiterate. However, this survey judged illiteracy in relation to the ability to read and write English. When adjusted to correspond to the census definition, the figure is closer to 8.2%, an increase of 7% over 1970.

[2] Data collected on 30 Sept.

[3] Per 10,000 population.

[4] Not available.

[5] 1930 figures do not differentiate among types of advertising. For 1988, figures include national and local advertising for newspapers, magazines, farm publications, television, radio, yellow pages, direct mail, business papers, outdoor, and miscellaneous.

For example, despite its ubiquity, we don't really know very much about the social uses of the telephone. Apart from pioneering studies by Colin Cherry, Martin Mayer, A. A. L. Reid, Emanuel A. Schegloff, and David Lester, we know little about the social uses of this 120 year-old medium.[4] If this is the case, it is hard to know how much telephonic communication directly substitutes for what was once accomplished by personal visits to others' homes, random meetings on walks through the neighborhood, or strolls around the town square. The best we can say is that the dramatic increase in telecommunications traffic by residential users indicates a change in communication patterns by individuals, much of which must be social communication.

In addition, the rapid increase in traffic via electronic networks, reflected in the statistics, implies a rapid increase in the total flow of personal communication. Still, we lack data of comparable reliability on the quantity of face-to-face communication during the same period. And since it is hard to construct any quantitative measure of face-to-face social communication, there is no real evidence of an increase or a decline. Thus, it might be argued that the total amount of interactions has not changed, only an increase in the percentage which is mediated. But if this were so, increased use of electronic media as channels of social communication would represent a substitution of personal interactions by mediated forms. In itself this would comprise a significant transformation in patterns of communication, as well as in the nature of social contacts—and it would comprise a key feature of interconnectedness. Yet there is no reason to believe that the number of interactions experienced by individuals today remains at the level experienced at the beginning of the century. Conventional wisdom points to increased interactions.

Ron Rice has described this proliferation of contacts and suggests that it offers a perceived advantage by making use of the maximum number of sources of information.[5] Since technologies such as computer bulletin boards, electronic mail, and voice messaging make it possible to stay in touch with a large number of people, the competitive professional person can develop a network of contacts who are viewed as potential information resources in the pursuit of career advancement. Rice points out that this strategy tests the ability to stay in touch with people encountered outside of the normal routine of meetings. But now an individual may exploit new technologies to develop numerous information-sharing relationships with people never actually met in person. In these new relationships the goal is neither the person nor the relationship, but information. For example, regular participants in computer bulletin boards sometimes know each other by aliases and communicate over long periods without ever meeting in person, talking on the phone, or even knowing each other's real names. The value of such relationships is in the information which is shared. Of course, a bulletin board is an extremely public communication medium, where every participant can read every comment, without necessarily replying. Nevertheless, each contributing member is motivated to contribute, since the nature of a bulletin board is transactional. One's compensation for contributing information comes from the information contributed by others.

Yet in the big picture, the desire to monitor as much information as possible leads frequently to information overload. As a result, techniques and tools for screening information become the only means of coping—and one screening technique is simply to demand reciprocity of information flow. With electronic mail and voice messaging systems, the advantages of sharing stand out with even greater clarity. People who do not regularly return messages or do not contribute fairly to the exchange tend to be dropped from other people's distribution lists. Those who do not give as much as they are given are cut off, though exceptions may be made for those of substantially higher status or power. In such a case, having the ear of the powerful may be as important as getting their input.

Other likely screening techniques have less to do with equity than with having the time to review the information on hand. Typically professionals and executives subscribe to periodicals which pile up unread on their desks or bookshelves. At best they may hope to scan the tables of contents of every issue. In response, executives in many industries now receive expensive newsletters electronically or in hard copy. Crammed with brief syntheses from data sources and trade literatures, their purpose is to advance awareness of important developments. Yet these, too, despite their cost, often go unread or even unopened. Whatever the screening techniques—even if they are irrational— the resulting selection process leaves the individual with a pattern of sources of information and contacts, each varying in degree of impersonality and idiosyncrasy. It is with regard to these strategies, stimulated by the need to cope with overflowing information, that life in the information age has changed fundamentally. In chapter four we discuss the motivating logics for screening information in media environments.

Still, it should be noted that the experience of depending on strangers did not arise with the information age. The effects of urbanization, the institutional substitution of functions once performed by the extended family, and the effect of job mobility on family and community ties, have long been observed in industrial societies.[6] Now as then, the trend continues toward more relationships of less depth, in which we receive little identification from others and provide little of ourselves.

Yet, if interconnectedness is a hallmark of the information society, how can it be that isolation is so prevalent? Back before the old industrial workforce gave way to the information workforce, and before the popularization of the idea of information, Robert Ezra Park—a mentor to Harold Innis at the University of Chicago; and, therefore, an intellectual ancestor to Marshall McLuhan—examined the range of interpersonal interactions emerging in the new urban settings created by industrialization.[7] He studied interactions on the basis of their depth and distinguished between primary and secondary relationships.

In primary relationships, individuals connect within a "primary group," where the individual defines his or her personality through the set of identifications experienced within the group. For example, members of a long-standing office work group will come to know a good deal about each other's family lives and past experiences, along with work performance, so that individuals in a primary group experience the other members in all or most of their roles. On the other hand, secondary relationships are those in which individuals are linked with regard to only one role relationship. They have a unidimensional quality although they may have relatively long duration, as well as significance in the lives of the individuals thus connected. Year after year, a commuter may exchange pleasantries with the same conductor of the same train or the vendor at the corner newsstand. Over time, the conductor and the news vendor may even provide the commuter with special favors. Similarly, in large organizations two individuals may play out a pair of interdependent roles for most of their lives and never go beyond the limits of that one interaction with each other. Park's point is that our dealings with each other are of different depths. We relate to some people in such a variety of ways that we come to know them as complete individuals, sharing aspects of personality with significant depth. Others we relate to only in one kind of interaction, knowing them with regard to only one of their roles. Park observed that urban settings were particularly characterized by a high proportion of secondary relationships.

Analyzing the same urban phenomena, Talcott Parsons referred to the same range of interactions as particularistic versus universalistic.[8] Particularistic relationships occur when we engage someone whom we know. That is, whatever the depth of our knowledge of an individual with whom we connect, we know we are interacting with a particular individual. By contrast, Parsons referred to universalistic interactions as anonymous relations where we do not distinguish the particular individual who is playing a role from any other who might be in it. That is, we simply treat the interaction as one between ourselves and the role. Though they both addressed the growing importance of relations between strangers, Park focused on the depth of knowledge we carry about those with whom we interact, while Parsons concentrated on individuality versus anonymity.

Park and Parsons formed their theories at a time when the information workforce was invisibly overtaking the industrial workforce, and their ideas influenced several generations of social observers. But as the information society has become visible, Erving Goffman's theories have dominated. Goffman refers to individuals who are involved in a relationship as its "ends." He further distinguishes between "anchored relationships"—in which each person identifies the other and is, in turn, identified—versus "anonymous relationships"—in which a pattern of mutual treatment is socially called for despite the fleeting and impersonal nature of the interaction. By accentuating the anchors, Goffman builds on Park's concept of primary and secondary relationships.

As long as society remained agricultural and small in scale, most individuals experienced a pattern of interactions where primary relationships outnumbered secondary relationships. But the coming of industrialization drew farmers from the countryside into the cities and into the new workforces concentrating there. Interconnectedness in these emerging urban environments shifted the mix of relationships and increased the total number of potential interactions. In his analysis of industrial society and the increasingly specific division of labor that came with it, Ferdinand Toennies took a different tack from Goffman when he observed a decrease in the number of primary relationships coupled with an increase in the number of secondary, or unidimensional, relationships.[9] The movement from agricultural villages and clan societies to urban industrial societies led to an increase in the numbers of people with whom one individual was forced to interact, along with a decrease in the complexity of relationships and the time spent in them.

Toennies's observations of the effect of the industrial revolution on communities described the transition from a Gemeinschaft society—in which individuals share primary relationships in an organic community, i.e., one which exists regardless of purposes being pursued—to a Gesellschaft society—in which there is a reason for the existence of the community in the form of a shared purpose. As a result of this change individuals relate to each other in secondary relationships, in terms of their roles with regard to the pursuit of their shared purpose.

In the information age, the drift away from primary relationships raises further questions about the nature of community. At the same time as electronic media have allowed us to communicate without regard to time and distance, we have become more purposive about the nature of our relationships. We are no longer limited to membership in the community of those physically around us, but are capable of defining the nature of the group, i.e., community with which we share common interests and purposes. In fact, we find it possible to define ourselves as citizens of a number of different communities. These communities may be professional, avocational, political, recreational, or organized around any interests shared with others.

The web of communication which binds these new communities together may be supported by occasional meetings and frequent electronic communication, or solely by some communication medium such as an electronic bulletin board. To be sure, we still experience organic communities around family, ethnic identification, and neighborhood. It is also true that friendships and other characteristics of organic communities may develop within the most purposive communities. But the trend which Toennies observed appears accelerated by increasing demands on individuals to seek information across widening horizons from sources whose relationships with us will remain "anonymous," in Goffman's terms, and "universalistic," in Parsons's terms, and to whom we can only relate through the communication media which support information age interconnectedness.

One final point needs to be made on the phenomenon of micro-interconnection. There is no evidence—nor should it be inferred from what is written here—that new methods of social interaction made possible by a variety of communication media are replacing face-to-face relationships. People still need direct social contact with those around them. Instead, the trend is toward developing relationships through the use of communication media, and adding them to those which are face-to-face. We increasingly find it necessary to extend our contacts and relationships beyond our physical surroundings, in order to do our jobs and to feel that we understand our world. As we increasingly share our purposes—be they professional, political, recreational or any other—with a dispersed group of individuals, we turn to new technologies, and seek to transform those individuals into a community. By exploiting various media, we develop secondary relationships that were previously impossible.

The combination of communication technologies and urban environments forces us to deal with anonymous relationships to which we would otherwise never have been exposed. It may even be that, because we have the capacity for developing purposive communities without regard to time and distance, we will have fewer secondary relationships which are face-to-face. After all, we can choose those with whom we interact for specific purposes from among a larger audience and may select distant partners for interaction over those close at hand. In addition, by using electronic media to overcome the limitations of time and distance, we can maintain some primary relationships which would otherwise have become impossible.

If the overall pattern is one of adding new relationships rather than replacing face-to-face interactions with mediated interactions, then from the point of view of the individual, increased interconnectedness is perceived as a rise in the number of electronically-mediated social interactions, especially in terms of secondary and anonymous relationships. What Park, Parsons, Goffman, and Toennies did not fully anticipate is that a growing proportion of secondary and anonymous contacts are with people seldom, if ever, met face-to-face.

Interconnectedness at the Meso Level

Just as an increase in interconnectedness can be observed at the micro or individual level, a parallel increase can be observed at the meso level, i.e., within and among organizations, especially business firms. Also facilitated by information technologies, meso interconnectedness results from organizational responses to changes in the economic environment.

The consequences of growing interconnectedness in organizations were noted in the early 1980s, though hints had surfaced at least a decade earlier in the writings of Galbraith and Bell.[10] In a pioneering article, George P. Huber drew attention to interconnectedness as a key to the success of organizations operating in changing environments.[11] Though he does not suggest a change in the dominant paradigms of capitalism and industrialism, he assumes that "post-industrial society will be a radically different environment for organizations than was industrial society," and that "the designs of organizations in post-industrial society will be qualitatively different from those of previous organizations."[12] Though his adoption of the language of post-industrial theory confuses the background to his thesis, his point is that successful organizations will be characterized by, "more and increasing knowledge, more and increasing complexity, and more and increasing turbulence."[13] His insight underscores the significance to interconnectedness.

Organizations seeking to adapt to this new environment will find that their structures and processes for information acquisition and distribution will have to become more managed, more continuous, and more elaborate. Likewise, their structures and processes for decision making will have to become more streamlined, in order to make decisions more frequently and faster; and, the turbulence of competition will require that innovations in organizational structures and processes be implemented more quickly and more frequently. From this perspective, firms must develop new information strategies to reduce uncertainties in the environments in which they compete. However, organizational responses vary by role. With the responsibility for tactics, managers perceive themselves under direct pressure from the rigors of competition. With the responsibility for strategy, senior executives share a widespread perception that firms are locked in a struggle for a relatively finite set of global resources, leading to an increasingly organized market. Belief in a steady increase in the level of organization of the market is not news and can be traced all the way back to Durkheim.[14]

Not surprisingly, managers of business organizations view information as an economic good, or, more specifically, as a resource to be exploited in the pursuit of profit. They adopt the economist's view of information as equal to the reduction of uncertainty. They focus on the potential for reducing uncertainty in an environment of increased information complexity as the key to the survival of firms in the information age.[15] Thus, in the most recent reformulation of the business world, information emerges as a key resource compelling managers to seek the optimum balance in the distribution of information assets. For their part, management experts, such as Paul R. Lawrence and Davis Dyer, or Michael Hammer and James Champy, conclude that success demands a balance between two kinds of information systems—those that maintain efficiency by integrating control, and those that maintain innovativeness by facilitating market relations among differentiated divisions.[16]

In fact, in one more instance of the persistence of paradigms tied to industrialism this theme of a balance between integration and differentiation represents the reinvention of a discourse going back to the theories of Max Weber. Weber addressed it in his classic study of the sociology of industrialism, *The Theory of Social and Economic Organization*, and it is also a principal theme in Parsons' and Smelser's analysis, *Economy and Society*.[17] More recently, it has figured in a debate over the most efficient technology of economic organization. The enduring question is how to maximize profits. Should managers develop organizational hierarchies designed to gather and process information necessary for integration, coordination, and control; or, should they rely on internal and external market relations that encourage firms—and divisions within firms—to generate information and create knowledge, in order to innovate and specialize?[18]

Although the language of capitalism stresses the virtues of the free market as the most efficient distributor of resources, corporate managers are loath to trust the vicissitudes of the marketplace. They prefer to rely on the power of their own organizations. In so doing, they maximize control over resources within their firms, with the intent to extend that control to the marketplace in what Galbraith called the management of demand.[19]

Chandler documented this tension at mid-century, at a time when managers were opting for differentiation by adopting divisional organizational structures in place of line and staff models.[20] He observed that in some large firms, controlling the business through an integrated line and staff hierarchy resulted in excessive delay and imposed the weight of orthodoxy on operational units, thereby reducing the firm's ability to innovate and to adapt to its environment. Divisional structures offered a response to this problem, by delegating responsibility for adaptation and innovation to the divisional units, while maintaining overall responsibility at the level of the general offices or corporate headquarters. Classic examples of this pattern of organizational change can be seen in the development of a divisional structure at General Motors, in the 1920s, to compete with an integrated Ford, or in the development of a divisional structure at General Electric in the 1950s.[21]

In the 1970s and '80s, more extreme examples of the divisional model have been noted, such as at the Dana Corporation, where management organized their general offices to employ a tiny number of people and to act as internal consultants to a large number of highly independent wholly-owned subsidiary companies.[22] Even more recently, the Asea Brown Boveri conglomerate has attracted attention for a similar organizational design.[23] In effect, divisional structures foster the advantages of innovative market behavior by means of competition within and among relatively independent divisions, while, at the same time, capturing many of the efficiencies of integration through hierarchical control from the head office.

Perhaps the most recently celebrated attempt by a large organization is IBM's creation, in the early 1980s, of an entirely independent unit to develop the personal computer, after a series of failures to develop such a product in the same divisions which had developed their more traditional lines of mainframe computer machinery.[24] Currently, the computer giant has taken a page from Asea Brown Boveri's book and is in the process of restructuring itself entirely into divisions.

As profoundly as the application of the divisional model has shaped the structure of corporations, it was only a first step in a series of attempts to respond to the information needs of simultaneous integration and differentiation. By 1975, when Chandler revisited the debate, he concluded that the divisional structure created its own problems. For example, general offices often had little if any access to information, other than what they got from the divisions.[25] Moreover, general office executives were likely to have been promoted from—and to maintain sympathy with—the divisions, thereby compromising the original intent of detachment. Consequently, leadership in the general office found it difficult to exercise independent review of, and control over, the divisions. Instead, general officers were placed in the position of ratifying the divisions' policies ex post facto.

However, at the very moment of Chandler's pessimistic reassessment, information and telecommunication technologies were being deployed, which made it possible for general office staffs to reassert themselves by accessing information independently of the divisions. Once executives comprehended these advantages, the subsequent demand for information has driven the development of all manner of information technologies, which, in turn, have further encouraged the restructuring of firms like the Dana Corporation and Asea Brown Boveri. In the twenty years since Chandler wrote, international data networks, distributed databases, and decision support systems have been implemented to provide general offices with exactly the kind of independent sources of information for which he noted the need.[26]

The matrix organization represents one response to these developments. In this model, project teams come together to solve previously defined problems. Highly independent in their operations, the specialist members of each team, nevertheless, reports to a manager within their functional group, as well as to a team leader. In this context, dual reporting and dual responsibility is designed to foster independence in the project teams while maintaining integration in the organization as a whole, by consciously violating the old dictum of hierarchical organizations that each employee should answer to one—and only one—supervisor. Drucker, among others, has speculated that the matrix organization represents an evolution toward an even more ad hoc organizational structure—one which he says cannot yet be named, diagrammed, or fully described because of its novelty.[27] To some commentators, it appears that the nature of these new structures is so dependent on the application of new information technologies that the proper place to observe their incubation is in the research groups in firms that design and manufacture those technologies.[28]

At its furthest extension, the trend toward interconnectedness in business organizations goes beyond the boundaries of individual firms to involve cooperative arrangements among firms. These arrangements themselves may take various forms, but they commonly exist somewhere between the negotiation-at-arm's-length of a market relationship, and the authority-cum-integration that occurs when one firm simply buys another and absorbs it. Of the specific technologies facilitating these patterns, some, like electronic data interchange (EDI) are specifically designed to expedite market relations. But other electronic messaging services, like the Internet, are showing rapid adoption for use in traffic among firms.[29] Furthermore, this increased flow of information among organizations parallels the increased flow within, as managers push for greater coordination and innovation.[30] In other words, the potential rewards for exploiting information resources in turbulent markets means that firms must become learning organizations, and the shortest path to the knowledge they need often leads to cooperation with other firms which have some of that knowledge.[31] Thus are formed alliances where the firms involved may be each others' suppliers, customers, or competitors. In some cases, such as in the practice of bench marking, the two firms may have no formal relation except for the desire to interact and learn together.

At the heart of this experimentation lies the need for rapid, innovative, and flexible responses, as well as efficient, coordinated, and integrated responses. As a result, one common trend in all of these experiments with organizational structure is that the number of both internal and external channels of communication increases at the same time that the flow of information becomes more complex. Therefore, as most managers perceive an ever growing demand for information, they are actually experiencing an increase in interconnectedness.

In the last third of the century, the twin pursuit of differentiation and integration has led to innovations that have tended to flatten organizational structures by replacing the main source of information gathering and processing—middle management—with information technologies. But contrary to the interpretations most often heard in popular analyses of American business, the motivation for reducing layers of middle management has not been driven by an inexorable tide of computer development.[32] Rather, the replacement of middle-level managers by information systems has resulted from conscious decisions made by higher level executives seeking to adapt their organizations to the particular demands made on them by their specific markets—in much the same ways that their predecessors approached the problems of scale and administration in the last decades of the 19th century.[33] In fact, one lesson to be drawn from the recurrence of technology replacing labor is that information occupations once thought to be relatively high status, such as those held by middle managers, are industrial in nature. For although society perceives the external trappings of managerial work as separating those who perform it from those who do factory work by the gulf of class, in fact middle-managers and assembly-line workers lose their jobs according to the same hard calculus by which work tasks are subdivided and mechanized.[34] Long seen as different in kind because of their locus in white collar work, the loss of unprecedented numbers of information jobs in the current recession has exposed the industrial essence of managerial information occupations.

Living through a time of change allows us to observe the unfolding patterns first hand. However, being within those patterns, we inevitably watch the course of change from a poor vantage point. Even so, we can already discern some aspects of advancing interconnectedness at the meso level. Organizations, especially business firms, are required to constantly restructure and reinvent themselves. In each successive change they find themselves in more need of information about themselves and their environment, including other organizations. Satisfying this need they become increasingly interconnected, and increasingly turn to new and more capable information and communication technologies. The flow of organizational information grows unabated; its goal, to coordinate and integrate, to innovate and specialize.

Interconnectedness at the Macro Level

Global interconnectedness has been a feature of images of the information society at least since Marshall McLuhan predicted the arrival of the global village.[35] Promoted into orthodoxy by the mass media, the current version holds that the world is becoming smaller and more interdependent. As realization of the value of information resources has grown in tandem with observations of ever increasing use of information media in the households of the industrial nations, global interdependency has come to be associated with communication and the flow of information.

During the Cold War era conventional wisdom visualized the organization of international politics and economics as a bipolar system.[36] Each nation traveled in the orbit of one or the other superpower, careening between gravitational attractions. The two powers created and dominated the institutions of coordination and control for their separate spheres. And no nation remained unaffected. Whether the regime was ever truly bipolar continues to be a matter of controversy; but with some exceptions, there existed two largely exclusive sets of institutions and processes aimed at achieving global social organization, each one based on distinct agreements among national units of sovereignty.

On the market side, the Bretton Woods agreements, along with institutions such as the World Bank, the International Monetary Fund, many of the constituent institutions of the United Nations, and private sector institutions like the New York Stock Exchange, served the role of coordination. Among the controlled economy countries the Soviet Gosplan, the Council for Mutual Economic Assistance (sometimes referred to as CMEA or COMECON), and the International Bank for Economic Cooperation (IBEC) served a similar function.[37] Each super power sought to center capital aggregation and infrastructure development on its own industrial base. In addition, each sought to further coordinate interactions among individuals, organizations, and nations within its sphere of influence by exploiting social and material technologies for gathering, processing, and communicating information. Two sets of legal and financial institutions grew up as parallel global alternatives, each of them necessary to capitalize and manage parallel infrastructures of information, telecommunication, transportation, and energy.

But now, one of these sets of institutions has crumbled; and, given the bipolar conceptualization of global relations in the Cold War era, politicians account for the collapse of the governments of the Communist bloc in the rhetoric of triumphant combat. Bipolar images, thus, dominate the "postwar" dialogue—images such as the victory of freedom over enslavement, capitalism over communism, democracy over dictatorship, and the market over central planning. Yet, without necessarily challenging the validity of these bipolar images, they have held deep meaning for billions of the world's inhabitants for over fifty years. We may gain new insights by examining the collapse of the Soviet bloc as parts of a pattern of increased global interconnectedness.

By viewing this collection of events from the perspective of interconnectedness, it appears that the controlled economies reached and exceeded the limits of central planning. That is, once the governments of the Soviet bloc overreached their abilities to coordinate and control their societies and economies, they experienced a gradual loss of order, a deterioration in their forms of social organization, and a resultant loss of popular confidence—the onset of societal entropy, if you will.[38] So, although the struggles of the Cold War severely strained the organizational difficulties of the Warsaw Pact countries, the essence of their collapse revolves around their failure to control and coordinate increasingly complex and turbulent interactions on a global scale. Soviet planners fell short in their attempts to influence the global economy; they proved unable to coordinate the production and distribution within and among their client states; and, they eventually failed to ensure the material well being of their own state—as badly as did their predecessors the Czars. In other words, the disintegration of the Soviet Union may not necessarily indicate a "victory" of the free-market bloc, but rather an internal failure of coordination and integration.

Applying the lessons inherent in the example of the Soviet bloc collpase, it may be possible to enhance our understanding of the challenge posed by the growing need for interconnectedness in the surviving international market system. After all, it is now up to this system, whether or not one views it as victorious, to coordinate and control an increasingly tumultuous global economy that has been expanded by the addition of the former controlled economies—with all of the problems of reorganizing and integrating them. And there is evidence that as a set of institutions for global coordination and control, the surviving system may also be straining at the limits of its effectiveness—or, indeed, may already have exceeded them.

One obstacle to further coordination may stem from the need to aggregate sufficient capital. The development of truly global markets in goods and services is requiring the construction of a new infrastructure. Much like the push to extend the railroads from coast to coast across every continent, a new movement is underway to interconnect the globe with the technologies of communication. And, as was the experience of governments in the 19th century, the aggregation of capital necessary to build these new telecommunication and information systems exerts a heavy strain on public institutions. In Latin America and Eastern Europe, governments are privatizing their infrastructures and selling them off to foreign investors in order to attract the capital for modernization. Russia, Hungary, Mexico, Argentina, and New Zealand, among others, have sold some portion—or all—of their telecommunication systems to multinational companies. On the other hand, countries such as Brazil, which have sought to exclude foreign companies, by borrowing the capital necessary to develop their own infrastructures, have frequently defaulted, contributing to a global capital shortage and a reluctance to lend money for development projects.[39] In other words, the global financial system seems to be straining to develop and fund the infrastructure necessary for global interconnection.

Nevertheless, in recognition of the interconnectedness of the worldwide market for capital, trading on stock and commodities exchanges now occurs around the world and around the clock.[40] Moreover, though mostly invisible to the public at large, this is one area where technological progress might well be thought of as revolutionary. In financial transactions which are accomplished electronically, the idea of a "float"—the time between an agreement to transfer funds and the actual transfer of funds—has all but disappeared because information technologies, by raising the virtual speed of transactions to the speed of light, have made it possible to realize the centuries-old dream of bankers. Yet, precisely because of these advances, the expanded volume and rate of transmission of financial information may well have overtaken the capacities of existing institutions to oversee and regulate the system in order to prevent abuse, fraud, and corruption.

National systems, intended to prevent abuse by setting and policing restrictions on the behavior of players in financial markets, cannot keep up with the volume of instantaneous transactions. On the New York Stock exchange alone, the volume of shares traded swelled from 4.5 trillion in 1970, to 54.2 trillion in 1989.[41] As a result, those whose pursuit of self-interest is supposed to make the global market work efficiently find themselves tempted by their knowledge of the social and material technologies of the electronic marketplace—technologies which they know intimately and which operate so rapidly and with such complexity that individual transactions have become virtually invisible. The Boesky, Milken, and Savings and Loan scandals in the United States, the Japanese securities brokerage scandals, and the worldwide BCCI scandal occurred because insiders with special knowledge manipulated the system to their own advantage. Admittedly, each incident was ultimately discovered and punished to some degree; but, in every case, there was financial loss to investors and consequently a decline in confidence on the part of the other members of the system and the public at large. Although the particular details of abuse vary, all point to large scale failures by the existing regime to adequately enforce the rules of fair exchange. And, just as in the Soviet Bloc, when the loss of order leads to a loss of confidence, the system finds itself in jeopardy.

The integration of international markets encourages firms to behave like global players and further strains global coordination as firms act independently of the nations in which they operate. To be sure, this is not the first time that commercial enterprises have challenged the nations in which they operate. "Companies of exploration and trade"—enterprises such as the Hudson's Bay Company, and the British East India Company—traded globally, but acted as representatives of a nation-state. That clashes between governments and businesses occurred can be seen in the history of the British East India Company. For example, in the late 18th century the British government attempted a reform of the East India Company's army. That the Company maintained its own army is of interest in itself apart from the example of corporate versus national interests. After an intense political struggle spanning from England to India, the Company's officers defeated the attack on their organization. Yet though the history of the long relationship between the British government and the East India Company exhibits extreme complexity, allegiance was never doubted by either side.[42] In the early 20th century, large firms—such as Standard Oil and the United Fruit Company—routinely interfered with the internal politics of Arab or Latin American states, but their allegiances were clearly American as were their expectations of government support. In practice, this meant sending the U.S. Marines to Nicaragua as counters against the implied threat to United Fruit's profits imposed by Agusto César Sandino's movement. In all of these historical examples, the firm operating on a global scale identified itself as a representative of the nation, even though it frequently came into conflict with governments, including the government of the nation with whose nationality it identified.

Now, in the information age, the evolution that led firms to look beyond their national boundaries and then leave them behind is complete. Today, multinational firms speak with a voice not heard in the boardrooms of the British East India Company or the United Fruit Company. Percy Barnevik, the President and CEO of Asea Brown Boveri, with headquarters in Switzerland, speaks for his class when he says, "You optimize globally, you call the shots globally and you have no national allegiances."[43] Still, Barnevik's implications of a power struggle between business and government is not new. Child labor laws and workplace safety laws, which exist in all industrialized countries, stem from the fact that business interests sometimes harm citizens and that, from time to time, governments challenge business interests in order to protect the welfare of the citizenry. As corporate identities echo governments' abilities to gather, process, and communicate information on a truly global scale, however, governmental systems for regulating corporate behavior are experiencing frustration. In other words, by operating in many nations, multinational corporations possess the flexibility of resources to avoid constraints imposed by any single government. So, for example, when firms of the early industrial era contested with governments over child labor, workplace safety, or inadequate health care for workers, long-term investments in capital assets forced firms to concede these issues. But as assets become more informational, firms can exploit the inherent transportability of information by shifting operations away from countries where workers challenge corporate policies, to countries where governments oppose labor activism.[44]

In a sense, nations and firms increasingly deal with each other as equals and as competitors; or, from another perspective, the more firms act internationally, the less they experience accountability.[45] Therefore, as the information economy expands globally, it is forcing a new kind of economic and political organization upon the players. In this new organization there will be structures and institutions, such as the newly emerging free trade agreements, in which nations and global business organizations participate as equals. Consequently, the existing international system, based as it is on agreements among sovereign states, and deriving its authority from those states, displays its inadequacy.

The emergence of new economic and political alignments suggests that economic organization progresses through stages, and that the transitions are understandable in terms of cycles affected by the application of existing infrastructural technologies. Joseph A. Schumpeter was one of the first to attempt an explanation when he argued that, on the one hand, new infrastructural technologies are a response to the demand for new institutions and processes for economic coordination, while, on the other hand, the availability of innovations creates opportunities for change in scale and scope of organization.[46] Economies go through periodic reorganizations, resulting from the introduction of new technologies of production, with the diffusion of each new innovation occasioning dislocations and disjunctures in the existing social system. It is a view that assumes economies, and social organization in general, do not tend toward a static equilibrium but are dynamic—thus rejecting the equilibrium assumption of classical economics. According to Schumpeter, as the level of organization increases, new technologies—in the broad sense of ways of doing things as well as in the narrow sense of technical tools—become necessary, in order to move beyond each successive plateau of development. As a result, interpretations of macro interconnectedness by economists of the Schumpeter school have led to proposals that we are currently going through just such a period of global economic and social reorganization. They point to the mutual relationship between the technologies of the information age and the change in scale and scope of economic organization currently underway.[47]

But even if one doesn't subscribe to Schumpeter's theory of long cycles, the evidence argues for a characterization of the information age as a period of transition, during which demand for increased levels of global social organization interacts with the impacts of increasingly capable information technologies. Examples supporting such a characterization grow in abundance. The international order of things is changing, and those changes make events in every corner of the world increasingly relevant for all of us.

Of course, it is impossible to predict, much less to describe, the eventual regime. Yet evidence of macro interconnectedness points to other even larger flows of economic, political, and military information used to support the coordination of interactions among people, firms, and nations on a global scale. The pressures which are bringing the "ancien regimes" to a close constitute the formative context within which new institutions and processes will grow.

What we now experience as macro interconnectedness is the expanding flow of information for purposes of global social and economic coordination—evidence of which also contributes heavily to theories positing the arrival of an information society. The new regime will emerge when these flows become institutionalized and codified.

Both in content and in conduit, the global flow of information which serves the functions of interconnection is becoming increasingly apparent; and along with it, there is the one consistent perception that interconnectedness grows among economic, social and cultural communication systems around the world. This phenomenon, taken together with increases in interconnectedness among firms and among individuals, makes up a large part of the popular perception of the information society. Thus, Thoreau's question persists. Yet, ironically, the drive for interconnectedness shows that it needs no answer. Interconnectedness grows because social organization demands it and technology allows it.

Notes

1. Thoreau, H. D. (1854/1942). *Walden; Or life in the woods.* New York: New American Library, p. 40.
2. Smelser, N. J. (1976). *The sociology of economic life.* Englewood Cliffs, NJ: Prentice Hall, p. 55.
3. Table 58 (1990). Statistical abstract of the United States: 1990. Washington DC: Bureau of the Census.
4. Cherry, C. (1977). The telephone system: Creator of mobility and social change. In I. d. S. Pool (Ed.), *The social impact of the telephone* (pp. 112-126). Cambridge, MA: MIT Press. Lester, D. (1977). The use of the telephone in counseling and crisis intervention. In I. d. S. Pool (Ed.), *The social impact of the telephone* (pp. 454-472). Cambridge, MA: MIT Press. Maddox, B. (1977). Women and the Switchboard. In I. d. S. Pool (Ed.), *The social impact of the telephone* (pp. 262-280). Cambridge, MA: MIT Press. Mayer, M. (1977). The telephone and the uses of time. In I. d. S. Pool (Ed.), *The social impact of the telephone* (pp. 225-245). Cambridge, MA: MIT Press. Reid, A. A. L. (1977). Comparing telephone with face-to-face contact. In I. d. S. Pool (Ed.), *The social impact of the telephone* (pp. 386-414). Cambridge, MA: MIT Press. Schegloff, E. A. (1977). Identification and recognition in interactional openings. In I. d. S. Pool (Ed.), *The social impact of the telephone* (pp. 415-450). Cambridge, MA: MIT Press.
5. Rice, R. E. (1987). New patterns of social structure in an information society. In J. R. Schement & L. Lievrouw (Eds.) (1988), *Competing visions, complex realities: Social aspects of the information society* (pp. 107-120). Norwood, NJ: Ablex.
6. For a variety of views on the social changes wrought by industrialization, see Ashton, T. S. (1948). *The industrial revolution 1760-1830.* London, UK: Oxford University Press. Badham, R. (1984). The sociology of industrial and post-industrial societies. *Current sociology: La sociologie contemporaine, 32*(1), 1-135.

Badham, R. J. (1986). *Theories of industrial society*. London: Croom Helm. Engels, F. (1845/1987). *The condition of the working class in England* (Wischnewetzky, Florence, Trans.). Harmondsworth, UK: Penguin. Friedman, G. (1955). *Industrial society*. New York: The Free Press. Fromm, E. (1955). *The sane society*. New York: Holt, Rinehart and Winston. Galbraith, J. K. (1967). *The new industrial state*. New York: The New American Library. Harrison, J. F. C. (1973). *The birth and growth of industrial England 1714–1867*. New York: Harcourt Brace Jovanovich Inc. Harvey, E. B. (1975). *Industrial society: Structures, roles, and relations*. Homewood, IL: Dorsey Press. Katz, M. B., Doucet, M. J., & Stern, M. J. (1982). *The social organization of early industrial capitalism*. Cambridge, MA: Harvard University Press. Marx, L. (1967). *The machine in the garden: Technology and the pastoral ideal in America*. New York: Oxford University Press. Mayo, E. (1945). *The social problems of an industrial civilization*. Cambridge, MA: Harvard University Press. Polanyi, K. (1944). *The great transformation: The political and economic origins of our time*. Boston, MA: Beacon Press. Veblen, T. (1899/1918). *The theory of the leisure class: An economic study of institutions*. New York: The Modern Library.

7. Park, R. E. (1916). The city: Suggestions for the investigation of human behavior in the urban environment. *American Journal of Sociology, 20*, 577–612.

8. Parsons, T. (1951). *The social system*. New York: Free Press.

9. Toennies, F. (1971). *On sociology: Pure, applied, and empirical*. Chicago, IL: University of Chicago Press (pp. 62–72).

10. Bell, D. (1976). *The coming of post-industrial society*. New York: Basic Books. Galbraith, J. K. (1967). *The new industrial state*. New York: The New American Library.

11. Huber, G. P. (1984). The nature and design of post-industrial organization. *Management Science, 30*(8), 928–951.

12. Huber, G. P. (1984) p. 929.

13. Huber, G. P. (1984) p. 931.

14. Durkheim, E. (1933). *The division of labor in society*. New York: Free Press (pp. 369–370).

15. Arrow, K. J. (1974). *The limits of organization*. New York: W. W. Norton. Arrow, K. J. (1979). The economics of information. In M. L. a. M. Dertouzos Joel (Eds.), *The computer age: A twenty-year view* (pp. 306–317). Cambridge, MA: MIT Press. Hirshleifer, J. (1973). Economics of information: Where are we in the theory of information? *American Economic Association, 63*(2 (May)), 31–39. Knight, F. H. (1921). *Risk, uncertainty, and profit*. Boston, MA: Houghton, Mifflin. Lamberton, D. M. (Ed.). (1971). *Economics of information and knowledge*. Harmondsworth, UK: Penguin.

16. Hammer, M., & Champy, J. (1993). *Reengineering the corporation: A manifesto for business revolution*. New York: Harper Business. Lawrence, P. R., & Dyer, D. (1983). *Renewing American industry*. New York: Free Press.

17. Parsons, T., & Smelser, N. J. (1956). *Economy and society*. Glencoe, IL: Free Press. Weber, M. (1947). *The theory of social and economic organization* (Henderson, A. M. and Parsons, Talcott, Trans.). New York: Oxford University Press. See, especially (pp. 284–293) in Parsons and Smelser.

18. Hayek, F. A. v. (1945). The use of knowledge in society. *American Economic Review, 35*(4), 519–530. Malone, T. W., Yeates, J., & Benjamin, R. I. (1987). Electronic markets and electronic hierarchies. *Communications of the ACM, 30*(6), 484–497. Ouchi, W. G. (1980). Markets, bureaucracies, and clans. *Administrative Science Quarterly*(March). Thorelli, H. B. (1986). Networks: Between markets and hierarchies. *Strategic Management Journal, 7*(1), 37–52. Williamson,

O. E. (1975). *Markets and hierarchies, analysis and antitrust implications: A study in the economics of internal organization.* New York: Free Press.

19. Galbraith, J. K. (1967).
20. Chandler, A. D. J. (1962). *Strategy and structure.* Cambridge, MA: MIT Press.
21. Chandler, A. D. J. (1977). *The visible hand: The managerial revolution in American business.* Cambridge, MA: Harvard University Press (pp. 455-463, 475-476).
22. Peters, T. J., & Waterman, R. H. (1982). *In search of excellence: Lessons from America's best-run companies.* New York: Harper & Row.
23. *NY Times,* (2 March 1992) pp. C-1 et seq.
24. De Voney, C. (1983). *IBM's personal computer.* Indianapolis, IA: Que. Freiberger, P., & Swain, M. (1984). *Fire in the valley.* Berkeley, CA: Osborne/McGraw-Hill.
25. Chandler, A. D. J. (1975). The multi-unit enterprise: A historical and international comparative analysis and summary. In H. F. Williamson (Ed.), *Evolution of international management structures* Newark, DL: University of Delaware Press.
26. For an analysis of the scope and kinds of implementation see, Antonelli, C. (Ed.). (1988). *New information technology and industrial change: The Italian case.* Dordrecht, Neth.: Kluwer Academic Publishers, especially Chapters 1 and 2.
27. Drucker, P. F. (1988). The coming of the new organization. *Harvard Business Review, 66*(1), 45-53. Drucker, P. F. (1989). *The new realities.* New York: Harper & Row.
28. Brown, J. S. (1991). Research that reinvents the corporation. *Harvard Business Review, 69*(1), 102-111. Zuboff, S. (1991). Can research reinvent the corporation? *Harvard Business Review, 69*(2), 164-175.
29. Anthes, G. H. (1991). Internet society to guide research net. *Computerworld, 25*(31), 42. Shorrock, T. (1991). EDI service poised for major growth, commerce department predicts. *Journal of Commerce and Business, 390*(27633), 3B.
30. Hart, P., & Estrin, D. (1990). Inter-organization networks in support of application-specific integrated circuits: An empirical study. At the *8th International Conference of the International Telecommunication Society,* Venice, Italy, March 18-21.
31. Ciborra, C. U. (1992). Innovation, networks, and organizational learning. In C. Antonelli (Ed.), *The economics of information networks* (pp. 91-102). Amsterdam, Neth.: North-Holland.
32. Taylor, J. R., & Van Every, E. J. (1993). *The vulnerable fortress: Bureaucratic organization and management in the information age.* Toronto, Ont.: University of Toronto.
33. Beniger, J. R. (1986). *The control revolution.* Cambridge, MA: Harvard University Press. Brownlee, W. E. (1974). *Dynamics of ascent: A history of the American economy.* New York: Knopf. Chandler, A. D. J. (1977). *The visible hand: The managerial revolution in american business.* Cambridge, MA: Harvard University Press. Galbraith, J. K. (1967). *The new industrial state.* New York: The New American Library. Heilbroner, R. L., & Singer, A. (1984). *The economic transformation of America: 1600 to the present* (2nd ed.). New York: Harcourt Brace Jovanovich. Schement, J. R. (1989). The origins of the information society in the United States: Competing visions. In J. Salvaggio (Ed.), *The information society* (pp. 29-50). New York: Lawrence Erlbaum. Yates, J. (1989). *Control through communication: The rise of system in American management.* Baltimore, MD: Johns Hopkins Press.
34. Braverman, H. (1974). *Labor and monopoly capital: The degradation of work in the twentieth century.* New York: Monthly Review Press. Carlton, R., & Christina, S. w. (1987). *Dreams betrayed: Working in the technological age.* New York:

Lexington Books. Chamot, D. (1987). Electronic work and the white-collar employee. In R. E. Kraut (Ed.), *Technology and the transformation of white-collar work*. (pp. 23–33). Hillsdale, NJ: Lawrence Erlbaum Associates. Gilchrist, A. e. a. (1987). Information technology and information work. *Aslib Proceedings, 39*(10), 313–326. Kraut, R. E. (1987). *Technology and the transformation of White-collar work*. Hillsdale, NJ: Lawrence Erlbaum Associates. Mills, C. W. (1951/ 1956). *White collar*. Oxford, UK: Oxford University Press. Schement, J. R., Curtis, T., & Lievrouw, L. A. (1985). Social factors affecting the success of introducing information technology into the workplace. In *48th Annual Meeting of the American Society for Information Science*, (pp. 278–283). Knowledge Industry Publications Inc. U.S. Congress (1987). The electronic supervisor: New technology, new tensions. In *Office of technology assessment*, Washington DC: U.S. Government Printing Office.

35. McLuhan, M. (1962). *The Gutenberg galaxy: The making of typographic man*. New York: New American Library. McLuhan, M. (1964). *Understanding media: The extensions of man*. New York: New American Library. McLuhan, M., & Fiore, Q. (1967). *The medium is the massage*. New York: Bantam.

36. Morgenthau, H., J. (1985). *Politics among nations*. New York: Alfred A. Knopf.

37. Holzman, F. D. (1976). *International trade under communism*. New York: Basic Books.

38. Brucan, S. (1987). *World socialism at the crossroads*. New York: Praeger.

39. Fadul, A., & Straubhaar, J. (1991). Communications, culture, and informatics in Brazil: The current challenges. In G. Sussman & J. A. Lent (Eds.) (1991), *Transnational communications: Wiring the third world*. Newbury Park, CA: Sage.

40. Hamelink, C. J. (1983). *Finance and information: A study of converging interests*. Norwood, NJ: Ablex.

41. Table 841, (1991) Statistical abstract of the United States: 1991. Washington DC: Bureau of the Census.

42. Braudel, F. (1979). *Civilization and capitalism 15th–18th century: The wheels of commerce*. New York: Harper & Row. Braudel, F. (1979). *Civilization and capitalism 15th–18th century: The structures of everyday life*. New York: Harper & Row. O'Connell, R. L. (1989). *Of arms and men: A history of war, weapons, and aggression*. New York: Oxford.

43. Item in the business section. *NY Times,* (2 March 1992) pp. C-1 et seq.

44. Clearly, firms, especially those culturally rooted in the United States, never accepted workplace safety nor healthcare as permanent concessions. Recent management-labor disputes verify the continuing vulnerability of these worker benefits. For discussions of the issues affecting management-labor conflict in the U.S., both historical and current, see: Blauner, R. (1964). *Alienation and freedom: The factory worker and his industry*. Chicago, IL: University of Chicago. Braverman, H. (1974). *Labor and monopoly capital: The degradation of work in the twentieth century*. New York: Monthly Review Press. Carlton, R., & Christina, S. w. (1987). *Dreams betrayed: Working in the technological age*. New York: Lexington Books. Chamot, D. (1987). Electronic work and the white-collar employee. In R. E. Kraut (Ed.), *Technology and the transformation of white-collar work*. (pp. 23–33). Hillsdale, NJ: Lawrence Erlbaum Associates. Downing, H. (1981). Word processors and the oppression of women. In T. Forestor (Ed.), *The microelectronics revolution* (pp. 275–287). Cambridge, MA: MIT Press. Edwards, R. (1979). *Contested terrain: The transformation of the workplace in the twentieth century*. New York: Basic Books. Fromm, E. (1962). Alienation under capitalism. In E. Josephson & M. Josephson (Eds.), *Man alone: Alienation in modern society*

(pp. 56-73). New York: Dell. Gordon, D. M., Edwards, R., & Reich, M. (1982). *Segmented work, divided workers.* Cambridge University Press. Hartmann, H. I., Kraut, R. E., & Tilly, L. A. (Eds.). (1986). *Computer chips and paper clips: Technology and women's employment.* Washington Dc: National Academy Press. Hochschild, A. R. (1983). *The managed heart: Commercialization of human feeling.* Berkeley, CA: University of California. Howard, R. (1985). *Brave new workplace.* New York: Penguin. Lehrer, R. N. (1957). *Work simplification.* New York: Prentice-Hall. Mills, C. W. (1951/1956). *White collar.* Oxford, UK: Oxford University Press. Moore, T. S. (1985). The class patterning of work orientation. *Social Science Journal, 22*(2), 61-76. Murolo, P. (1987). White-collar women and the rationalization of clerical work. In R.E. Kraut (1987), *Technology and the transformation of white-collar work* (pp. 35-51). Hillsdale, NJ: Lawrence Erlbaum Associates. Noble, D. F. (1977). *America by design: Science, technology, and the rise of corporate capitalism.* Oxford, UK: Oxford University Press. Office of Technology Assessment (1984). *Computerized Manufacturing Automation: Employment, Education and the Workplace.* No. OTA-CIT-235). Congress of the United States. Olson, M. H. (1987). Telework: Practical Experience and Future Prospects. In R.E. Kraut (1987), *Technology and the transformation of white collar work* (pp. 135-152) Hillsdale, NJ: Lawrence Erlbaum Associates. Roethlisberger, F. J., & Dickson, W. J. (1939). *Management and the worker.* Cambridge, MA: Harvard University Press. Solomon, W. S. (1985). From craftspeople to production workers: Video display terminals and the devaluation of newspaper copy editing. *Communication, 8,* 207-224. U.S. Congress (1987). The electronic supervisor: New technology, new tensions. In *Office of technology assessment,* . Washington DC: U.S. Government Printing Office. U.S. Department of Commerce (1985). *Automation of America's offices, 1985-2000.* No. PB-185055).Office of technology assessment, Congress of the United States, National Technical Information Service. Whalley, P. (1984). Deskilling engineers?: The labor process, labor markets, and labor segmentation. *Social Problems, 32*(2), 117-132. Zimbalist, A. (1979). *Case Studies on the Labor Process.* New York: Monthly Review Press. Zuboff, S. (1988). *In the age of the smart machine: The future of work and power.* New York: Basic Books.

45. Melody, W. (1985). The information society: Implications for economic institutions and market theory. *Journal of Economic Issues, 19*(2), 523-539.
46. Schumpeter, J. A. (1939). *Business cycles.* New York: McGraw Hill.
47. Dosi, G., Freeman, C., Nelson, R., Silverberg, G., & Soete, L. (Eds.). (1988). *Technical change and economic theory.* London, UK: Pinter.

3

Information Work

The annual labor of every nation is the fund which originally supplies it with all the necessaries and conveniences of life which it annually consumes, and which consist always either in the immediate produce of that labor, or in what is purchased with that produce from other nations.

According, therefore, as this produce, or what is purchased with it, bears a greater or smaller proportion to the number of those who are to consume it, the nation will be better or worse supplied with all the necessaries and conveniences for which it has occasion.—Adam Smith[1]

As fewer Workers in the rich nations have engaged in physical production, more have been needed to produce ideas, patents, scientific formulae, bills, invoices, reorganization plans, files, dossiers, market research, sales presentations, letters, graphics, legal briefs, engineering specifications, computer programs, and a thousand other forms of data or symbolic output. This rise in white-collar, technical, and administrative activity has been so widely documented in so many countries that we need no statistic here to make the point. Indeed, some sociologists have seized on the increasing abstraction of production as evidence that society has moved into a 'post-industrial' stage.—Alvin Toffler[2]

Toffler evokes an image most Americans take as fact. The basis for the image rests upon the impression that we are entering a new age—the information society—which may be observed by following the course of three recent events: the emergence of the information economy; increased reliance on information technology; and greater numbers of individuals engaged in information work. In this chapter, we address the conventional view of the information workforce and suggest that the data have been misread. We also analyze the nature of information work and its unfolding patterns. However, to understand those developments we must begin with Marc Porat.

His pioneering work, *The Information Economy*, is the original source of data for most interpretations of work in the information society and underlies the majority view, which links his findings to Bell's theory of post-industrial society.[3] Most studies rely on Porat's premise that information work became

Portions of this chapter are based on an earlier research article: Schement, J. R. (1990). Porat, Bell, and the information society reconsidered: The growth of information work in the early twentieth century. *Information processing and management,* 26(4), 449–465.

the dominant kind of work in the U.S. at about the same time that the information sector of the economy became the largest economic sector. They tie these events to the development and diffusion of the computer. The dominant image in the literature pictures the late twentieth century as an era when the economy and the labor force underwent a paired transformation, probably driven by a revolution in computing technology. As one leg on this tripod, information work forms a key component in this explanation, because it reflects daily life most directly and represents the actual activities of the members of society.[4]

Approaches to the Definition and Measurement of Information Work

Determining precisely what is information work and who is an information worker presents a severe test to the social scientist. Obviously all human activities require some measure of information processing or manipulation. Humans continuously filter information in order to adapt to their social and physical environments and every human task, no matter how routine, depends on an intellectual capacity. In the case of manual work, for example, the goal of these information activities is to facilitate the performance of a physical task. The assembly line worker must interpret what he or she sees and interpret management's directives in order to carry out the appropriate task, even if it is no more complicated than fitting a washer onto a bolt.

Machlup was the first to enter this field and he sought to define knowledge in order to further his analysis of the knowledge economy.[5] To do so, he required a model of what he called the knowledge workforce, in order to answer questions derived from his attempt to redefine the GNP. But in a ten chapter book, his survey of knowledge workers filled one chapter. Not surprisingly, his analysis of the labor force lacked the thoroughness of his analysis of the knowledge sector of the economy. While his other studies on the nature of knowledge and information shed light on these complex phenomena, his conceptualization of knowledge production continues to be awkward.[6]

For example, he experienced difficulty in defining the production of "new knowledge." He identified one kind of knowledge producer as an "original creator" who, although drawing on a rich store of information received messages of all sorts, adds so much of his own inventive genius and creative imagination that only relatively weak and indirect connections can be found between what he has received from others and what he communicates.[7] In principle Machlup resisted any interpretation of original creators as confined solely to those in the "upper strata" [his phrase]; but he limited his group of original creators to scientists and engineers, though he acknowledged that the bulk of time spent doing scientific and engineering work involves little original creation in the above sense. He did concede that original creativity could also be present in the work of a newspaper columnist but he could not say exactly how. Even so, he found that workers who produced knowledge constituted 31.6% of the labor force in 1959 (see figure 3-1).[8] Yet though Machlup popu-

FIGURE 3-1

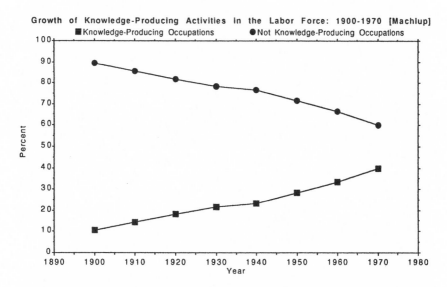

Source: Machlup F. and Kronwinkler T. (1975), Workers who produce knowledge: a steady increase, 1900 to 1970. *Weltwirtschaftliches Archiv. 37*, pp. 752–759. Their source: *1900–1950: Historical statistics of the United States*, pp. 75–78.

FIGURE 3-2

Source: Bell, D. (1976), *The coming of post-industrial society.* pp. 134, 137. New York: Basic Books.

larized the concept, the problems he experienced in his attempts to operationalize information work continue to plague researchers.

Bell noted the rise of the service workforce and its importance to the shape of a post-industrial society (see figure 3-2). He proposed the existence of a newly-emerging knowledge class, composed primarily of professional and technical workers with a scientific elite at its core.[9] According to his theory, the knowledge class will lead post-industrial society as a class of technocrats. But he ignores the possibility that workers outside the elite class might also originate, synthesize, and apply information in order to produce "new knowledge." That the triumph of bureaucratic reason did not come about in the '80s, nor does it appear on the horizon in the '90s, does not by itself negate the theory, although his exclusive focus on technocrats diverted researchers from examining the full extent and composition of information work.

It was Porat who first broke away from the conceptual constraints of operationalizing new knowledge. He did so by introducing the more inclusive term "information" and by concentrating on the extent to which the production, processing, and distribution of information goods and services contributes to the U.S. GNP. He squarely answered the criticism that information processing is present in all work by reframing the controversy.

> We are trying to get at a different question: Which occupations are primarily engaged in the production, processing, or distribution of information as the output, and which occupations perform information processing tasks as activities ancillary to the primary function?[10]

He aggregated the number of "information workers" as a new sector of the economy (see Table 3.1 and figure 3.2). For this reason, Porat's study is brilliant—yet at the same time limiting.

His re-analysis of the economy uncovered the strength and presence of information activities. He altered our thinking about economic activity to such an extent that the phrase "information economy" has entered the literature as well as popular speech. The idea of an information sector within the economy has taken firm hold. His focus on "information" rather than "knowledge" avoids Machlup's conceptual pitfall, and imposes a broader, more realistic framework for measuring the extent of this kind of work. On the other hand, Porat admitted that information work might occur outside of the information sector, in some agricultural occupations for example. But since these were located outside of the information sector he could not analyze them and keep to his framework. On this issue he continued in the tradition of Machlup and found that information workers earned 53% of all labor income in 1967.[11]

Shortly after Porat published his study, the Expert Group at the Organization for Economic Cooperation and Development (OECD) attempted an even more thorough analysis of information work as an occupational behavior occurring in any economic sector, rather than as an activity present solely within an information sector of the economy. They constructed a typology of information occupations, utilizing the 1968 International Standard Classification of Occupations (ISCO) as their point of departure. Then, they divided information work into four groups of occupations: 1) information producers; 2) information processors; 3) information distributors; and 4) information infrastructure occupations. Because OECD identified information occupations, rather than directly aggregating information workers as did Machlup and Porat, they provided the opportunity for comparison of empirical data from numerous countries. As a result of the Expert Group's breakthrough, researchers have begun to accumulate data on information occupations and workforces in many countries.[12]

Schement and Lievrouw studied the informational content of work.[13] They assumed Porat's given, that "intellectual content is present in every task, no matter how mundane."[14] But beyond this basic recognition, they observed that information activities are increasingly integrated into many occupations, even traditional ones. For example, an automobile mechanic at Sears routinely fills out numerous forms prior to performing any work on an automobile brought in for service. As car diagnostics become computerized a greater proportion of the mechanic's work time is spent processing information. Taxi drivers also spend significant amounts of time communicating with dispatchers, processing directions, and maintaining logs of their transactions. Yet it must be noted that from the 1880s, mechanics were already performing information functions at lower levels of intensity than they do now. But until the 1980s, the informational task was not abstracted or packaged in visible forms; it was embedded in the total experience of work. In fact, all occupations, even very traditional ones, contain patterned information activities as part of the work task, and some traditional occupations contain surprisingly high levels of information processing.

But with information occupations, manipulation of information defines product, task, and worker. Schement and Lievrouw identified three primary categories of workers: (1) information producers; (2) information recyclers; (3) information maintainers; as well as two categories of secondary information workers: (4) information technology producers; and, (5) information technology maintainers.[15] Their content analysis of the Dictionary of Occupational Titles (DOT), the basic document for describing occupations, reinforced the hypothesis that information work occurs across all sectors of the workforce. They found, as one would expect, that nearly all of the information sector (divisions 00-29) fell within their definition of information occupations. Similarly, they determined that 50% of those occupations in the service sector (30-38) could be considered informational. But they also found that information occupations comprised 25% of the industrial sector (50-99) and 26% of the agricultural sector (40-46). While the Department of Labor correctly identified an information sector within the labor force, its definitions were excessively narrow since other sectors also contained significant numbers of information occupations. Information jobs made up 40% of the total occupations in the U.S. labor force, an indication that information work takes place in all areas of the economy.[16]

Bell, Porat, OECD, and Schement and Lievrouw are only a few who have grappled with the concept of information work since Machlup first attempted an economic analysis of the production of knowledge. In the intervening years, despite the disagreements, a general picture has emerged, so that nearly all definitions of information work encompass a basic set of behaviors, as summarized in the following definition.

> *Information work* occurs when the worker's main task involves information processing or manipulation in any form, such as information production, recycling, or maintenance. The consequence of information work is information, whether in the form of new knowledge or repackaging existing forms. Unlike the assembly line worker, an information worker—such as a telephone operator—processes and manipulates information as an end in itself. Information defines the task, the product, and the worker.

Porat's Study and Its Misinterpretations

Machlup's data indicates a steady growth of knowledge workers throughout the twentieth century. If one extrapolates the trend depicted in figure 3-1, then knowledge workers would have passed the 50% mark around 1980 or soon thereafter. Rubin and Huber, with Taylor, carried forth a project begun by Machlup—but unfinished at the time of his death in 1983—and updated his 1962 findings by carefully adhering to his classification scheme of occupations. They found all knowledge producing workers to comprise 41.23% of the total economically active population in 1980.[17] This falls considerably below Machlup's earlier estimate. But because Machlup's scheme is not as inclusive as Porat's and others, he and his followers consistently give lower figures for the share of information work. Neither Machlup, nor Rubin et al., attempted a breakdown into four workforce sectors, i.e., agriculture, industry, service, information.

Bell's more qualitative approach proposes that the growth of the service sector, made up of professional and technical workers, comprised 12.2% of the total workforce in 1963 (see figure 3-2).[18] Bell's subsequent writings, like most others, rely on Porat's data and his now famous four sector grouping.[19]

Porat took his data from the Bureau of Labor Statistics and addressed the task of defining those occupations in which some workers primarily manipulate information (see figure 3-3). In particular, he saw that certain service occupations, e.g., physicians and registered nurses, underwent rapid changes in the 1960s and '70s, so that they might reasonably be considered informational in the near future. But at the time of Porat's research he recognized

TABLE 3-1
Porat's (1977) Typology of Information Workers

Markets for Information

1. Knowledge producers (scientific and technical, producers of private information services).
2. Knowledge distributors (educators, public information disseminators, communication workers).

Information in Markets

3. Market search and coordination specialists (information gatherers, search and coordination specialists, planning and control workers).
4. Information processors (non-electronic based, electronic based).

Information Infrastructure

5. Information machine workers (non-electronic machine operators, electronic machine operators, telecommunication workers).

TABLE 3-2
Occupations Allocated 50% to Service and 50% to Information

Physicians	Hucksters
Registered Nurses	Sales Clerks, Retail Trades
Dietitians	Misc. Clerical Workers
Health Record Technologies	Managers, Retail Trade, Salary
Radiological Technologies	Managers, Personal Services, Salaried
Counter Clerks, exc. food	Managers, Personal Services, Self-Employed
Officers, Pilots, Pursers on Ships	Managers, Business Services, Salaried
Officials of Lodges, Societies, Unions	Managers, Business and Repair Services, Self-Employed
Demonstrators	Receptionists

Source: Porat, 1977, p. 119.

TABLE 3-3
Occupations Allocated 50% to Industry and 50% to Information

Foreman, NEC

Inspectors, Scalers, Graders, Lumber

Chainmen, Rodmen (Surveying)

Checkers, Examiners, Inspectors (Manufacturing)

Graders and Sorters (Manufacturing)

Source: Porat, 1977.

TABLE 3-4
Service Occupations Allocated to Industry

Railroad Brakemen	Truck Drivers
Barge Captains	Glaziers
Plumbers	

All skilled crafts whether based in factories or not.
All occupations involved in the transport of bulk commodities.

Source: Porat, 1977, p117.

them as occupations in transition. He attempted to sift out the information work portion by splitting eighteen occupations, allocating one half of each occupation to the information sector and one half to either the service sector (see Table 3.2) or the industrial sector.[20] He therefore challenged the utility of traditional definitions and opened for consideration the possibility that information work might occur in occupations that did not conform to intuitive definitions. He argued that lumping together foremen who were information workers with foremen who were industrial workers confused occupational labels, thus implicitly challenging Bell's identification of the knowledge workforce.[21]

Porat's radical departure from earlier schemes solves the problem of acknowledging occupations in transition, but leaves the impression that some occupations have always had significant numbers of information workers. For example, an argument can be made for classifying general practitioner (GP) physicians as information workers, when working with data from the 1960s, 1970s and 1980s. Today, a typical GP meets the patient in a clinical setting and elicits information about the suspected illness. The GP then diagnoses the illness and prescribes treatment. The patient takes the prescription to a pharmacist who interprets the physician's instructions and physically dispenses the medication. The patient then performs self-treatment by ingesting the medication. The pharmacist and the patient perform the physical aspects of the treatment. The physician performs the informational components of data collection and diagnosis. Diagnosis stands at the core of the medical profession's definition of itself. Porat's claim considering GPs information workers is valid for recent decades. However, in the first half of the century GPs performed surgery, dispensed medication, gave injections, and took blood samples, in addition to performing diagnoses. It is unlikely that even 50% of all GPs were primarily information workers prior to the 1960s, the decade when doctors quit making house calls and providing individual treatment. Porat faces the same problem with some industrial occupations, which he also split. Foremen, for example, have increasingly assumed tasks of coordinating activities, and collecting and disseminating information. Throughout the twentieth century automation and unionization resulted in converting many foremen from industrial workers into information workers. However, this transformation did not occur at a uniform rate. Some foremen, especially those in small construction businesses, continue to play the role of lead worker. Porat recognized these occupations as containing a significant amount of information work. But his decision to allocate half of their numbers as information workers gives the false impression that, in the first half of the century, these occupations contained large counts of information workers. So, for a researcher attempting to understand the long-term growth of the information workforce, accepting Porat's scheme means accepting an amplifying distortion as one probes farther back in time. Porat would have achieved greater accuracy by judging the presence of information work on a decade-by-decade basis. In this way, he might have compensated for the uneven rate of change. But as we shall see later, such detailed analysis would have been virtually impossible.

Of more profound effect was his decision to shift some occupations from the service sector to the industrial sector, in order to construct his four sector scheme (see Table 3-6). He chose to redefine these occupations (e.g., plumbers and glaziers) as industrial, reasoning that, since these workers manipulated physical objects, their occupations should be considered industrial. Furthermore, he also reallocated some transportation occupations on the premise that "transportation of bulk commodities is an essential feature of an industrial economy."[22] By assigning plumbers, glaziers, railroad brakemen, truck drivers, and all skilled crafts—whether factory-based or not—to the industrial sector, he inflated the industrial workforce while deflating the service workforce, thus contributing to the illusion that industrial workers dominated the workforce well into the 1950s. With these seemingly innocuous changes, he effectively redefined the meaning of "industry," resulting in even greater confusion than the decision to split occupations between sectors. Changing the grouping of the occupations but leaving the traditional labels intact has led subsequent researchers to assume that the curve for the industrial sector (in figure 3-3) reflects only those occupations conventionally thought of as industrial.

In fact, few social scientists have explored beyond Porat's results to analyze his data or categories, so that his novel groupings have created the basis for a popular misunderstanding. Certainly, this was not Porat's intention. He wrote *The Information Economy* as his dissertation and probably performed the reassignment of occupations in response to suggestions from committee members seeking a more rational basis for differentiating occupations in the industrial sector from those in the service and information sectors. After all, the allocation of occupations to sectors involves some arbitrariness.[23] The point is that Porat's shuffling of occupational categories made perfect sense within the goals of his study. He discussed the reasoning behind his decision in the first volume of *The Information Economy*. But the brief explanation on operationalizing occupations within the industrial sector lies buried in the text and rarely noticed.[24] Since the main purpose of the report is to measure the extent of information activity in the U.S. economy, the discussion of the workforce is supplementary and limited to chapter 7.

In Porat's analysis, information workers overtook service workers in 1920, and surpassed agricultural workers at the end of the same decade. But they did not reach parity with industrial workers until 1955. According to Porat, information workers did not come into their own as the primary workforce group until the late fifties. The timing of the trend-line for information workers coincides with the period when computers were proliferating and the information economy was growing in visibility—the late '50s and early '60s. Not surprisingly, he interpreted the coincidence of these trends as reflecting the coming of an information society.

Bell's theory of post-industrial society provides a similar interpretation of the growth of the service sector and influenced Porat. His service sector includes most of Porat's information workers. But then, Porat influenced Bell. Writing a review of Porat's research in 1979, Bell supported Porat's interpretation and equated post-industrial society with the information society by incorporating Porat's results.[25] Bell expanded on his original thesis arguing that the explosion in information technology, along with the recency of the information economy and information workforce, presents strong evidence that the information society is a post-industrial society. Faced with evidence of converging trends and the recency of these developments, most researchers interpreted the data as confirming the passing of the old industrial society. Consequently, they moved on to studies framed within post-industrial theory. However, one supposed factual basis for this interpretation—the recent rise of the information sector of the workforce—may not be so.

Reanalyzing the Labor Force Data

Schement conducted a reanalysis of the U.S. workforce, in order to test Porat's data, something no one else had attempted.[26] He chose two approaches designed to reduce the systemic bias built into Porat's study. First, he reevaluated the census data in an attempt to accurately measure the proportional representation of information workers in those composite occupation groups containing both information and non-information workers that became more information orientated between 1900 and 1980 (see tables 3-2 and 3-3). Second, he reversed Porat's reassignment of service occupations to the industrial sector (see table 3-4) so as to maintain conventional groupings of occupations.

Although his design was clear, the gross nature of occupational statistics gathered by the census presented a major challenge. For one thing, the census combined or divided occupational categories in 1910, 1920, 1950, 1960, and 1970 making it difficult to calculate the numbers of information workers within the affected categories. For example, *musicians and music teachers* disappear

FIGURE 3-3

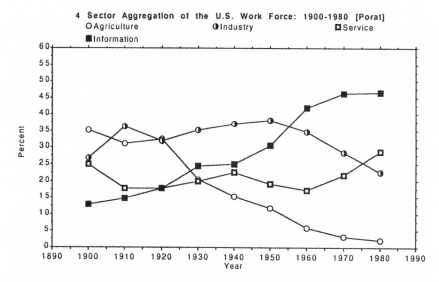

Source: Porat, M. U. (1977), *The information economy: Definition and measurement.* (OT Special Publication 77-12 [1]). p. 121. Washington, DC: Office of Telecommunications, U.S. Department of Commerce.

as a separate group beginning with the 1970 census, their numbers being sub-
sumed within the total for *professional, technical, and kindred workers.* On
the other hand, *express messengers and railway mail clerks,* suddenly appear

TABLE 3-5
Percentages of the United States Workforce by Sector(Porat, Bell): 1900–1980

Year	Agriculture	Industry	Service	Information
1900	35.3	26.8	25.1	12.8
1910	31.1	36.3	17.7	14.9
1920	32.5	32	17.8	17.7
1930	20.4	35.3	19.8	24.5
1940	15.4	37.2	22.5	24.9
1950	11.9	38.3	19	30.8
1960	6	34.8	17.2	42
1970	3.1	28.6	21.9	46.4
1980	2.1	22.5	28.8	46.6

Source: Bell, D. (1979), "The Social Framework of the Information Society," in M.L. Dertouzos and J. Moss (Eds.), *The computer age: A twenty-year view,* pp. 163–211. Cambridge, MA: MIT Press.

in 1910 in large numbers, as do *foremen, construction;* and *motion picture projectionists.* These insertions give the impression that groups of information occupations came into existence suddenly where none existed before. Foremen pose problems when trying to separate information from non-information workers. For the 1940 census, foremen in non-railway transportation industries were divided into *foremen, transportation except railroad,* and *foremen, telecommunications, utilities, and sanitary services.* Then in the 1970 census, they were recombined into one group to also include *foremen, railroads and railway express service.* In some cases, information workers could not be separated from non-information workers. For example, *jewelers, watchmakers, goldsmiths and silversmiths; fruit, nut, and vegetable graders and packers, excluding factory;* and *airplane pilots and navigators;* include both information and non-information workers. The case of jewelers and watchmakers is difficult because watchmakers produce information devices. Similarly, vegetable graders generate information but packers do not. In both cases, cycles of automation and foreign trade have affected information and non-information workers differentially, making it difficult to determine the proper ratio for one census period, much less nine. In the case of the commercial airline industry a stable ratio of around 2 pilots to 1 navigator has existed since 1920, but even this cannot be determined without resorting to numerous outside sources. Lastly, the 1950, 1960, and 1970 censuses show discrepancies between the numbers of workers in the occupations listed and the subtotals for occupation groupings. For example, when one adds the number of workers listed in the 1970 census for all occupations comprising *professional, technical, and kindred workers,* the sum is 7,897,000. But the general total given by the census is 11,561,000. Three million six hundred and sixty-four thousand workers were "lost" because the census total included persons for whom occupations were not reported. Undoubtedly, information occupations fell within these unspecified subtotals. However, upon review of the possibilities for resolving the problems inherent in the census data, no solution promised greater accuracy in determining the number of information workers. Schement's task was akin to painting a portrait with a house painter's brush. So, ultimately, all attempts to measure the numbers of information workers hidden in suspected occupations were defeated.

Schement's goal was to test Porat's 4 sector construction of the workforce; therefore, he chose a conservative approach. Of those composite occupations listed in tables 3-2 and 3-3, only *managers; checkers, examiners, inspectors (manufacturing)* ; and *and sorters (manufacturing),* were considered information workers. All occupations identified in table 3-4 were placed within the service sector. Conventional assumptions were further maintained regarding the "industrial nature" or "service nature" of an occupation. In so doing, the revised industrial and service sectors avoided the systematic bias which exaggerated the size of Porat's industrial sector.

When compared, the data from all three studies Machlup's, Porat's, and Schement's revision—show an increase in the percentage of information workers. Porat's and Schement's data show information workers overtaking agricultural workers during the 1920s. Similarly, the studies indicate that information occupations experienced little growth during the depression years. Porat found a diminished rate of growth for information workers from 1960 to 1970, and the findings in Schement's reanalysis support him. All of the studies show information workers approaching 50% of the workforce in the 1980s.

However, while Porat's data (figure 3-3 and table 3-5) indicate that the percent of information workers reached a level higher than the percent of industrial workers in the 1950s, with the service sector increased beyond the industrial sector in the mid-1970s, Schement's reanalysis shows that the information work sector overtook the industrial work sector by 1930, and that the service work sector intersected the industrial work sector during the 1940s. By correcting for the systematic biases in Porat's work categories, the data in figure 3-4 and table 3-6 show important workforce shifts occurring during the 1920s and 1930s. They show the information work sector rising to primacy by 1930, stalled during the depression, and continuing to grow after 1940.

The crucial decades for the emergence of the information workforce were 1920–1940. In this period, the United States passed the threshold into a workforce where information workers formed the single largest group. At the same time, service workers reached near parity with industrial workers, and farm workers finally fell below the other major groups. Throughout the post World War II era, the industrial work sector placed third and diminished steadily. Information workers surpassed 50% after 1980, becoming the majority of the workforce.

Based on the growth trend between his 1960 and 1970 data, Porat forecast a leveling off of the information workforce after 1970. He implied that information work might reach a point of saturation as it approached 50% of the workforce. Collected twelve years later, the data in figure 3-4 and table 3-6 show no actual leveling. During the seventies the growth rate of the information sector approximated that of the booming fifties. From 1980 to 1986 growth slowed to a rate similar to that of the sixties. As of 1986, the information portion of the labor force continued to gain against other sectors and stood at 52% of the total workforce. While no leveling off has been observed, there can be no doubt that the information work sector will peak at a point somewhere beyond 50%.

The differences are significant because Porat's data show the information work sector reaching primacy in the years after World War II and the industrial work sector succumbing to the service work sector more recently. Taken at face value, his body of data provides evidence for a recent shift to a workforce dominated by information workers and reinforces a view of the information

FIGURE 3-4

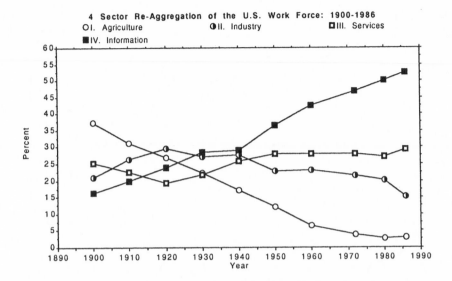

Source: Table 627, *Employed Persons, by Sex, Race, and Occupation: 1986*. U.S. Bureau of the Census. *Statistical Abstract of the United States: 1988* (108th Ed.). Washington, DC, 1987. Table 675. *Employed Persons by Sex, Race, and Occupation: 1972 and 1980*. U.S. Bureau of the Census. *Statistical Abstract of the United States: 1981* (102nd Ed.). Washington, DC, 1981. Series D 233-682. *Detailed Occupation of the Economically Active Population: 1900 to 1970* U.S. Bureau of the Census. *Historical Statistics of the United States, Colonial Times to 1970*. (Bicentennial Ed.). Part 1. Washington, DC, 1975.

society emerging after 1955. By contrast, Schement's reanalysis suggests that the information work sector surpassed the other work sectors by the end of the third decade of the century. Although the post-war rise of the information economy and computer technology certainly affected the expansion of the information workforce, they cannot be considered primary causes, since the pattern of information work was set decades before the emergence of the information economy or the diffusion of the computers. Instead of a post-industrial phenomenon, the growth of information work can best be seen as a manifestation of the forces that created industrial society. To misperceive this connection is to fail to see industrialization behind the layoffs of white collar workers in the 1990s. For that reason, rise of the information workforce needs to be understood in the context of the history of industrial society in the United States.

The Dynamics and Formation of Information Work

The powerful forces that propelled information work to the forefront of the American economy converged in the earliest decades of this century, during

TABLE 3-6
Percentages of the United States Workforce by Sector(Schement):
1900–1980

Year	Agriculture	Industry	Service	Information
1900	37.5	20.9	25.3	16.4
1910	31.1	26.4	22.5	20
1920	26.9	29.6	19.5	24
1930	22.4	27.1	21.9	28.6
1940	17.3	27.6	25.9	29.1
1950	12.2	23	28.1	36.7
1960	6.6	23.1	27.9	42.4
1972	3.7	21.5	28	46.8
1980	2.8	20.2	27.1	50
1986	2.9	15.2	29.3	52.6

Source: Table 627, *Employed Persons, by Sex, Race, and Occupation: 1986.* U.S. Bureau of the Census, *Statistical Abstract of the United States: 1988* (108th Ed.). Washington DC, 1987. Table 675. *Employed Persons by Sex, Race, and Occupation: 1972 and 1980.* U.S. Bureau of the Census. *Statistical Abstract of the United States: 1981* (102nd Ed.). Washington, DC, 1981. Series D 233–682. *Detailed Occupation of the Economically Active Population: 1900 to 1970.* U.S. Bureau of the Census, *Historical Statistics of the United States, Colonial Times to 1970* (Bicentennial Ed.). Part 1. Washington, DC, 1975.

the height of the "industrial" period. They did so in response to the problems posed by industrialization itself in the previous century. In the earliest decades of the 19th century, firms on both sides of the Atlantic operated with minuscule information workforces. Charles Dickens' portrait of the firm of Scrooge and Marley typifies these small enterprises. Attached to the firm's warehouse, the main office took up two rooms: the counting house from which Scrooge directed the business; and a small alcove occupied by his clerk, Bob Cratchit, charged with maintaining external communications by pen and foolscap.[27] Such firms contained little margin for growth.

By the middle decades of the 19th century, however, entrepreneurs had discovered economies of scale and were building empires on this principle.[28] But as we saw in chapter 2, the very size of these empires presented immense problems of control for their directors. The solution relied on information as the foundation resource.[29] So when Alfred P. Sloan Jr. conducted an organization study of General Motors in 1920, and recommended that each GM division develop statistics for determining the relation between net return and invested capital in order to assist senior management in deciding the allocation of resources to each division, he set in motion the building of a vast information infrastructure within the corporation. In 1921, before the implementation of Sloan's organization study, GM contained 40 separate corporate staffs and 14 manufacturing divisions each with its own staff. By 1925,

TABLE 3-7

Comparison of Selected Information Workers to Selected Government
Information Workers [in thousands]: 1900, 1930, 1960

Year	1 Clerical*	2 Professional**	3 Total[1+2]	4 Government[†]	5 Gvt. %[4÷3]
1900	877	1,234	2,111	239	11.3%
1930	4,336	3,311	7,647	601	7.8%
1960	9,617	7,336	16,953	2,398	14.1%

Source: Machlup, F., & Kronwinkler, T. (1975), Workers who produce knowledge: a steady increase, 1900 to 1970, *Weltwirtschaftliches Archiv.*, *111*(4), 752–759, Series Y, 308–317. *Paid Civilian Employment of the Federal Government 1816 to 1970.* U.S. Bureau of the Census, *Historical Statistics of the United States, Colonial Times to 1970* (Bicentennial Ed.), part 1. Washington, DC, 1975.

*Clerical = Clerical and kindred workers.

**Professional = Professional, technical and kindred workers.

[†]Government = Total federal government employees [including non information workers].

with the reorganization of GM well underway, there were 41 corporate staffs and an additional 32 manufacturing divisions with staffs organic to their operations.[30] The invention of organizations based on the flow of information occurred in every large industry. As of 1902, the directors of the United States Rubber Company received information from 36 corporate level staffs and 51 divisions, while the directors of Armour & Company, in 1907, reported 23 corporate staffs, and 9 divisions containing 71 separate staffs.[31]

American managers like Sloan had discovered that the profitability of large corporations depended on efficient management, and that efficient management depended on information. As a result, the number of information workers employed by large corporations grew rapidly in the first decades of the twentieth century (see Table 3-7). For example, clerical and kindred workers increased by nearly 500% between 1900 and 1930 and then increased again by 220% between 1930 and 1960. The numbers of professional, technical and kindred workers increased by nearly 270% from 1900 to 1930; between 1930 and 1960, their numbers increased by 220%.[32]

Yet one might reasonably argue that in order to judge the relative importance of corporate bureaucracies in creating the information workforce, it is necessary to know something of the extent to which the rise of information work was influenced by the growth of government civil service. After all, if the curve for information workers in figure 3-4 and table 3-6 mostly reflects civil servants, then it invalidates an explanation based on the expansion of corporate bureaucracies.

The data show that between 1900 and 1930, total federal government employees—including non information workers—increased by 360%; whereas their numbers increased by 400% between 1930 and 1960. Nevertheless, during the first decades of the century, the percentage of federal government employees shrank in relation to all clerical, professional, technical and kindred workers as the growth of corporate bureaucracies outdistanced the growth of the federal government (see table 3-7).[33] In 1900, federal civil servants made up 11.3% of all clerical, professional, technical and kindred workers. In 1930, the first census year to record the primacy of the information work sector, their share dropped to 7.8%. By 1960, in the wake of government growth due to World War II and the Cold War, federal civil servants rose to 14.1%. In short, government information workers were not the major source of growth for the information workforce in the first decades of the century.

That the growing ranks of information workers were interdependent with the industrial workforce can be seen in figure 3-4 and table 3-6. During the Great Depression, the effect of shutting down factories was felt by both industrial and information workers. Industrial workers lost jobs directly from the factory floor. But less obviously, information workers lost jobs since they also figured into the calculus of corporate profitability. Thus both the industrial and information workforces stagnated between 1930 and 1940, ironically underscoring the point that the information workforce of 1930 was the direct result of industrial production.

Showing that information work arose prior to World War II removes one of the three conceptual legs of post-industrial theory. That is not to say that important economic and technological changes did not occur over the last 30 years. By the 1980s, the information workforce contained a source of production in its own right—the producers of information commodities. It is simply to say that any theory of the information society must accept a more complex view and explain the growth of the information workforce in the '20s and '30s, as well as the changes that occurred in the '60s, '70s, and '80s. Theories of the information society that limit their explanations to the recent past do not explain very much.

Perhaps the oversight is not so surprising. In contrast to the visibility of material technologies like the railroad or the computer, the diffusion of the social technology of modern management took place with less public notice. That it happened in offices and behind closed doors means that today we see it in the background rather than in the foreground of history. But what is not seen clearly may have profound effects. Consequently, we are just now learning about the underlying dynamics that stimulated the proliferation of new information occupations in the first half of the century. Still, it is one thing to statistically analyze the macro pattern of information work and quite another to understand the occupations themselves.

Information Occupations

To gain a clearer picture of the emergence of information work, one must also examine the growth trends of representative occupations. Scientists and

engineers, librarians, electronics technicians, computer operators, and telephone operators represent occupations of varying status, spread throughout
the economy, and exhibiting the range of behaviors that constitute information work. Along with managers discussed in chapter 2, a review of these
occupations provides insight into the emergence of a distinct information
workforce.

Scientists and engineers generate the new knowledge that underlies most
process or product innovations, and are major contributors to the information
base. Their intellectual output results in a major stimulation to the information economy with resulting repercussions on the organization of the information economy. In fact, all accounts of the rise of the information age place
them at the heart of the plot , and their growth reflects the changing importance of information itself. As a group, scientists and engineers grew from
557.000 in 1950, to 4,372,000 in 1986, an increase of nearly 800% (see figures 3-5 and 3-6). By the late 1980s, their numbers roughly equaled the entire
information workforce of 1900. But, while scientists and engineers constituted 12% of the information workforce in 1950, in the 1980s they dropped
to 8%.

That such dramatic increases in their numbers resulted in a decrease in
their percentage of the labor force illustrates the remarkable growth of the
entire information workforce. First, the rise of the military-industrial complex
grew out of a scientific-engineering nucleus and demanded growing numbers
of information occupations and workers for its expanded workforce.[34] In 1987,
32% of the $124.2 billion spent by the federal government on R&D went to
defense and space-related research, most of it in private industry.[35] Even with
the wind-down of the Cold War, and despite Eisenhower's farewell warning,
the military-industrial complex remains a large employer of scientists and
engineers.[36] Secondly, nearly all other industries now depend on scientific
knowledge as both a primary economic resource and as a product. As illustrated in figure 3-6, the private sector employed 74% of all scientists and
engineers.[37] Third, as the great size and complexity of many markets encourages data gathering and formal analysis, while at the same time discouraging
intuitive decision making, corporate managers make use of social scientists to
provide information about the demand for their products, further swelling the
ranks of the information workforce.[38] Fourth, the labor force, as a system,
continues to respond to the demands of science and engineering by creating
support occupations.

Perhaps the most central of these support occupations, electronics technicians and computer operators have experienced considerable growth, with
computer operators, in particular, showing spectacular increases in numbers
(see figure 3-7). As recently as 1970, neither of these groups was distinctly
identified in the labor force. Yet sixteen years later, computer operators approached 1 million in number. Like the locomotive engineer and fireman of

FIGURE 3-5

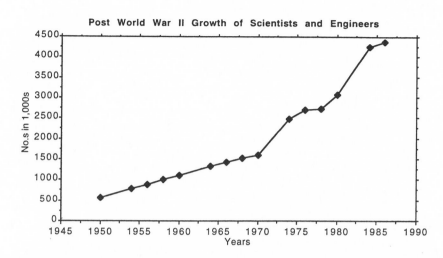

Source: Series W 168–180 (1975), *Historical statistics of the United States, Colonial Times to 1970* (Bicentennial Ed.). Washington DC: GPO. Table 1042 (1981). *Statistical Abstract of the United States: 1981.* Washington DC: U.S. Bureau of the Census. Table 961 (1987), *Statistical Abstract of the United States: 1988.* Washington, DC: Bureau of the Census.

FIGURE 3-6

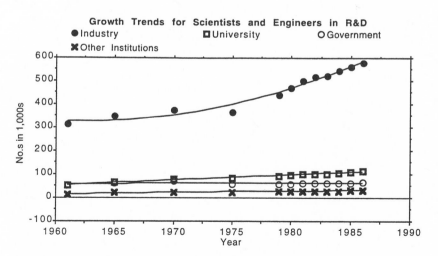

Source: Table 1041 (1981). *Statistical Abstract of the United States: 1981.* Washington, DC: U.S. Bureau of the Census. Table 960. (1987). *Statistical Abstract of the United States: 1988.* Washington, DC: Bureau of the Census.

FIGURE 3-7

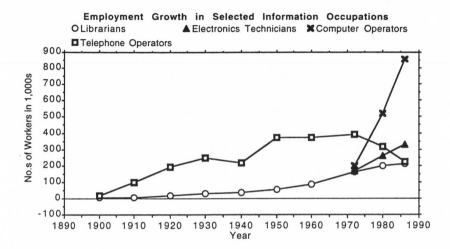

Source: Series D 233-682 (1975). *Historical Statistics of the United States, Colonial Times to 1970* (Bicentennial Ed.). Washington DC: GPO. Table 675 (1981), *Statistical Abstract of the United States: 1981*. Washington, DC: U.S. Bureau of the Census. Table 627. (1987). *Statistical Abstract of the United States: 1988*. Washington, DC: Bureau of the Census.

an earlier era, the computer operator and the electronics technician reflect the human link to technological change; for without the operator and the technician, technological innovations remain prototypes. But once the technology takes hold, the rise or decline of the occupation is dominated by the cycle of the technology—that is, by both the positive and negative outcomes of mechanization.

On the other hand, librarians and telephone operators, having their roots in the nineteenth century, are two of the oldest information occupations examined here. Though the function of librarian can be discerned in documents from ancient Sumer, modern professional librarianship has its roots in the nineteenth century public library.[39] The occupation of telephone operator can be directly traced to the opening of the first telephone exchange in 1878.[40] In the second half of the twentieth century, demand for librarians grew beyond the public library into the private sector, especially as corporations became more dependent on sources of readily available information. Librarians' traditional expertise for building and maintaining collections of books provided a professional pool of labor as corporations began to establish their own information collections and special libraries—including information stored in forms other than books. Telephone operators have been part of the labor force since the establishment of the first telephone exchange in New Haven, Connecticut.

The first operators were boys with experience as telegraphists. But in September of 1878, Emily Nutt was hired in Boston as the first woman operator, and management soon saw women operators as a godsend. Not nearly as rude or abrasive as the boys, they worked for a fraction of a man's pay; so that, within a year, women had swept the boys from the job.[41] For a century, telephone operators represented an ideal opportunity for young women seeking to enter the white collar labor force.

In the 19th century, few possibilities existed for young women who wanted or needed work outside the home. Store clerking, sewing, and librarianship were acceptable for girls, though the opportunities were limited since these occupations also appealed to men. Factory work might appeal to respectable girls in the early part of the nineteenth century when mill owners offered supervised boarding houses, but by the 1870s the pressure of the industrial revolution and the flood of immigrant labor had turned factories into gaping maws swallowing up workers in 12 hour shifts, 7 days a week.[42] For young women from modest backgrounds, telephone work, as it was called, offered salvation from the degradation of the factory floor. Fortunately, demand grew apace with the spread of the telephone. In 1900 there were 19,000 operators, and roughly 18 telephones per 1,000 population. By 1970, the peak year of employment, there were 420,000 operators. Telephone availability had soared to 583 per 1,000 population, a growth rate of 3,250 percent.[43]

However, because telephone operators are employed as one component in a mechanical communication process, their jobs are sensitive to technological innovations that substitute mechanical switches for human labor. Continued introduction of progressively sophisticated mechanical and electronic switches has boosted the productivity of the individual operator and diminished demand for her services. Therefore, by 1970 the ratio of operators to telephones was 1/335, down from a ratio of 1/50 in the beginning.[44] The number of operators began to decline after 1970, and will continue to decline into the twenty-first century. From the vantage point of the present, the rise and fall in the employment curve of telephone operators seems obvious. Even when paid at women's wages, their expense as a labor cost prompted the search for suitable mechanical substitutes. The success of that search can be seen in the curve's decline (see figure 3-7). For computer operators, on the other hand, the future appears limitless, as their burgeoning numbers testify. But management's motivation to cut labor costs among computer operators functions as a constant of industrialism, just as it did for telephone operators. The rising cost of hiring computer operators compels managers to seek mechanical ways to increase productivity, thus tempering demand for additional operators. Thus, the shape of the employment curve for telephone operators informs us of the long-term employment path for computer operators. To be sure, telephone operators thrived as an occupation for one hundred years, and are hardly scarce today. Yet their numbers have fallen to the level of the 1920s. The pressure to automate was always there, as it must also be for computer operators, especially when one considers their higher salaries. Both occupations symbolize the fusion of human and machine necessary to run the information society.

While some occupations such as scientists, engineers, and librarians have found their niche in response to the fundamental needs of the information economy, others seem to be as susceptible to mechanization as factory jobs. In fact, the human-machine balance, evident in the experience of telephone operators, reflects the interplay of labor cost, productivity, and profit present in all modern occupations. As long as managers face the calculus of maximizing profits and minimizing costs, occupations, whether information or otherwise, will continue to come under the scrutiny of job rationalizers.

Yet work means more than productivity ratios. In order to better understand the social dimension of information work, it is necessary to explore less quantifiable territory.

The Meaning of Information Work

That a sizable percentage of working individuals do not contribute directly to the production and distribution of material goods is a novel experience in human history. The industrial revolution produced a society where a sizable percentage of its members no longer labored at producing food. Yet at no time did the numbers of Americans actually employed in manufacturing exceed 27% of the total labor force.[45] While America's industrial output soared, advances in the technologies of production and organization acted to reduce the numbers of factory workers. As recounted in chapter 1, these same advances laid the foundations for the information workforce of today. But though information workers have predominated for most of the 20th century, until recently the language of work has tended to reflect the shop floor more than the office desk, as illustrated by these examples from *Working* by Studs Terkel.

> I noticed somebody talking on the phone the other day, one of the older guys. He said he was at the office. It dawned on me when a guy says, "I'm at the office," it means, "I don't dirty my hands." He wasn't at work, he was "at the office."[46]

> The company I work for doesn't make a product. We provide a service. Our service is auditing.[47]

Terkel himself displayed a related blind spot. Of the 133 workers who constitute the subjects of his book, he interviewed 61 information workers (46%) without realizing it. That *Working* , published in 1974, received no serious criticisms on this point indicates how recently we have come to recognize the fact of information work. So perhaps it is not surprising that information work is misunderstood or viewed with suspicion.[48] After all, we have only just begun to understand the idea of information, while many workers have yet to recognize that information forms the focus of their labor.

The divide between information work and physical work exists because information work takes place within a cognitive context to a much larger degree than physical or factory work. Even with highly routinized information work, such as filing and key punching, recognition of recorded symbols and intellectual judgment guide the work activity and define the product. Verbs such as *analyze, classify, compose, diagnose, estimate, evaluate, organize, plan, predict, record, schedule, search, summarize, synthesize, and tell*, characterize information work; whereas, *adjust, align, assemble, attach, clean, construct, fabricate, insert, and wire*, more typically describe physical work.[49] So, though a narrow boundary exists between manual work and some information occupations, it is the intellectual dimension that dominates information work. Information work also falls between physical and service work when it comes to the power of the worker to influence the rate of production. For example, when factory workers threaten to strike, managers can prepare by stockpiling inventory in order to avoid a loss of sales during the period of non-production. By contrast, service workers can deny management the product simply by staying off the job, since there is no way to stockpile services. However, information work resembles both. Like service workers, information workers can deny management the part of their labor that constitutes an intellectual service. For example, the verbal instructions provided by receptionists cannot be saved for later use. However, some kinds of information can be stockpiled just like any material good. Managers of a database operation can continue to deliver data should the key punchers go on strike, even though the database cannot be updated—although, in many cases, the database would decrease in value if the strike proved of long duration. For those industries where the information product is delivered on a storable medium, management faces the same options as it does in manufacturing. Information work contains characteristics of both factory work and service work, depending on the nature of the final product.

But from the point of view of the worker, information occupations contain their own distinct logic. For one thing, because the work is largely mental, it may seem devoid of any lasting product. Writing a policy, giving directions, planning a meeting, answering the phone, arranging a schedule, sending a memo, and facilitating a sale leave subtle traces. By contrast, factory and construction workers can point to a final product and recount their small contribution to the assembly of the parts. When the final product is unclear, as it is for many middle managers, the movement of information becomes an important focus. Under these circumstances, information workers may identify with the distribution of information and derive satisfaction from keeping up with the flow. But unlike identification with a final product, identification with the distribution of information denies the worker a sense of closure, especially when job related tasks are indistinct and merely a part of the general flow of the organization. Granted, some information products bring high recognition.

Authors who publish books receive some acclaim—no matter how minor—and they are, thereafter, publicly identified as authors. Members of a team that produced a successful ad campaign develop a reputation within their field and the same is true for some engineers, artists, actors, and scientists. But for the secretaries, clerks, and middle managers who also contribute to the programs, designs, and campaigns, their lot is to remain anonymous. Though they may receive informal recognition, they usually achieve no public identification with the product. So for most information workers the end result is not the product, but the process. When the final product is information workers may find themselves adrift in a sea of abstractions. That is, when the output is not clear, the individual derives meaning from the work experience. For such workers, connection to the product may simply be memories—memories without proof.

In the case of professional cultures with a heavy emphasis on the intellect as the source of production, this priority carries with it profound claims on the participants. Aspiring professionals must adapt to ways of thinking appropriated by the professional culture and shared by its members. The socializing process begins as soon as the individual enters a graduate program of study and is exposed to the special language and perspective of the profession. An aspiring individual learns to think like a lawyer, doctor, engineer, scientist, librarian, or professor and develops a world view shaped by the values of the profession. So strong are professional cultures that popular stereotypes often overemphasize "typical" characteristics e.g., lawyers are aggressive; doctors pretend to be omniscient; engineers are socially awkward; scientists are absent-minded; librarians are orderly; and, professors are either impractical or pedantic, or both. But whether the stereotypes are "true" or not, professions do affect the attitudes and values of their members because the paradigms of the professions become the perspectives through which the members view their work and eventually the world. This phenomenon will become increasingly prevalent as the information economy expands and as more individuals become information workers. More individuals will experience the cognitive blend between occupational values and world view, the combination traditionally experienced by professionals. Granted, many information workers will suffer the confinement of the industrial system, even though they work in non factory settings. Nevertheless, what distinguishes the information worker is the reliance on symbols, as the basic ingredients for constructing the product. As the economy demands more information products, more workers will merge their intellects with the production process. So, when seen on a continuum—from industrial-assembly line to intellectual-professional—those occupations falling closer to the professions will demand more intellectual effort; and, in so doing, will impart a world view. In this way occupationally-reinforced ways of thinking, that peculiar privilege and trap of the professional, will become commonplace.

Alienation and the Meaning of Information Work

If an information worker's brain acts as the means of producing information goods and services, and if this arrangement also influences the worker's cognition in a kind of mental convergence, then a new relationship may be emerging as mind and work fuse.

By contrast, the old relationship was marked by dissonance, as Friedriech Engels noted when observing the condition of the English working class.

> Another source of demoralization is their being condemned to work. As voluntary, productive activity is the highest enjoyment known to us, so is compulsory toil the most cruel, degrading punishment. Nothing is more terrible than being constrained to do some one thing every day from morning until night against one's will. And the more a man the worker feels himself, the more hateful must his work be to him, because he feels the constraint, the aimlessness of it for himself. Why does he work? For love of work? From a natural impulse? Not at all! He works for money, for a thing which has nothing whatsoever to do with the work itself. [50]

As Engels astutely discerned, the discipline of industrialization forced workers to become separated from their own labor; so, though they might produce something with their own hands, they had no claim to it. By selling their labor, rather than the products of their labor, workers came to regard themselves as commodities. Once in the factory, a worker's behavior was regulated by an imposed division of labor until each man or woman behaved like a cog in a mechanized process.[51] For many workers their role in production became so small and abstract that identification with the manufacture of the entire product became impossible. The condition that estranged and then subordinated the worker to the 'reified' product of his labor, Marx called *alienation*.[52]

Perhaps rooted in the Protestant Ethic or in the Judeo-Christian notion of the dignity of labor by one's own sweat, the expectation that work should provide some moral satisfaction left the worker in conflict when confronted with the new forms of industrial work.[53] But once the labor process, i.e., the material assets necessary to produce the product plus the organization of the work became the property of the capitalist, the worker lost all control over the work activity and the product.[54] The new work relationship now dominated the worker's life, as in the coal miner's lament.

> Sixteen tons, what do you get, another day older and deeper in debt.
> Saint Peter don't you call me cause I can't go, I owe my soul to the company store.[55]

No longer expecting physical, emotional, or moral fulfillment from work, industrial workers came to regard work as a means to an end.

Yet, though alienation threatened to reduce the worker to the status of an animal, the worst nightmares did not come to pass. For one thing, even the most alienating work contains some potential for pleasantries with co-workers. In addition, most workers can extract some meaning from even the most repetitive jobs.[56] For that matter, humans possess an astounding capacity for adapting to their environments, and it is this adaptability that carried most individuals through the traumatic transition from pre-industrial to industrial life. Today, the industrial revolution hovers in the indistinct shadows of history for most Americans, while the conditions observed by Marx now constitute the norms accepted by nearly all workers in the United States.[57] Even high status information workers like engineers and middle managers experience forms of alienated work. In modern society, characterized as it is by video leisure, as well as government protection from the worst excesses of capitalist employment and unemployment, alienation is rendered bearable. But as the environment of the factory fades against the environment of the office, will the tide of alienation abate? It might.

Since information work depends on the manipulation of symbols, it can create a buffer between the act of work and the physical world. The worker comes to depend on symbols and abstractions for his or her livelihood and these come to hold a significant place in the worker's world view.[58] It seems fairly clear that for an elite, information work offers the chance to reintegrate meaning with labor and thus to achieve the satisfaction missing from alienated work. These workers, e.g., some writers, academics, professionals, et al. can exploit the symbolic essence of information work for purposes of self-actualization. Still, industrial principles of organization, with their emphasis on formulistic efficiency, have also made their appearance in the office, where accumulating evidence indicates that in some—perhaps many—information occupations, the scrutiny of the efficiency expert and the calculus of productivity has resulted in deskilling and automation.[59] Today, corporate leaders are exploiting the advantages of new information technologies, in order to reduce employment in white collar occupations. So although the symbolic quality of information work opens new vistas, it has not proved immune to encroachment by the industrial system.[60]

Nevertheless, we may yet confuse the fuzzy boundaries between information work and information leisure as affirmation of a decline in alienation and miss the truly integrating possibilities. We would do well to keep in mind Aristotle's observation that happiness consists of striving after perfection through the use of the intellect because information work comes closest to his ideal, especially when it requires major intellectual involvement.[61] In the balance, it appears that information work may break down some aspects of alienation while intensifying others. Thus, rather than resolving the issue, the information age has only given it a new twist.

For the first time, large numbers of individuals—not just the elites—make a living by acts of the mind where processing information is the product of their work. As information work becomes the standard against which other forms of toil are compared, it will alter the way we think about work. Whereas, executives, lawyers, and engineers, still talk of "rolling up their sleeves," "getting their hands dirty," and "working up a sweat," their expressions hark back to an era when work was primarily physical, soiling, and exhausting of body. In the 21st century, new images will dominate the language of work and they will be drawn from the technologies and processes of the manipulation of symbols. Still, just as the image of a computer programmer working at Fairchild Electronics is familiarly etched in the public consciousness, so too should be the image of a 1920s distribution clerk, routing crates of apricots picked on land that now houses Fairchild Electronics. Both images capture the essence of information work, even as one image fades.

Notes

1. Smith, A. (1776/1902). *An inquiry into the nature and causes of the wealth of nations.* New York: American Home Library, p. 39.
2. Toffler, A. (1980). *The third wave.* New York: William Morrow, p. 186.
3. Porat, M. U. (1977). *The information economy: Definition and measurement* No. OT Special Publication 77-12 (1)). Washington DC: Department of Commerce/Office of Telecommunications. The following citations illustrate the widespread reliance on Porat's findings. Bell, D. (1981). The social framework of the information society. In T. Forestor (Eds.), *The microelectronics revolution* (pp. 500–549). Cambridge, MA: MIT Press. Dizard, W. P. J. (1982). *The coming information age: An overview of technology, economics, and politics.* New York: Longman. Katz, R. L. (1988). *The information society.* New York: Praeger. Nora, S., & Minc, A. (1980). *The computerization of society: A report to the president of France.* Cambridge, MA: MIT Press. Ochai, A. (1984). The emerging information society. *International Library Review, 16*(4), 367–372. Toffler, A. (1980). *The third wave.* New York: William Morrow. Williams, F. (1982). *The communications revolution.* Beverly Hills, CA: Sage.
4. Only data presented for the 20th century are presented in this chapter, because they are the most relevant to the questions asked here. Although Porat's analysis goes back to 1860, data for the 19th century are not of sufficient reliability to be of use to our discussion.
5. Machlup, F. (1962). *The production and distribution of knowledge in the United States.* Princeton, NJ: Princeton University Press.
6. Machlup, F., & Mansfield, U., Eds. (1983). *The study of information: Interdisciplinary messages.* New York: John Wiley & Sons.
7. Machlup, F. (1962) p. 33.
8. If one includes students ninth grade and up as members of the labor force, the figure increases to 42.8%. Machlup, F. (1962) pp. 349, 386.
9. Bell, D. (1976). *The coming of post-industrial society.* New York: Basic Books (pp. 228–232).
10. Porat, M. U. (1977) p. 105.
11. Porat, M. U. (1977) pp. 8, 117.
12. Katz, R. L. (1988). *The information society.* New York: Praeger. Singlemann, J. (1978). *From agriculture to services.* Beverly Hills, CA: Sage. At about this time, Debons, King, Mansfield, and Shirey were conducting their survey of information professionals. They also followed an occupational approach, but limited their

analysis to "professionals" only in their definition of those whose occupations required them to hold a bachelor's degree or higher. Thus, their analysis shed useful light on the characteristics of information professionals within the labor force, but did not attempt to study the pattern of distribution of information work. Debons, A., King, D. W., Mansfield, U., & Shirey, D. L. (1981). *The information professional: Survey of an emerging field.* New York: Marcel Dekker, Inc.

13. Schement, J. R., & Lievrouw, L. A. (1984). A behavioral measure of information work. *Telecommunications Policy, 8*(4), 321-334.
14. Porat, M. U. (1977) p. 105.
15. Schement, J. R., & Lievrouw, L. A. (1984).
16. In the DOT, 55% of all occupations were found in the industrial sector. The preponderance of industrial occupations, in contrast to the actual number of industrial workers, can be attributed to the longer period of time available for industrial occupations to subdivide and specialize, as well as to the pro-industrial bias built into the DOT at its inception during the Depression years. The information work sector was already the largest sector during the Depression. Yet the idea of information work would not arrive for 40 years. Schement, J. R. & Lievrouw, L. A. (1984) (pp. 330-333).
17. Rubin, M. R., & Huber, M. T., with Taylor, E.L. (1986). *The knowledge industry in the United States 1960–1980.* Princeton, NJ: Princeton, p. 196.
18. Bell, D. (1976). *The coming of post-industrial society.* New York: Basic Books, p. 217.
19. Bell, D. (1981). The social framework of the information society. In T. Forestor (Eds.), *The microelectronics revolution* (pp. 500-549). Cambridge, MA: MIT Press.
20. Porat, M. U. (1977) p. 119.
21. Bell, D. (1976). Other researchers, such as Schement and Lievrouw, pursued this line of questioning by studying the extent to which information work behavior had penetrated the entire work force. Schement, J. R., & Lievrouw, L. A. (1984).
22. Porat, M. U. (1977) p. 117.
23. Personal communications recorded in December 1976, and November 1977.
24. Porat, M. U. (1977) p. 117.
25. Bell, D. (1979). The social framework of the information society. In M. L. Dertouzos & J. Moss (Eds.), *The computer age: A twenty-year view* (pp. 163-211). Cambridge, MA: MIT Press, pp. 180-186.
26. Schement, J. R. (1990). Porat, Bell, and the information society reconsidered: The growth of information work in the early 20th century. *Information processing and management, 26*(4), 449-465.
27. Dickens, C. (1843/1939). *A christmas carol.* New York: Washington Square Press (pp. 13, 16, 17, 30).
28. Chandler, A. D. J. (1977). *The visible hand: The managerial revolution in American business.* Cambridge, MA: Harvard University Press (pp. 240-244). Heilbroner, R. L., & Singer, A. (1984). *The economic transformation of America: 1600 to the present* (2nd ed.). New York: Harcourt Brace Jovanovich (pp. 175-176).
29. Beniger, J. R. (1986). *The control revolution.* Cambridge, MA: Harvard University Press (pp. 219-287) Chandler, A. D. J. (1977). *The visible hand: The managerial revolution in American business.* Cambridge, MA: Harvard University Press, pp. 81-187. Heilbroner, R. L., & Singer, A. (1984). *The economic transformation of America: 1600 to the present* (2nd ed.). New York: Harcourt Brace Jovanovich (pp. 143-167). Schement, J. R. (1989). The origins of the information society in the United States: Competing visions. In J. Salvaggio (Ed.) (1989). *The information society* (pp. 29-50). New York: Lawrence Erlbaum, pp. 41-44.

30. Sloan, A. P. J. (1963). *My years with General Motors*. New York: Doubleday (pp. 53-54, 56, 115).
31. Chandler, A. D. J. (1977) pp. 436-437, 394-395.
32. Machlup, F., & Kronwinkler, T. (1975). Workers who produce knowledge: a steady increase, 1900 to 1970. *Weltwirtschaftliches Archiv., 111*(4), 752-759. For an excellent treatment of the social and political dynamics affecting the 19th and 20th century growth of the professional work force, see Abbott, A. D. (1988). *The system of professions: An essay on the division of expert labor*. Chicago, IL: University of Chicago.
33. State and local government employment figures were either incomplete or unreliable for 1900-1930; most state and territorial governments—Oklahoma, Arizona, and New Mexico—were small in numbers of employees. The inclusion in these numbers of federal government employees who were not information workers appears to be a reasonable compensation for the absence of figures on state and local government employees.
34. Galbraith, J. K. (1967). *The new industrial state*. New York: The New American Library (pp. 297-303, 332-349).
35. Table 948. (1987). In *Statistical abstract of the United States: 1988*. Washington DC: Bureau of the Census.
36. Eisenhower, D. D. (1960). Farewell radio and television address to the American people, January 17, 1961. In *Public papers of the presidents of the United States, Dwight D. Eisenhower, 1960-61* (pp. 1035-40). Washington D.C.
37. Table 960. (1987). In *Statistical abstract of the United States: 1988*. Washington DC: Bureau of the Census.
38. Schement, J. R., & Lievrouw, L. A. (1988). A third vision: Capitalism and the industrial origins of the information society. In J. R. Schement & L. Lievrouw (Eds.) (1988), *Competing visions, complex realities: Social aspects of the information society* (pp. 33-45). Norwood, NJ: Ablex, pp. 8-9.
39. Dalby, A. (1986). The sumerian catalogs. *Journal of Library History, 21*(3), 475-487. McArthur, T. (1986). *Worlds of Reference: Lexicography, Learning and Language from the Clay Tablet to the Computer*. Cambridge, UK: Cambridge University Press, pp. 21-23.
40. Brooks, J. (1975). *Telephone: The first hundred years*. New York: Harper & Row (pp. 65, 66).
41. Brooks, J. (1975) (pp. 65, 66). Maddox, B. (1977). Women and the Switchboard. In I. d. S. Pool (Ed.), *The social impact of the telephone* (pp. 262-280). Cambridge, MA: MIT Press.
42. Heilbroner, R. L., & Singer, A. (1984). pp. 220-223.
43. Table D 233-682, Table R 1-12. (1975). *Historical statistics of the United States, colonial times to 1970* (Bicentennial Ed.). Washington DC: GPO. Table 881. (1987). In *Statistical abstract of the United States: 1988*. Washington DC: Bureau of the Census. Total number of telephones in the U.S. in 1900: 1,005,000; in 1970: 120, 218,000; in 1982: 151,000,000 (est.).
44. Table D 233-682. Table R 1-12. (1975). *Historical statistics of the United States, colonial times to 1970* (Bicentennial Ed.). Washington DC: GPO.
45. U. S. workers employed in manufacturing reached their peak percentages in 1920, and then again in 1950 and 1970. Note the following percentages for 1870-1988— 1870: 19%; 1880: 19%; 1890: 19%; 1900: 20%; 1910: 22%; 1920: 27%; 1930: 20%; 1940: 20%; 1950: 24%; 1960: 23%; 1970: 24%; 1980: 20%; 1988: 17%. Table Series D 167-181. (1975). *Historical statistics of the United States, colonial times to 1970* (Bicentennial Ed.). Washington DC: GPO. Tables 635, 658. (1981). *Statistical abstract of the United States: 1981*. Washington DC: U.S.

Bureau of the Census. Tables 624, 650. (1990). *Statistical abstract of the United States: 1990*. Washington DC: Bureau of the Census.

46. Terkel, S. (1974). *Working*. New York: Pantheon, p. 451.

47. Terkel, S. (1974) p. 263.

48. In other times, individuals performing information work were seen as parasites because they were considered non-productive. For example, Edmund Burke's comment from the edge of the Enlightenment rues the passing of a romantic age and the coming of a new age with its representatives. "But the age of chivalry is gone. That of sophisters, economists, and calculators, has succeeded; and the glory of Europe is extinguished forever." From *Reflections on the Revolution in France*, Burke, E. (1790/1910). *Reflections on the revolution in France*. London, UK: J. M. Dent & Sons Ltd, p. 73.

49. Adapted from Schement, J. R. and Lievrouw, L. A. (1984) *A behavioral measure of information work*. *Telecommunications Policy, 8*(4), Table 4, p. 327.

50. Engels, F. (1845/1987). *The condition of the working class in England* (Wischnewetzky, Florence, Trans.). Harmondsworth, UK: Penguin (pp. 145–146).

51. Durkheim, E. (1933). *The division of labor in society*. New York: Free Press, (pp. 374–381).

52. Marx, K. (1886/1906). *Capital: A critique of political economy*. New York: The Modern Library. But see also: Bier, W. C. (Ed.). (1972). *Alienation: Plight of modern man*. New York: Fordham University Press. Blauner, R. (1964). *Alienation and freedom: The factory worker and his industry*. Chicago, IL: University of Chicago. Braverman, H. (1974). *Labor and monopoly capital: The degradation of work in the twentieth century*. New York: Monthly Review Press. Fromm, E. (1962). Alienation under capitalism. In E. Josephson & M. Josephson (Eds.), *Man alone: Alienation in modern society* (pp. 56–73). New York: Dell. Geyer, R. F., & Schweitzer, D. (Eds.). (1981). *Alienation: Problems and meaning, theory and method*. London, UK: Routledge & Keegan Paul. Heilbroner, R. (1980). *Marxism: For and against*. New York: W. W. Norton. Marcson, S. (Ed.). (1970). *Automation, alienation, and anomie*. New York: Harper & Row. McLeod, J., Ward, S., & Tancill, K. (1965). Alienation and uses of the mass media. *Public Opinion Quarterly, 65–66*, 583–591. Postman, N. (1985). *Amusing ourselves to death: Public discourse in the age of show business*. New York: Penguin. Weber, M. (1958). *The protestant ethic and the spirit of capitalism* (Parsons, Talcott, Trans.). New York: Charles Scribner's Sons.

53. "By the sweat of your face shall you get bread to eat." Genesis 4:19; "There is nothing better for man than to eat and drink and provide himself with good things by his labors. Even this, I realized, is from the hand of God." Ecclesiastes 3:24; "And with misspent toil he molds a meaningless god from the self-same clay." Wisdom 15:8. (1983). *The New American Bible* (Translated from the original languages by the Catholic Biblical Association of America, Trans.). New York: Thomas Nelson Publishers. See also John Paul II. John Paul II (1981). *On human work: Laborem exercens*. United States Catholic Conference. Berger, B. M. (1963). The sociology of leisure: Some suggestions. In E. O. Smigel (Ed.), *Work and leisure: A contemporary social problem* (pp. 21–40). New Haven, CN: College and University Press.

54. Braverman, H. (1974). *Labor and monopoly capital: The degradation of work in the twentieth century*. New York: Monthly Review Press, pp. 56–57. Heilbroner, R. (1980). *Marxism: For and against*. New York: W. W. Norton, pp. 70–73. Marx, K. (1962). Alienated labor. In E. Josephson & M. R. Josephson (Eds.), *Man alone: Alienation in modern society* (pp. 93–105). New York: Dell, pp. 95, 96, 98, 100, 101.

55. Travis, M. (1947). "Sixteen tons". New York: Capitol Recording. Later popularized by Tennesee Ernie Ford in 1955 and also recorded on Capitol Records.

56. Blauner, R. (1964) pp. 24–34.

57. Today, one can still observe the human dimension of the coming of industrialization. In the Favelas of Sao Paolo, Brazil, and in the Black townships of South Africa, one may encounter individuals who have traveled the distance from self-contained farm to urban factory. But even there, the inquirer would most likely miss the element of novelty and shock that confronted the first English and American textile workers.

58. Zuboff, S. (1988). *In the age of the smart machine: The future of work and power.* New York: Basic Books (pp. 76, 81, 185).

59. Kraut, R. E. (1987). *Technology and the transformation of white-collar work.* Hillsdale, NJ: Lawrence Erlbaum Associates (pp. 14, 90, 101). Solomon, W. S. (1985). From craftspeople to production workers: Video display terminals and the devaluation of newspaper copyediting. *Communication, 8,* 207–224. Sydow, J. (1984). Sociotechnical change and perceived work situations: Some conceptual propositions and an empirical investigation in different office settings. *Office: Technology and People, 2,* 121–132. Zimbalist, A. (1979). *Case Studies on the Labor Process.* New York: Monthly Review Press, pp. 1, 51, 103, 193, 242. But see also Peter Whalley for an analysis of engineers that argues that various organizational cultures treat these professionals differently, not always in an alienating manner. Whalley, P. (1984). Deskilling engineers?: The labor process, labor markets, and labor segmentation. *Social Problems, 32*(2), 117–132.

60. A variation of this theme can be seen in the production of information and its distribution within organizations, where, as noted in chapter 1, the growth or maintenance of bureaucracies results. The very bigness of these structures and their dependence on documentation results in abstraction of the organization's relationship to its members—as well as to its clients. And, since bureaucracies typify the information society, their brand of alienation is especially noteworthy. For classic comments on this phenomenon, see Fromm, E. (1955). *The sane society.* New York: Holt, Rinehart and Winston (p. 116).

61. Aristotle (350 B.C./1927). *Aristotle: Selections.* New York: Charles Scribner's Sons, pp. 224–226, 279–282.

4

Media Environments

Suppose that by the twenty-first century every human on earth who has a wrist-mounted communications device can be in contact with any other human via a satellite communications network; that home television has over 100 channels, many of them interactive; that most home appliances are programmable or controllable by our voice; that most mail is sent electronically; that small discs for our home players can hold many thousands of pages of textual information; that an electronic network makes available a university education for anyone willing to pursue it; and that we can join our communities for work, play, education, health care, or inspiration electronically? What then?—Frederick Williams[1]

On the Saturday afternoon of the future while the children play *Star Wars* on the screen, the head of the household may be immersed in sport. He watches one game on the big screen while a printer at his side spatters news of other games. With his keyboard he can request the results of other games to be displayed on the screen. He can freeze a frame of the televised play at any moment and examine it.—James Martin[2]

However, the most popular goodies in this high-tech community are electronic consumer products: personal computers, video recorders, home communication systems, video games.—Everett M. Rogers and Judith Larson[3]

How do we adapt our private lives to the information society? We have chosen to rephrase the more frequently asked question that asks how people will experience leisure in the information society. Leisure is a problematic notion. It is often equated with private life and posed as the opposite of work, which is often equated with public life. But as the information society introduces forms of work that take place in the home, the familiar dichotomy creates a shallow analysis, at once oversimplifying the interplay of emerging tendencies. In this chapter we explore the fuzzy boundaries experienced by individuals as they accommodate the private sphere to the information society.

Living, as we do, in a culture that reveres technology, most Americans think of the information society as a parade of newly developed technologies. This assumption sets the baseline for popular expectations of what the information society has to offer the individual. Williams' view of the future where a computerized nerve center frees the individual of many reasons to leave home is typical; and Martin's scenario, where the latest television technologies deliver a sports fan's fantasy—access to every game played everywhere—

is a regular story line in the popular media. In the 20th century's last decade, neither of these predictions seems so strange. We have largely assimilated their images and expectations. Yet they only make sense because they carry within them a set of cultural assumptions that we take for granted.

Both scenarios imply a kind of progress resulting from new inventions of machine technology. They make sense because Americans embrace an optimistic technological determinism that anticipates new technologies in the belief that they will elevate the quality of life.[4] Therefore, if greater quality of life is the reward, then the goal in these scenarios is personal convenience for the individual. Society, as imagined here, ends at the front door and begins again at the office when the telecommuter's product appears on office screens or fax machines. Within this logic, the individual represents the sole component of society and, by implication, personal convenience equals fulfillment.

Both scenarios describe a personal environment dense with channels for receiving information. But neither hints at how the individual will cope with the flow into the home, nor does each suggest whether the information will arrive in some intelligible context or as so many fragments. In fact, by introducing significant work into the home, the first scenario blurs the boundaries between work activities and non-work activities like leisure. The individual in the first scenario emerges as an information seeking professional actively charting a course through the technological landscape of the information society. But in the second description, we imagine a sedentary male—in a rather traditional household—encircled by technology for consuming sports information and seemingly buffered from the rest of his family. In both scenarios, the information choices one makes may serve to distinguish one from one's peers. Consequently, apparent differences in patterns of information use might become the basis for defining oneself as an individual unique from the rest. If so, then information consumption, rather than some activity or contribution to society, will become the new basis for defining the individual.

Information as a Consumer Good

To ask what kinds of information Americans "consume" makes some sense in a consumer culture but it misrepresents the nature of information. After all, the reading of a newspaper produces no deterioration in the information itself. Granted, the value of the information may decrease as it loses its timeliness for the reader. However, the measure of value derives from the user, not from the information. In addition, the paper itself degrades with use and time, but this constitutes consumption of the medium or package, not of the information. Neither of these consequences cause "exhaustion" or "depletion" of the information, nor match the experience of consuming material goods like food or clothing.[5] Yet the concept of "consumption" is an appropriate one for understanding how we make use of information, because patterns of information consumption bear virtual similarities to those for consuming material goods. For example, in the course of learning to be consumers, individuals adjust their information demands in response to marketing and advertising. They master the evaluation, purchase, replacement, and display of information exactly as they do for other goods. They purchase many information goods in the same markets in which they purchase material goods.

Can there be conspicuous consumption of information? Americans certainly demonstrate ingenuity in the public exhibition of their material possessions. Yet information, because it is symbolic and ephemeral, poses a challenge to the culture of display. How then can one show off to advantage that which is mental in its pure state? The solution to this dilemma of status lies in packaging the information. Concurrent with the evolution of a consumer culture of information came elaborate packaging and rituals of display. Whether subtle, as in the commuter who parades the Wall Street Journal under her arm on the train, or overpowering, as in a wall decorated with audio and visual electronic equipment, the range of opportunities depends on the creativity of the individual and the customs of one's relevant audience. The latest spate of decorator phones gives some indication of the conspicuous display potential of a device which for 100 years stood for utilitarian design.

In this regard, the widespread adoption of elaborate media environments can be traced to the more general adoption of consumer values. The emergence of a consumer culture centering on information has been growing for the last 100 years. Expenditures on information goods and services have risen as a share of total expenditures, so that all Americans now spend significant portions of their disposable incomes on maintaining media environments. The rapid penetration of VCRs and cable further indicate the acceptance of a value defining information consumption as leisure. By contrast the slower acceptance of home personal computers might indicate the relative familiarity of the concept of leisure versus that of personal productivity. Though both concepts represent an extrapolation of the idea of information, for most individuals Martin's scenario is easier to relate to than Williams'. Yet though Americans continue to add on to their media environments and evolve new uses for them, we know little of that experience. Outside of a few media like film and television that have attracted both anecdotal comment and research, little systematic analysis exists to provide us with a broad view of this American taste for information.

Tables 4-1 and 4-2 on the availability of information goods and services indicate the relative cornucopia already on the market in 1900. Of the categories of information goods and services for sale today, 61% could be purchased by turn-of-the-century Americans.[6] We can, therefore, imagine the 20th century as a period when a rich menu of information goods and services became richer. However, one should not interpret tables 4-1 and 4-2 as implying that Americans generally consumed all of the goods and services available. In

TABLE 4-1
Some Information Goods Available to Consumers

art supplies*	paintings & sculptures*
audiocassettes	personal computers
audio compact discs	photo cameras*
audio records*	photo processing equip.*
audio tape	photographic film*
binoculars*	photos and posters*
books*	projection screens*
calculators*	radios
calendars	satellite antennas
catalogues*	sheet music*
computer software	signal decoders
eye glasses*	slide projectors*
fax machines	stereo equipment
film	surveillance devices
film cameras	telephones*
film projectors	TV sets
film screens	typewriters*
greeting cards*	VCR cameras
hearing aids*	VCR purchases
letters*	VCR tape purchases
magazines*	video cassettes
musical instruments*	video discs
newspapers*	video, computer games
	writing supplies*

* = Information goods available to consumers in 1900.

TABLE 4-2
Some Information Services Available to Consumers

cinema performances*	opera*
computer bulletin boards	photo developing services*
concerts*	professional training*
dance performances*	religious activities*
education, post secondary*	satellite services
education, primary*	self improvement services*
education, secondary*	sports events*
electronic mail	telephone services*
live/popular theater*	TV cable subscriptions
museums, expositions, etc.*	VCR rentals
online data services	VCR tape rentals

* = Information services available to consumers in 1900.

1900, just as in 1994, most households could afford only a subset of the total array of goods and services. These lists represent the limits of an individual's possible purchases, then and today.

The 20th century marks the move by Americans toward the consumption of information goods. The integration of national markets for material goods set the stage for the availability of information goods—and services—and their inclusion in the consumer culture appearing at the turn of the century. Americans embraced the new information products and services as they became available throughout the 20th century. At first glance, the level of expenditures (see Figures 4-1 and 4-2) may seem low—5.4% in 1986 doesn't sound like much—even for a limited selection of information goods. But in the course of the century, Americans increased their expenditures for information goods and services against other types of expenditures. In 1930, for example, Americans spent one dollar on information for every six dollars spent

FIGURE 4-1
Total Personal Consumption Expenditures: 1935–1986

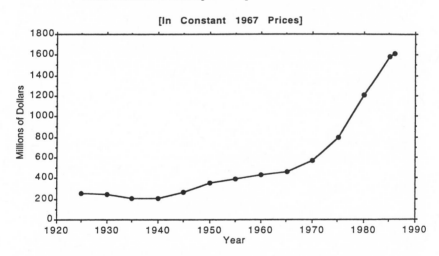

Source: Compiled from Series E 135-166 (1975). *Historical Statistics of the United States, Colonial Times to 1970* (Bicentennial Ed.). Washington DC: GPO. Table 738 (1987). *Statistical Abstract of the United States: 1988.* Washington, DC: Bureau of the Census.

[1] "Personal consumption expenditures represent the market value of purchases of goods and services by individuals and nonprofit institutions and the value of food, clothing, housing, and the rental value of owner-occupied houses, but does not include purchases of dwellings, which are classified as capital goods" (p. 218).

[2] Constant Price = Current Price multiplied by Consumer Price Index expressed as percent of the base year price. All prices in the formula are for a given year. Constant prices do not generally express qualitative change in the economy. Furthermore, constant prices tend to underestimate short-run fluctuations in prices. Increases after 1967 tend to be slightly over estimated.

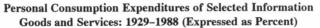

FIGURE 4-2
Personal Consumption Expenditures of Selected Information
Goods and Services: 1929–1988 (Expressed as Percent)

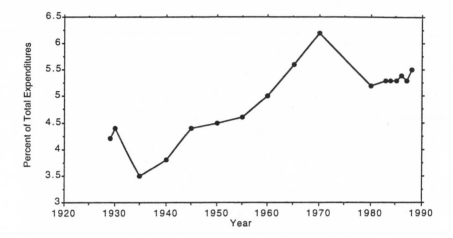

Source: Compiled from Series G 416–469 (1975). *Historical Statistics of the United States, Colonial Times to 1970.* Washington, DC: GPO. Table 708 (1981), *Statistical Abstract of the United States: 1981.* Washington, DC: U.S. Bureau of the Census. Table 676 (1987) *Statistical Abstract of the United States: 1988.* Washington DC: Bureau of the Census.

[1] Information goods and services include the following: telephone services, radio and television sets [including repair expenditures], records and musical instruments, books, maps, magazines, newspapers, sheet music, private education and research, jewelry and watches (Watches were estimated at 1/3 of the total for this category).

[2] Comparable data for 1971–1979 is not available. Clearly this is an important period since the percentage of total personal consumption expenditures spent on information goods and services dropped for the first time since the Depression. For now, the curve of the slope between 1970 and 1980 cannot be determined.

[3] Percentages beginning with 1960 include data for Alaska and Hawaii.

on food. By 1986, they spent one dollar on information for every 3.5 dollars spent on food.[7] Lower percentages of expenditures on information goods and services during the '80s probably indicate dropping prices for electronic equipment against a backdrop of declining real income. The pattern is complex; however, in general, Americans changed their disposable income spending to include more purchases of information related devices, and services.

The enthusiasm with which Americans consume information goods and services is really quite remarkable. In 1925, 10% of all households owned radios (see Figure 4-3).[8] By 1930, ownership stood at 46%. Ten years later, having suffered the privations of the Depression, Americans still managed to increase ownership of radios to 82% of all households. They bought radios at an astonishing rate, especially when one considers that the Depression forced personal expenditures on information goods and services to drop from 4.4% of all personal expenditures in 1930 to 3.5% in 1935, not recovering the 1930 level until 1945 (see Figure 4-2). In addition, radio technology of the time meant that when Americans decided to purchase a radio, many of them bought an expensive piece of furniture. A 1939 Philco console, for example, stood 40 inches high, 30 inches across, and came encased in high quality laminated mahogany. Despite these obstacles, radio achieved virtual saturation by 1950, just in time for the arrival of the next wave—television. Less than one household in ten owned TVs in 1950. However, fifteen years later, less than one household in ten remained without a TV. Television's complete adoption took less time than radio. Arriving in the '80s, Video Cassette Recorders (VCRs) have diffused along a growth curve as dramatic as that for television; VCR ownership increased from 1.1% of households in 1980 to 64.6% in 1989. When they first came on the market, purchases of radio and television sets—and VCRs—represented significant first-time costs. But as demand rose, technology advanced, and economies of scale took hold, prices dropped so that most households in the 1990s own, on the average, five radios and two TV sets.

FIGURE 4-3
Household Penetration of Selected Media 1920–1989

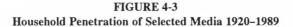
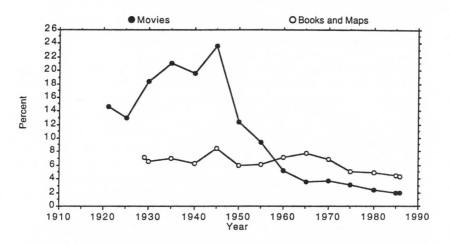

Source: Compiled from Series H 878-893, R 93-105, R 1-12 (1975), *Historical Statistics of the United States, Colonial Times to 1970.* Washington DC: GPO. Table 363, 878, 951 (1987). *Statistical Abstract of the United States: 1988* Washington, DC: Bureau of the Census. Table 914 (1989), *Statistical Abstract of the United States: 1990.* Washington, DC: Bureau of the Census.

Information services present a somewhat different pattern. Cable, for example, emphasizes a different set of choices. Unlike radio and TV, the decision to purchase cable services means continuous payments. Plus, an extensive wired infrastructure must exist prior to the delivery of services. Not surprisingly, the diffusion curve for cable looks less steep. But as with radio, cable penetration grew even through the sharp recession of 1982–83; and, by 1989, 53% of all households subscribed to cable services. Telephone services are similar in that they require the decision to pay a monthly fee, and the building of an infrastructure in order for the connection to function. In contrast to cable, the telephone infrastructure was built from scratch. So the adoption curve for the telephone looks more gradual. From 1878, when George W. Coy established the first practical exchange, 80 years passed before three out of four households boasted a telephone.[9] Though the adoption of radio sets proved immune to the Depression, telephone penetration dipped in correlation with personal expenditures. Telephones reached saturation by 1970, with 93% of households holding steady. But for households on the margin, the monthly payment structure of telephone service places the telephone beyond their means. The 7% of households without telephone service have become a serious policy issue as the switched telephone network underpins the computer-based technology for the next generation of enhancements, e.g., computer networks, fax machines, etc. Therefore, the one-time cost characteristic of radio and TV— allowing them to circulate second and third-hand—forms the core of the media environment for everyone—99% for radio, 98% for TV.

Figure 4.4 depicts the one major counter-current to the tendency toward more dense personal media environments. Like the telephone, daily newspaper circulation fell along with personal expenditures during the Depression. Circulation climbed as Americans recovered economically; so, in 1950, for example, when 9% of Americans owned televisions, daily newspapers circulated at a rate of 514 per 1,000 adults—virtual saturation if one accepts a figure of two adults per household in that year. But once television took off, newspaper circulation fell again. Throughout the '50s, as TV ownership climbed, the dailies faltered. By 1970, the year of television's complete penetration, newspaper circulation sank to 459 per 1,000. It never recovered. As of 1985, circulation had dwindled to an all time low of 356 per 1,000. A simple extrapolation of the curve indicates a future of lower circulation and readership. The social problem, of course, is that newspapers provide more detailed information of current events than does television, even with the advent of all-news cable channels. By spurning newspapers, Americans abandon a source of information in depth in favor of sources of more simplistic information like television and radio.

Figure 4-5 describes conditions of two other media that have fared enigmatically as Americans enhanced their media environments. Motion picture theater attendance generally rose from 1925 to 1945, the golden age of Hollywood. If anything, the Depression years stimulated theater attendance as audiences sought some escape from the monotony of poverty. The combination of television and the new family lifestyles of returning World War II veterans, knocked movie theater attendance into a 30-year decline. The curve indicates a turning away from public entertainment in favor of entertainment in the home. Where once theaters and movies were synonymous, in the '50s movies began to appear on TV. In the '80s tapes and VCRs converted the home into a movie theater with a customized schedule of showings.

The diffusion curves in figure 4-3 indicate the astonishing speed with which Americans augmented the media environments in their homes with each new electronic device on the market. The new electronic environment centered on television and, as cable and VCRs expanded TV's possibilities, they crowded out the daily newspaper. Furthermore, the economic support structure of the radio and television industries meant that Americans reorganized themselves into a consumer audience for mediated messages; but in so doing, they delivered themselves, as a commodity, for sale by media executives to advertisers.[10] Their comfort with this arrangement opened the way for cable services requiring continual payment.

Even before television eclipsed newspapers, radio led the way. It altered social patterns within the home by presenting a source of continuous messages requiring directed attention. Before radio, the phonograph introduced home entertainment

FIGURE 4-4

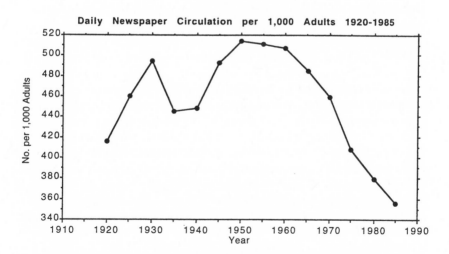

Source: Compiled from Series A 29-42, R 224-231 (1975), *Historical Statistics of the United States, Colonial Times to 1970 (Bicentennial Ed.).* Washington, DC: GPO. Tables 13, 878 (1987), *Statistical Abstract of the United States: 1988.* Washington, DC: Bureau of the Census.
Note: Adult population includes individuals 18 years of age and over.

FIGURE 4-5

Admissions to Motion Picture Theaters, and Purchases of Books and Maps, as a Percent of Total Personal Consumption Expenditures for Recreation: 1921–1986

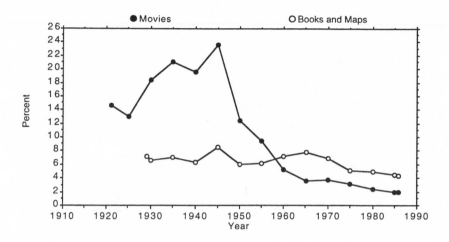

Source: Compiled from Series H 878-893 (1975), *Historical Statistics of the United States, Colonial Times to 1970* (Bicentennial Ed.). Washington DC: GPO. Table 396 (1981), *Statistical Abstract of the United States: 1981.* Washington, DC: U.S. Bureau of the Census. Table 363 (1987), *Statistical Abstract of the United States: 1988.* Washington, DC: Bureau of the Census.

[1] The Bureau of the Census combines books and maps. No consistent figures for books alone were found.

[2] Percentages for 1970-1987 reflect revisions to Personal Consumption Expenditure categories introduced in 1981.

where the technology became the focus of recreation. But, when the operator and the supply of cylinders—later discs—set the cadence of the phonograph, radio supplied sounds endlessly. In their turn, TV, VCRs, and cable exploited the environment originally created by radio. So, though we often associate television with a revolution in American lifestyles, the revolution began with radio. In fact, TV, VCRs, and cable are better thought of as enhancement technologies for radio. Their rapid rates of diffusion reflect the ease with which people added them to their existing media environments. That individuals easily understood the potential advantages of each new medium speaks to a cultural adaptation accomplished by the introduction of radio.

Television and the Media Environment in the Home

We have no precise picture of the total media environment in the home, though we have many snapshots of the central experience—television. TV

FIGURE 4-6
Personal Computers in Use: 1981–1988

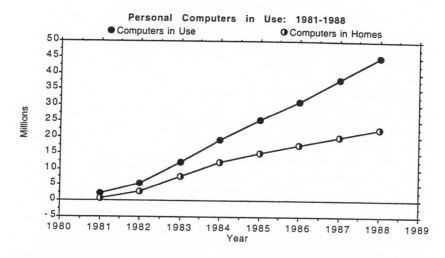

Personal Computers in Use: 1981-1988

Source: Compiled from Table 1340 (1989), *Statistical Abstract of the United States: 1990.* Washington DC: Bureau of the Census.
[1] Trendline for "Computers in Use" excludes data for multi-user personal computers.

has formed the core of American's involvement with media for the second half of the 20th century. Yet from its first bloom at the 1939 New York World's Fair, the new medium came under harsh scrutiny. Critics charged television with failure to materialize as the great educator of the masses or the herald of high culture to the common people. They wondered whether television eroded American morality, values, taste. At a time when barely one home in ten owned a set, commentators equated television with the atomic bomb as an influence on American culture.[11] Parents fretted over their children's viewing habits and asked if TV expanded knowledge or spread ignorance. Arriving at a time when Americans sought to erase memories of the Depression and prove to the world the virtues of a capitalist democracy, the possibility that television might debase the values or sensibilities of youth raised a serious challenge. Some wondered whether steady ingestion of TV fare might cause premature loss of innocence or even lead to criminal tendencies. The more psychologically-oriented hypothesized that television might cause abnormal behavior such as viewing addiction or withdrawal from social interactions.[12] Many parents accused television of ruining the eyes of their children.

By the end of its first decade in American homes, popular wisdom held that television had failed its promise. Newton Minow, chairman of the Federal Communications Commission, spoke for many when he addressed the National Association of Broadcasters in 1961 and charged that watching TV on a daily basis meant tuning in to a vast wasteland.[13] Yet by the time of Minow's speech, Americans had already reorganized their lives around television. Radio had been relegated to the kitchen or the bedroom, and television stood as the focal point of family leisure—the anchor for the new media environment. Holding their unease in check, Americans established television as the hearth of a new electronic castle.

Those early public debates over the merits of television indicate profound uneasiness and bewilderment. To vacillate in one's assessment between uplifter and debaser displays a lack of judgmental perspective. Alarm that television might cause children to lose their innocence or seek a life of crime hints at a desire for a fantasy world at odds with reality. One might make this case for the '50s in general. At once, Americans conferred tremendous importance on television and held it in deep suspicion.[14] The very contradictions apparent in these reactions stimulated research by psychologists and communications researchers. Two pivotal studies from this era offer portraits of Americans' involvement with television in its first full decade.[15]

The earliest, conducted between 1958 and 1960, focused on children. Wilbur Schramm, Jack Lyle, and Edwin B. Parker responded to the strongest theme in the television debate and investigated children's uses of television by conducting 11 separate studies, later synthesized in *Television in the Lives of Our Children*.[16] Children's response to television proved significant. When TV became available, purchases of sets occurred about twice as often in homes with children under 12, than in those without children. Even in a town where less than 20% of households owned televisions, over three fourths of the town's children reported watching TV on a regular basis. Television's effect was dramatic and visible to any parent. Movie going, radio listening, and reading decreased noticeably. Even comic books gave way to television watching, although children did not abandon the other media for television, like moths drawn to a candle. Instead, once the novelty of TV faded, a reallocation of participation in mass media took hold. Children accommodated the other media, so that total time spent with mass media went up. By 1951, a pattern emerged whereby children in Ann Arbor schools averaged 24 hours per week of television viewing. The pattern held, so that at the end of the decade, children in San Francisco schools averaged 22 hours. In addition, the researchers found no evidence that TV ruined children's eyes, even when they racked up viewing hours in excess of our per day. More likely, children with weak eyes discovered their conditions as a result of TV viewing. Schramm and his colleagues also found that viewing television at an early age contributed to learning vocabulary and general knowledge, an advantage noticeable in the first grade. By the time the child reached the higher grades, no television advantage could be discerned between viewers and non-viewers.[17]

Presaging the decline of newspaper readership, children claimed more trust in what they saw on television than what they heard on the radio or read in the paper. They rated television more trustworthy than either parent by a ratio of 2 to 1. Researchers wondered if this might not be a function of age and suggested that trust in TV might decline as these children approached adulthood. It was not to be. Today, television continues as the most trusted medium. In their summary, the researchers noted that boys and girls learned how to use the new medium at an early age. Children learned strategies from personal experience, contact with playmates, and from participating in the family's viewing rituals. Looking back on what appeared to them to be the decade of television, Schramm, Lyle, and Parker, hoped that Americans would come to terms with television and shape the medium into an asset for child development.[18] Without intentionally observing it, they documented the shaping of a media environment with television at the center and other mass media arrayed in support.

If the 1950s saw a heated debate over the effects of television on children, the decade also witnessed one by adults about adults. Gary A. Steiner drew wide attention when he published *The People Look at Television* [1963].[19] Conducting his survey of adults in 1960, Steiner found a population customarily spending several hours a day in front of the set. Asked which household inventions of the previous 25 years contributed most to making life more enjoyable, adults voted overwhelmingly for television. They reported enjoyment with their experience and primarily associated television with relaxation. TV surpassed, reading, playing with children, golf, dropping in on friends, going to the movies, and visiting a bar, as a means of recreation. By 1960, television had become the most important part of a typical evening, and many declared television to be a facilitator of family togetherness. Others reported TV as the main source of pleasure during their favorite time of the day. Describing the effects of a broken set, one housewife reported, "We went crazy. My husband said, 'What did I do before TV?' "[20]

In the midst of these expressions of satisfaction came doubts. Americans also associated TV with laziness and felt that they wasted time by watching TV. Steiner concluded that television had not yet achieved a justification. His respondents, for example, associated golf with health, reading with mental stimulation, and liquor with reducing tension. But television was still in search of its niche, prompting Steiner to paraphrase viewer sentiments as, "... a perfect way to relax for lazy people who should be doing something else."[21] Still some years away from the era of remote controllers, multi channel screen inserts, mini-ads and sound bites, viewers complained that commercials broke up the mood of the program, making it choppy. Others felt disoriented when commercials interrupted the flow of the program. Americans had yet to learn to cope with large amounts of fragmented information.

The study also presents an image of Americans juggling attention among *sources* of information. For Steiner's adults, the newspaper retained a slight edge as the most trusted medium and the one offering the most detailed information. Adults still attended to radio, magazines, and movies. But TV now occupied the center of the individual's information web. In the important arena of politics, TV had taken over from the newspaper. Forty-two percent of the respondents felt that television gave, "the clearest understanding of candidates and issues in national elections."[22] Steiner's research revealed a public eager and in awe, but uneasy.[23] TV loomed so large in the imagination that it seemed ready to eclipse older media. As members of a society astonished by the speed with which television had penetrated American life, researchers saw the medium as a monolithic giant and set out to discover "the effects of television." Neither Steiner nor Schramm and his colleagues saw the complexities and uses of media environments created by individuals. They visualized the home as a TV theater.

In the 30 years after *Television in the Lives of our Children*, and *The People Look at Television*, hundreds of researchers have produced thousands of studies seeking to understand the public's involvement with television. Television researchers have drawn on competing paradigmatic traditions from: studies of propaganda effects during World War I; conceptualizations of the audience as active users seeking gratifications from the medium; television as text; and, the changing consciousness of the viewing state. They have explored social science methods, from the laboratory experiment to the public opinion survey.[24] More recently, researchers have called for naturalistic studies of the television experience.

Robert Kubey's and Mihalyi Csikszentmihalyi's extensive analysis of television viewing behavior in the home, *Television and the Quality of Life*, represents an example of this latest approach.[25] Their composite picture indicates that television watching is a significant activity which fills about 40% of all leisure time. Respondents report feeling passive and relaxed while watching TV. Viewing demands little concentration or alertness and offers few challenges. The same feelings continued after turning off the set, even to the extent of inhibiting subsequent concentration. For the most part, the more time spent watching, the less the enjoyment. In addition, heavy viewers disclose that they enjoyed television less than light viewers. Heavy viewers and alienated individuals are also more likely to use TV as a means of temporarily alleviating ongoing negative feelings. Kubey and Csikszentmihalyi suggest that heavy viewing might lead to psychological dependence for those who fall into a routine which relies on the time organization of television. Seen from this perspective, some people retreat into media environments because they offer a measure of control in an uncontrollable world.

The viewing experience makes an ambiguous contribution to the quality of family life. On the one hand, time spent together as a family might increase as a result of heavy viewing. On the other hand, general passivity associated with the viewing experience implies less involved interaction. The two researchers concluded that people often use TV to substitute for interactions with others, and to subdue loneliness. Thus, television is the medium of escape for some of the people, most of the time, and for most of the people, some of the time.[26]

With new studies and new methods, a clearer picture emerges of the role that television plays in the lives of Americans. But how Americans manipulate TV as one part of an increasingly dense home media environment remains unclear. For one thing, the evidence indicates that most people combine other activities with watching television about two thirds of the time. They also report watching television as a background activity 28% of the time.[27] From the data, and from our own anecdotal experiences, we may infer that individuals spend large portions of non work time manipulating more than one source of information at the same time. Most Americans, for example, indulge in dining and watching TV, perhaps skimming a magazine simultaneously. In households where eating is sometimes a solitary activity, the above combination seems common. Twenty-five percent of all households in the U.S. contain a single person. Although television stands at the center of the media environment in the home, people negotiate information through other media combinations. College students regularly report staying up late to write term papers while listening to recorded music. Many professionals take reports and briefs home, and they read them while watching or listening to the news. Among our own colleagues, some enjoy solving the Sunday *New York Times* crossword puzzle over a cup of coffee and classical music. That is the point of daily life besieged by media; people create complex media environments which they actively manipulate because they possess the capacity to simultaneously process information from numerous sources. They consume information from more than one medium at a time by learning to ignore the bulk of messages encountered, in order to pay attention to a small subset. They learn to cope with media density by developing an implicit strategy for negotiating the vast number of messages encountered daily.[28]

Contemporary Americans live amidst many media, and spend large amounts of time with these media, primarily with television but not exclusively. These media make up a significant ecology within the culture of the home, for it seems that individuals invest considerable portions of their disposable income to build media environments that they use to stay in touch but also to escape. It seems that a media environment is as necessary to rational and emotional health as is food and clothing.[29] In other words, for a house to be a home, food and shelter is not enough. There must also be media.

Alienation

So far, we have documented the continuing tendency to consume information, to construct evermore elaborate media environments in the home and, in one instance of a growing trend, to insinuate work into the domestic sphere.

An understanding of these trends provides a window on the culture of the information society. But can an analysis of media environments in the home lead us to an understanding of the condition of society? To do that, we must connect to a larger social theme—alienation.

Throughout most of the 20th century, philosophers and social observers saw alienation as the most pervasive condition of society.[30] In that view, alienated American workers sell their labor as a commodity; and, so disconnected from the end result are they, that to own the product of their labor they must purchase it at market prices. Consequently, they identify themselves by how much they earn, rather than by some measure of internal worth. Furthermore, these circumstances are taken as typical by most Americans.[31] Even highly paid information workers like engineers and middle managers experience work in versions of the above description. More subtly, advertising techniques encourage individuals to acquire goods and to project fulfillment, love, satisfaction, happiness, success, social advantage, revenge—the whole range of human emotions—onto those goods. Individuals, therefore, define themselves by what they purchase and measure their success by the televisions, VCRs, personal computers, and satellite dishes that they own. In this way modern individuals create their moral and spiritual identities on the basis of what they have acquired—experiencing an extension of alienation beyond work. As Erich Fromm observed in the 1950s,

> [the individual] 'consumes' ball games, moving pictures, newspapers and magazines, books, lectures, natural scenery, social gatherings, in the same alienated and abstractified way in which he consumes the commodities he has bought. He does not participate actively,.... The value of fun is determined by its success on the market, not by anything which could be measured in human terms.... In the alienated form of pleasure nothing happens within me; I have consumed this or that; nothing is changed within myself, and all that is left are memories of what I have done.[32]

Alienated consumption comes as part of the legacy inherited by the information society, but with a twist since the tendencies of the information society contribute to behaviors that are characteristic of an age of information. For example, in a trend beginning with radio, people created media environments in their homes that favored passive reception of messages. Though the conceptualization of "passivity" remains controversial among television researchers, it seems fairly clear that the act of watching TV demands less involvement than many activities that compete for leisure time.[33] Ironically, the home media environment also offers an easy retreat as individuals seek to escape from the alienation of work. But it may also impose its own form of alienation C. Wright Mills stressed in his critique of the mass media.

> The media provide much information and news about what is happening the world, but they do not often enable the reader or the viewer to truly connect his daily life

with these larger realities. They do not connect the information they provide on public issues with the troubles felt by the individual. They do not increase rational insight into tensions, either those in the individual or those of the society which are reflected in the individual.[34]

What is paradoxical is that the alienated consumption described by Mills is built on the idea of information. Yet though consuming information means consuming a pure abstraction, American consumerism is characteristically materialistic; and so, it imposes a distinctly non intellectual slant on the consumption of information. For example, the average information consumer derives little status from reading a good book or thinking a great thought. On the other hand, ownership of things broadcasts materialistic success. Consequently, the repeated demand for communication appliances illustrated in figure 4-5 also represents accrued status through the accumulation of material possessions. Seen from that perspective, a wall full of video and audio equipment measures more success than a head full of knowledge. Or, as proclaimed on a popular bumper sticker of the eighties, "Whoever has the most toys wins." Martin's vision attracts as much for its gadgets as for its promise of a video telecommunications sports orgy.

The drive to accumulate information goods as possessions also arouses the act of accumulating. Not surprisingly, in such an atmosphere shopping itself becomes a final goal. In Fromm's words, "The marketing orientation is closely related to the fact that the *need to exchange* has become a paramount drive in modern man.... In capitalistic society *exchanging has become an end in itself*." [his italics][35] Thus, Americans define themselves by their consumption of information goods.

A complex picture emerges of private life in the information age. The separation between work and home appears to be under renegotiation for a portion of the working population, especially information professionals. At the same time, the effects of alienation show up beyond the workplace in buying patterns characterized by the measurement of personal success according to one's possessions, a kind of alienated consumption. The consumption of information goods has emerged in the 20th century as a lifestyle whose values are promoted as ongoing themes in advertising.[36] Yet, the picture also contains possibilities for composing an inner directed life with values derived from sources other than capitalism—possibilities that require a closer examination of the media environment and the fragmented pattern by which it receives messages.

Fragmentation

When individuals rely on media for information about the world around them, they must acquire the devices necessary to receive, store, and display that information; they must, therefore, build a media environment in the home.

The more devices owned, the denser the media environment, so that most of us live our waking hours awash in messages. But when messages filtered through the media environment come unconnected, or as bits without organic integrity, the media environment exhibits fragmentation. A quick browse through a weekly news magazine illustrates the point; the juxtaposition of news stories with ads reveals little continuity. Similarly, tuning in to a contemporary radio station brings forth a stream of songs, commentary, news items and commercials, each unconnected—or loosely connected at best—to content aired previously or content following. Though the media environments we personally construct within our homes determine the sources and quantity of the messages we receive, the fragmented arrival of those messages directly affects the individual quality of private life. When individual situations are woven into the social fabric, fragmentation influences the climate of ideas within which we form values and construct reality. Fragmentation acts against interconnectedness. Consider the following examples.

In 1910, most middle class families lived in cities or towns. Home might be a brownstone of the kind still to be seen in northeastern cities. Depending on the tastes of the family members, they might subscribe to magazines, e.g., *Woman's Home Companion, Harper's Monthly, Scientific American, Collier's.* If the family lived in a small town, they might also subscribe to the Montgomery Ward catalogue, or to the Sears, Roebuck catalogue. Newspapers like the *New York Times*, or its competitor the *New York Herald*, would be available from news hawkers or at a corner stand. A family with intellectual interests would surely own a collection of books, perhaps even setting aside a room in the house as a library or study. The furniture may include a piano, played by one or more members of the family. The piano might be a dual function player piano requiring only the skill necessary to turn the wind-up crank. Music might also be supplied by a wind-up phonograph or Victrola. In northeastern cities with telephone service, a middle class family would subscribe and connect via a party line into a central exchange where calls were put through by operators.[37]

Into this home, the family accepted visitors, a common event given patterns of socializing in urban settings. On a typical evening, the guest might be a relative and the intent of the visit would be to talk. If the guest came with specific information, or to gather information, then that determined the topic of discussion. On an evening dedicated to a "sociable get together," the possible span of subjects depended on the interests of the guests. Therefore, most evening discussions ranged across several topics, and the depth of the conversation, as well as the involvement of the participants, might be quite intense. Over the course of a long evening, the guests might well pursue a topic at length, leaving it only when they were satisfied or exhausted. The participants themselves composed the subject by contributing stories, anecdotes, and relating personal experiences. If the evening took a lighter bent, someone might play the piano, in which event, the evening became a "sing along." Participants were expected to contribute and exceptional singers were prized. A "sociable" evening at the beginning of the 20th century depended on the members to contribute the content; for that reason, middle class children, especially girls, learned conversation as an art form. Yet many middle class families had already planted the seed of the media environment to come. Already in 1910, the phonograph contested with the piano for primacy in supplying music. Increasingly, families clustered around the "talking machine," and listened to the products of Tin Pan Alley engraved on the new 78 rpm discs, and, by 1920, passive entertainment began to replace active entertainment.

In 1991, middle class families are less likely to live in urban brownstones. Most live in single family dwellings in suburban or semi-urban communities. Print media of all kinds arrives via mail or direct delivery. Electronic devices dominate the home, beginning with a television set, as prominently displayed in the living room as was the piano in the salon. In addition, nearly every room contains some message reception device or devices. The kitchen has a radio and/or a television, plus a telephone. Bedrooms will likely contain telephones, radios, televisions, and music equipment. If the working members of the family are information professionals, there may be a study equipped with telephone, computer, and possibly more music gear. From the house, telephone and TV cable lines stretch to local trunk lines. In some communities, the silhouette of the dwelling includes a satellite dish antenna.

In contrast to an evening spent in the salon of a brownstone, the television schedule sets the range of potential subjects. With cable—a 50-channel system makes available 400 half-hour programs in the course of a four hour evening—the expectations expand considerably. However, programs arrive in a totally fragmented way, with the content from one showing no apparent connection to the next. If the watcher has lingering interest in a subject, there is no way to continue once the program ends. The total television experience is dictated externally, with minimal participation required of the viewer. In the course of a long evening, an individual might watch six to eight independent programs interlaced among 100 to 180 distinct commercials. The family members gathered around the TV might spend as much time together as the socializers of 1910, but they probably interact less.[38] Moreover, as Kubey and Csikszentmihalyi document, working individuals spend roughly two hours per day watching TV. For non working or older viewers, TV time varies considerably but consists of more hours.[39]

Beyond television, it seems likely that nearly all time spent at home falls within view or earshot of some media. With the arrival of new interactive technologies, perhaps the television will give way to the computer as the center of the household universe—or perhaps they will meld into a device with the characteristics of both but not easily recognizable as either one or the other. In a home dominated by interactive technologies, the members will probably become more proactive in their consumption of media—conceivably following the model proposed by Williams—but an interactive home will not likely reduce the mutual isolation of the individuals that is already noticeable. Negotiating daily life already consists of coping with a blur of messages; and, in the new interactive environment, this tendency will intensify. Messages will continue to arrive in a highly fragmented mode, sometimes simultaneously, each independent of the other and competing for the individual's attention.

The distance between 1910 and 1991 may appear cosmic. After all, standing around the piano singing "My Darling Clementine" contrasts sharply against an evening where some members of the family watch "The Cosby Show" in the den, while others play video games in the bedroom. Yet the record reveals great continuity. Figures 4-2, 4-3, and 4-6 show that for nine decades Americans built and consistently updated the hardware necessary for media environments in their homes. The attitudes that underlie this transformation spanned the century.

What motivates individuals to acquire so many media, especially when the messages arrive in so many fragments? From the 1930s to the 1950s, psychologists like Abraham Maslow sought to construct a theory explaining human motivations. Maslow proposed that humans experience three categories of basic needs. First and most important are physical needs: the fundamentals of survival—hunger, thirst, safety, and ordinary prudence, which might be overlooked in striving to satisfy hunger or thirst. Secondly, come social needs: belongingness and love—striving to be accepted by intimate members of one's family, as well as esteem, status, reputation, and prestige. Lastly, humans seek self-actualization—a desire to know, understand, systematize, organize, and construct a system of values.[40] Maslow's theories shaped psychology and formed the core of the principles for the marketing strategies that reinforce consumer culture and encourage us all to build media environments in our homes. But because Maslow's hierarchy of needs is fundamentally materialistic, it provides no overt consideration of information as a basic human need. More recently, human needs for information have received greater consideration, as indicated by Daniel Stern.[41]

> Over the past several decades, evidence has accumulated from many diverse areas that the infant, from birth, will seek out stimulation and even work for it. In fact, the seeking of stimulation has by now achieved the status of a drive or motivational tendency not unlike that of hunger, an analogy that is not farfetched. Just as food is needed for the body to grow, stimulation is needed to provide the brain with the "raw materials" required for the maturation of perceptual, cognitive, and sensorimotor processes. The infant is provided with the tendencies to look for and get this needed "brain food."

To withhold stimulation is to impose sensory deprivation; and, because stimulation is the basis through which humans receive information, to withhold information is to isolate a person from society.[42] But since Maslow implicitly located information seeking activities with self actualization, at the peak of his hierarchy, he overlooked humans as cognitive beings who must constantly interact symbolically in order to maintain their mental equilibrium.

There is no complete nor conclusive answer to the question of why Americans built media environments with such long running enthusiasm. But given the human compulsion for information, it may well be that such a course satisfied an innate need. For, though the social basis for an answer has long been provided by scholars who identified the growth of commercial consumer culture as affecting individual values and material desires, now a possible sociobiological basis must also be considered. Humans need stimulation—in the form of information—to be human.

One Information Society, Many Realities

Although the evidence implies widespread acceptance of information technologies as necessities for modern living, we cannot assume that they are, or have been, uniformly available. We may hypothesize that uses of media environments vary widely. Different social classes experience distinct circumstances of work and leisure; therefore, they construct their media environments accordingly. Nevertheless, no matter one's social standing, the media environment, once created, imposes some common experiences.

In most cases, the individual opens a window to an avalanche of messages. A torrent of potential messages spews into the filter of personal attention. The few messages that are actually attended to can still overwhelm an individual. Of those, fewer still are internalized. From the receiver's perspective, this is information overload, meaning that by far most messages are lost. Once the media environment is built, this outcome becomes inevitable—the denser the media environment, the more lost messages. While the human brain might appear as a severe bottleneck to an information scientist, the loss of most messages seems of little concern to Americans as they enthusiastically refine their media environments. If a motivating logic exists for most individuals, it goes something like this:

An increase in the number of information channels $\Rightarrow$
An increase in the number of messages $\Rightarrow$
An increase in the amount of new information $\Rightarrow$
An increase in the amount of knowledge $\Rightarrow$
An increase in perceived welfare.

Given the above reasoning, few Americans would argue that they are worse off for living in such a densely mediated environment. Besides, the strategy of inclusion appeals to the American sensibility that more is better. Yet coping with the modern avalanche of messages requires a new strategy that breaks with traditional behavior. In order to function while awash in messages, people intuitively develop a strategy of exclusion. They erect mental blinders to most messages and sift the remainder, often attending to several channels simultaneously. Remarkably, the strategy of exclusion seems understood at a very basic level. In fact, few people become immobilized when confronting a dense media environment. For the most part, Americans have made a smooth transition from a strategy of information inclusion to one of information exclusion. They required no formal training, not even passing the skill informally from parent to child. Admittedly, cases exist to the contrary; so, for example, when managers must make deadline decisions, information overload hinders efficiency. In general, however, the following logic appears increasingly common in the information society:

An increase in the number of information channels ⇒
An increase in the number of messages ⇒
An increase in filtering behavior ⇒
A decrease in messages received ⇒
A limited increase in the amount of new information ⇒
A limited increase in the amount of knowledge ⇒
An increase in perceived welfare.

It seems likely that the two logics co-exist. The old logic serves as an ideological umbrella. It says, "more information is better," and so individuals continue to expand their media environments. In addition, it serves to accommodate us to the information society. At the same time, the new logic becomes our algorithm for actually coping with the waves of messages we face everyday.

What kinds of information do individuals actually receive? For most, the media environment does not create an atmosphere like the one predicted by Williams. Rather than rationally accessing the information most appropriate to the decisions facing the user, the typical media environment probably comes closer to the model described by Martin—super entertainment presented as capitalist realism. Can such a climate provide information of use for successfully negotiating daily life? This is not a simple question; for, depending on the specific individual, the "Oprah Winfrey Show" may contain more useful information than the "McNeil/Lehrer News Hour." People increase their levels of personal knowledge from all media and from all genres.[43] The social scientist cannot predict that a particular message or genre will contain more useful information, thus giving it greater social value; for that matter, neither can the individual. The strategy of exclusion almost necessarily contains an inherent element of irrationality. Prior to its reception, no one can predict which message will be of greater use. Therefore, on what basis can one decide which to exclude and which to receive? The answer is none, and all. Since no single algorithm can provide the best tactic for all needs, a strategy of trial and error probably works best; and, interestingly, this is what people seem to do.

What little we know of life within a media environment indicates a complex phenomenon. In the first place, the old boundaries, between work and home, between public and private life, between labor and leisure, no longer appear so clear or so fixed. In part, the fuzziness stems from a century-long pattern of increased information consumption. In the 20th century, Americans made a remarkable commitment to build and expand a media environment in the home. Even at the depths of their greatest economic nightmare, they purchased the latest information technologies in astounding numbers. At the same time, they evolved new media use behaviors for negotiating simultaneous messages through multiple channels, and eventually built their media environments around the television set.

Some take the idea of a media environment further. They blur the geographic distance between work and home, while adopting new values of work and leisure. But by initiating this new work-home environment, they call into question the meaning of alienation. Whereas alienation from work, as identified in the 19th century, focused on conditions of work for its defining element, the alienation of the 20th century extends the malaise to other aspects of behavior, especially consumption. Advertising plays a significant role in creating an alienated society by reinforcing models of behavior that privilege materialism and consumerism over integrity and spirit. Those models of behavior, also known as capitalist realism, became dominant values transmitted through the media environment.[44]

At the beginning of the century, leisure revolved around social visits, discussions, and active contributions to entertainment. At the end of the century, entertainment depends more on passive exposure to a small portion of the many messages accessible through one's private media environment. Of equal importance, messages arrive into the home in numbers higher than ever before. They hold to no apparent pattern, each containing content unconnected from the next—a phenomenon known as fragmentation. In considering the motivations for expending so many resources on media environments, we also suggest that people do so to fulfill a basic human need for information. However, the relationship between this need and the involvement with media is little understood.

Also, a new strategy for filtering messages seems to be emerging. For the first time in human history, a strategy of information exclusion has become urgent. The new strategy relies on excluding the greater portion of the messages transmitted, so as to focus on a manageable few. But how these many strands intertwine is not clear. Even the theme of alienation that results from the adoption of consumer values cannot be accepted in a pure form, since, in the case of information consumption, some good seems to come from consuming information, no matter what the content. What is clear is that in the information age there are as many realities as there are individuals to imagine them.

Notes

1. Williams, F. (1982). *The communications revolution.* Beverly Hills, CA: Sage, p. 268.
2. Martin, J. (1981). *Telematic society: A challenge for tomorrow.* New York: Prentice-Hall (pp. 121–122).
3. Rogers and Larson describing disposable income expenditures on entertainment in Santa Clara County, California. Rogers, E. M., & Larsen, J. K. (1984). *Silicon valley fever: Growth of high-technology culture.* New York: Basic Books, p. 170.
4. Technological determinism is the belief that changes in technology drive changes in society. A critique of technological determinism as a basis for interpreting the information society can be found in chapter 6.
5. Of course information may be lost, as was, for example, the original organization chart drawn up by Daniel C. McCallum for the New York and Erie Railroad. When a record no longer exists, and no human remembers, then information is irretrievable.
6. Strict comparability poses problems. For example, the radio purchased in 1930 bears little resemblance to the "Walkman" given as a birthday present in 1991, either in form or pattern of use. The same can be said for the other media tracked in figure 4-5. Nevertheless, to view the array of goods and services available then and today provides us with valuable insights.
7. Series G416-469 (1975) *Historical statistics of the United States, Colonial Times to 1970* (Bicentennial Ed.). Washington DC: GPO. Table 676 (1987) In *Statistical Abstract of the United States: 1988* Washington DC: Bureau of the Census.
8. What is a household? According to the Bureau of the Census, "A household includes the related family members and all the unrelated persons, if any, such as lodgers, foster children, wards, or employees who share the housing unit. A person living alone in a housing unit, or a group of unrelated persons sharing a housing unit as partners, is also counted as a household.…

   'The figures for number of households are not strictly comparable from year to year. In general, the definitions of household for 1790, 1900, 1930, 1940, 1950, 1960, and 1970 are similar. Very minor differences result from the fact that in 1950, 1960, and 1970, housing units with five or more lodgers were excluded from the count of households, whereas in 1930 and 1940, housing units with 11 lodgers or more were excluded, and in 1790 and in 1900, no precise definition of the maximum allowable number of lodgers was made." (1975). *Historical Statistics of the United States, Colonial Times to 1970* (Bicentennial Ed.). Washington DC: GPO, p. 6.
9. Brooks, J. (1975). *Telephone: The first hundred years.* New York: Harper & Row, p. 65.
10. The first to recognize this seeming contradiction was Dallas Smythe. He understood that the exploitation of consumers occurred with their consent. See Smythe, D. (1977). Communications: Blindspot of western marxism. *Canadian Journal of Social and Political Theory* (Fall), 1–27. Smythe, D. (1981). *Dependency road: Communication, capitalism consciousness, and Canada.* Norwood, NJ: Ablex.
11. "Forward," Bernard Berelson, in Steiner, G. A. (1963). *The people look at television: A study of audience attitudes.* New York: Knopf (pp. vii–x).

12. Schramm, W., Lyle, J., & Parker, E. B. (1961). *Television in the lives of our children*. Stanford, CA: Stanford University (pp. 1-10).

13. Speaking directly to broadcasters and station owners, Minow caused a sensation. "But when television is bad, nothing is worse. I invite you to sit down in front of your television set when your station goes on the air and stay there without a book, magazine, newspaper, profit-and-loss sheet or rating book to distract you— and keep your eyes glued to that set until the station signs off. I can assure you that you will observe a vast wasteland." Minow, N. N. (1964). Address by Newton Minow to the National Association of Broadcasters, Washington D.C. May 9, 1961. In N. N. Minow (Ed.), *Equal time: The private broadcaster and the public interest* (pp. 48-64). New York: Atheneum.

14. At one time or another, parents and commentators leveled some of these same accusations at the phonograph, vaudeville, dime novels, movies, comic books, radio, magazines, and video games—not to mention popular toys such as cap guns. Since the emergence of an urban industrial culture, parents have displayed unease with the influence of popular media on the socialization of their children.

15. Over 2,800 television research studies have been published since 1946. Kubey, R., & Csikszentmihalyi, M. (1990). *Television and the quality of life: How viewing shapes everyday experiences*. Hillsdale, NJ: Lawrence Erlbaum, p. 25. Clearly, no broad analysis of the information society can represent this corpus in detail. Schramm, Lyle, and Parker (1961), summarized studies of TV and children, while Steiner (1963) reviewed research on adults during television's formative decade. Kubey's and Csikszentmihalyi's study focused on television as part of the total experience of daily life. We concentrate on these three because of their key positions in television research literature.

16. Schramm, W., Lyle, J., & Parker, E. B. (1961). *Television in the lives of our children*. Stanford, CA: Stanford University. Wilbur Schramm, author of short stories, speech writer for F.D.R., concert musician, and minor league baseball player, taught himself the techniques of the social sciences. His desire to understand the social effects of the mass media led him to found the two original communications research institutes, the first at the University of Illinois, the second at Stanford University.

17. The relevance of television's conferred advantage on students existed for only a short time in the United States. Today it is moot since nearly every child watches television from an early age. But in Eastern Europe, the former USSR, and some less developed countries, the question continues to stimulate inquiry.

18. Schramm, W. et al. (1961) pp. 11-16, 31, 24-56, 96, 147, 171.

19. Steiner, a psychologist in the Graduate School of Business at the University of Chicago, conducted his public opinion research at the Bureau of Applied Social Research, Columbia University, under a grant from C.B.S. Many pioneers of mass media research—Bernard Berelson, Sam Becker, Paul Lazarsfeld, Kurt Lange, Ithiel de Sola Pool, Wilbur Schramm, and Frank Stanton—advised on portions of the project.

20. Steiner, G. A. (1963). *The people look at television: A study of audience attitudes*. New York: Knopf, p. 25.

21. Steiner, G. A. (1963) p. 56.

22. Steiner, G. A. (1963) p. 31.

23. Steiner, G. A. (1963) pp. 30, 21, 22, 31, 47-48, 53-57, 229, 230, 210. This brief review of *The people look at television* focuses on those opinions which point to the emergence of mediated environments. The greater extent of the study concentrated on viewing preferences.

24. For a sampling of the range of analyses, see: Bauer, R. A. (1964). The obstinate audience: The influence process from the point of view of social communication. *American Psychologist, 19*, 319-328. Belson, W. (1967). *The impact of television*. London, UK: Cheshire. Bower, R. T. (1973). *Television and the public*. New York: Holt, Rinehart, & Winston. Comstock, G., Chaffee, S., Katzman, N., McCombs, M., & Roberts, D. (1978). *Television and human behavior*. New York: Columbia University. Davison, W. P., Boylan, J., & Yu, T. C. (1976). *Mass media: Systems and effects*. New York: Praeger. DeFleur, M. L., & Dennis, E. E. (1988). *Understanding mass communication*. Boston: Houghton Mifflin. Dorr, A. (1986). *Television and children: A special medium for a special audience*. Beverly Hills, CA: Sage. Feshbach, S., & Singer, R. D. (1971). *Television and aggression: An experimental field study*. San Francisco, CA: Jossey-Bass. Gerbner, G., & Gross, L. (1976). Living with television: The violence profile. *Journal of Communication, 26*, 173-179. Katz, E., Blumler, J., & Gurevitch, M. (1974). Uses of mass communication by the individual. In W. P. Davidson & F. T. C. Yu (Eds.), *Mass communication research: Major issues and future directions* (pp. 11-35). New York: Praeger. Klapper, J. T. (1960). *The effects of mass communications*. Glencoe, IL: The Free Press. Meyrowitz, J. (1985). *No sense of place: The impact of electronic media on social behavior*. Oxford, UK: Oxford University Press. Newcomb, H. (1979). *Television: The critical view*. New York: Oxford. Wartella, E. (Ed.). (1979). *Children communicating: Media and development of thought, speech, and understanding*. Beverly Hills, CA: Sage. Webster, J. (1986). The television audience/The new media environment. *Journal of Communication, 36*(3), 77-91.

25. Kubey, R., & Csikszentmihalyi, M. (1990). *Television and the quality of life: How viewing shapes everyday experiences*. Hillsdale, NJ: Lawrence Erlbaum.

26. Kubey, R., & Csikszentmihalyi, M. (1990) pp. 71, 157-158, 171-173.

27. Kubey, R., & Csikszentmihalyi, M. (1990).

28. Consumption of information for leisure also occurs outside the home. But unlike turn of the century urban life, the center of entertainment today is in the home. Other activities, like films and concerts, are chosen in relation to entertainment in the home.

29. Basch, M. F. (1988). *Understanding psychotherapy: The science behind the art*. New York: Basic Books. Berger, P. L., & Luckmann, T. (1966). *The social construction of reality*. Garden City, NY: Doubleday. Shiffrin, R. M., Castellan, N. J., Lindman, H. R., & Pisoni, D. B. (Ed.). (1975). *Cognitive theory: Volume one*. Hillsdale, NJ: Erlbaum. Stern, D. (1977). *The first relationship: Mother and infant*. Cambridge, MA: Harvard.

30. See, for example, Berger, B. M. (1963). The sociology of leisure: Some suggestions. In E. O. Smigel (Eds.), *Work and leisure: A contemporary social problem* (pp. 21-40). New Haven, CN: College and University Press. Bier, W. C. (Ed.). (1972). *Alienation: Plight of modern man*. New York: Fordham University Press. Blauner, R. (1964). *Alienation and freedom: The factory worker and his industry*. Chicago, IL: University of Chicago. Braverman, H. (1974). *Labor and monopoly capital: The degradation of work in the twentieth century*. New York: Monthly Review Press. Fromm, E. (1962). Alienation under capitalism. In E. Josephson & M. Josephson (Eds.), *Man alone: Alienation in modern society* (pp. 56-73). New York: Dell. McLeod, J., Ward, S., & Tancill, K. (1965). Alienation and uses of the mass media. *Public Opinion Quarterly, 65-66*, 583-591. Parker, S. (1971). *The future of work and leisure*. New York: Praeger. Parsons, T., & Smelser, N. J. (1956). *Economy and soci-*

ety. Glencoe, IL: Free Press. Rubin, L. B. (1976). *Worlds of pain: Life in the working-class family.* New York: Basic Books. Seeman, M. (1959). On the meaning of alienation. *American Sociological Review, 24,* 783–791. van den Haag, E. (1962). Of happiness and despair we have no measure. In E. Josephson & M. Josephson (Eds.), *Man alone: Alienation in modern society* (pp. 180–199). New York: Dell. Weber, M. (1947). *The theory of social and economic organization* (Henderson, A. M. and Parsons, Talcott, Trans.). New York: Oxford University Press.

31. Bellah, R. N., Madsen, R., Sullivan, W. M., Swidler, A., & Tipton, S. M. (1985). *Habits of the heart: Individualism and commitment in American life.* Berkeley, CA: University of California.

32. Fromm, E. (1955). *The sane society.* New York: Holt, Rinehart and Winston (pp. 124–125).

33. Kubey, R., & Csikszentmihalyi, M. (1990) pp. 36, 98, 154–155, 171–172. We have focused on television for many of our illustrations because the research literature contains much information on television-related behavior but little on other behaviors of information consumption. However, it should be noted that the mediated environment in the home may contain much more than television; e.g., newspapers, magazines, comic books, books, tapecassettes, compact disks, radio, video games, videotape recorders, personal computers, board games, drawing and painting materials, etc.

34. Mills, C. W. (1956). *The power elite.* Oxford, UK: Oxford University Press (pp. 214–215).

35. Fromm, E. (1955) pp. 132–133.

36. The desire for material possessions, though most clearly seen at the end of the 20th century, stems from roots that go back to the early decades of the republic. Alexis de Tocqueville commented on the universal desire for material possessions exhibited by Americans during his visit to the U.S. in the 1830s. Tocqueville, A. de (1835/1964). *Democracy in America* (Reeve, Henry, Trans.). New York: Washington Square Press, pp. 199–204. Thomas Jefferson's concern for the materialism of the growing industrial urban centers caused him to extol the virtues of the small yeoman farmer as the model for American economic development Padover, S. K. (Ed.). (1946). *Thomas Jefferson on democracy.* New York: New American Library (pp. 68–71).

37. Half a century later (1950), three of four households with telephones in the United States were still connected through party lines. Brooks, J. (1975) p. 267.

38. Kubey, R., & Csikszentmihalyi, M. (1990). *Television and the quality of life: How viewing shapes everyday experiences.* Hillsdale, NJ: Lawrence Erlbaum. Meyrowitz, J. (1985). *No sense of place: The impact of electronic media on social behavior.* Oxford, UK: Oxford University Press. Postman, N. (1985). *Amusing ourselves to death: Public discourse in the age of show business.* New York: Penguin. Webster, J. (1986). The television audience/The new media environment. *Journal of Communication, 36*(3), 77–91.

39. Kubey, R., & Csikszentmihalyi, M. (1990) pp. 70–75.

40. Maslow, A. H. (1954). *Motivation and personality.* New York: Harper & Row (pp. 80–106).

41. Stern, D. (1977). *The first relationship: Mother and infant.* Cambridge, MA: Harvard (pp. 52–53).

42. Basch, M. F. (1988). *Understanding psychotherapy: The science behind the art.* New York: Basic Books. Bruner, J. (1975). The ontogenesis of speech acts. *Journal of Child Language*(2), 1–19. Bruner, J. (1990). *Acts of meaning.* Cambridge,

MA: Harvard. Bruner, J. S. (1973). *Beyond the information given: Studies in the psychology of knowing.* New York: Norton. Stern, D. (1977). *The first relationship: Mother and infant.* Cambridge, MA: Harvard. At what point does stimulation become information? It may be hypothesized, for example, that the stimulation an infant receives from being held tightly by the mother contributes to its bonding, and is essentially non informational; while the stimulation an infant experiences by hearing language leads to the formation of symbols, the basis for information. So, it would appear that not all forms of stimulation elicit the changes in the brain that develop to process information and form thoughts. So, though it seems obvious that infants don't have fully formed thoughts, the transition from stimulation to information is anything but clear.

43. Comstock, G., Chaffee, S., Katzman, N., McCombs, M., & Roberts, D. (1978). *Television and human behavior.* New York: Columbia University. Davison, W. P., Boylan, J., & Yu, T. C. (1976). *Mass media: Systems and effects.* New York: Praeger. Dorr, A. (1986). *Television and children: A special medium for a special audience.* Beverly Hills, CA: Sage. Katz, E., Blumler, J., & Gurevitch, M. (1974). Uses of mass communication by the individual. In W. P. Davidson & F. T. C. Yu (Eds.), *Mass communication research: Major issues and future directions* (pp. 11-35). New York: Praeger. Wartella, E. (Ed.). (1979). *Children communicating: Media and development of thought, speech, and understanding.* Beverly Hills, CA: Sage. Webster, J. (1986). The television audience/The new media environment. *Journal of Communication, 36*(3), 77-91.

44. Schudson, M. (1984). *Advertising, the uneasy persuasion: Its dubious impact on American society.* New York: Basic Books. Schudson, M. (1989). How culture works: Perspectives from media studies on the efficacy of symbols, *Theory and Society 18*(2), 153-180.

5

Tensions

And though all the winds of doctrine were let loose to play upon the earth, so truth be in the field, we do injuriously by licensing and prohibiting to misdoubt her strength.—John Milton[1]

After such knowledge, what forgiveness? Think now
History has many cunning passages, contrived corridors
And issues, deceives with whispering ambitions,
Guides us by vanities.—T. S. Eliot[2]

Neither Milton nor Eliot would have recognized the phrase information policy; but, as these quotes from their writings illustrate, they understood some of the tensions that accompany the tendencies of the information society. In this chapter we address the tensions stirred by the changes described in the previous chapters, and the responses that are shaping policy thinking. In the first part, we examine the essential tension that underlies the information society—the traction between the ownership and exchange of information as a commodity versus the distribution of information as a public resource. But in a departure from most such discussions, we further consider the consequences of this debate for privacy and information needs. The second part of the chapter concentrates on the infrastructure of the political process by focusing on integration between big politics and big media in contrast to fragmentation at the level at which the individual receives the messages. The third part of the chapter comprises an analysis of distributional justice as it pertains to three of the main issues facing information policy makers—information poverty, literacy, and universal service. We end the chapter with a review of the underlying assumptions that often determine which policies succeed and which fail.

Throughout, we pay special attention to the constraints that cultural beliefs exert on policy behavior. In keeping with the macro perspective of the book, we do not analyze specific policies in detail; rather, we propose general directions in the belief that only by reconsidering the context will the question of balance return to public discourse on information.

The Basis of Information Policy

If policies are collectively agreed upon actions taken to maintain the organization of society, then information and communication policies are the most basic.[3] Communication is the process through which all cultural, political, and economic organization flows—and information is the stuff in the flow. As with matter and energy, they are complementary manifestations of the same phenomenon. So it should not be surprising that this most basic policy matter has been left implicit in our system. Fundamental issues—such as the meaning of participation—are neither easily articulated nor easily resolved. Seen from this perspective, the unwillingness of Americans to delineate a national information policy appeals to a certain logic. Instead, they have played out the logic of their assumptions by resolving the problems of the moment and by putting off the less tractable fundamental issues. Information and communication policies in the U.S. have therefore been limited to immediate problems and framed by existing technologies. It has always been so.

Rather than in the abstract, the responsibility of government to provide the communications infrastructure for an integrated and informed society is stated in Article I of the U.S. Constitution in terms of the technology of "Post Offices and post Roads." Freedom of speech, the press, assembly and petition, as described in the First Amendment, express the principle of participatory liberty in terms of the technologies of the time. Similarly, the Fourth Amendment definition of freedoms as restrictions on government protects individual privacy of communications against unreasonable searches but limits this protection to the security of "papers." The Communications Act of 1934 divides the world of regulated communications into common carrier by wire and radio, broadcast radio, and private radio. The two major amendments to this policy regime since 1934, the Satellite Communications Act and the Cable Communications Act, have also dealt with existing technologies as the basis for justifying new policies.

On the basis of this history, one might conclude that the task of information and communication policy-making is to keep up with technological change—an inference that often leads to despair. For if policy is supposed to reflect the relevant technologies of the moment, and if, as today, those technologies change momentarily, then the task of information policy-making has become the task of Sisyphus; although, among themselves, policy makers are more likely to refer to this dilemma in terms that allude to the task of Herakles at the stables of Augeas.

The fallacy which leads to this conclusion is the idea that it is the technologies that require policy responses. The technologies are simply the media. The real challenge for policy makers is that the turbulence of technological change militates against a continuation of our focus on the instant and neglect of the fundamental. In other words, if we continue to try to finesse any discussion of basic principles by proposing policy directions in terms of present technologies, the increasing numbers and complexity of information and communication technologies for which policies must be formulated will lead to overload and paralysis.

Yet though no explicit statement of an integrated national information policy exists, the basic themes may be interpolated from the pattern of outcomes in previous policy debates. To view information policy in this way—i.e., to make explicit the policy themes which have guided the resolution of transient information and communication regulatory issues—allows us to see the development of information policy right back to the dawn of the industrial age, even though policy makers of that time might not have recognized their participation in any long term process.

The Essential Tension

The most significant questions of information policy derive from the long running socioeconomic tension inherent in the drive to commoditize information goods and communication services. The first question asks how to maximize the flow of socially useful information; i.e., what is the social goal? The second asks what should be the proper roles for government and the market in order to meet the goal of the first question; i.e., how should the goal be implemented? The tension is institutionalized in the First Amendment of the Constitution and in the Copyright Law of 1790, but it pertains to any democratic state with a capitalist economy. If Americans have become aware of this tension only in recent decades, others have been more perceptive; de Tocqueville, for instance, observed and commented on the tendency among Americans to commoditize what he called scientific information,

> As they are always dissatisfied with the position they occupy, and are always free to leave it, they think of nothing but the means of changing their fortune, or increasing it. To minds thus predisposed, every new method which leads by a shorter road to wealth, every machine which spares labor, every instrument which diminishes the cost of production, every discovery which facilitates pleasures or augments them, seems to be the grandest effort of the human intellect. It is chiefly from these motives that a democratic people addicts itself to scientific pursuits,— that it understands them and respects them.[4]

From the beginning, when Benjamin Franklin argued successfully for the federal government to be granted power to provide a postal service, Congress has preferred provision in the private sector. This meant, that although Congress created and maintained a postal system, there was no monopoly on letter conveying until 1845, the same year that the postal service first faced competition from the telegraph, itself granted by Congress to a group of private investors over the objections of inventor Samuel Morse, Senator Henry Clay, and the Postmaster General.[5] In the case of the press, though the private sector position seems clear, the tension persists; government subsidized early newspapers; and later, with the invention of broadcasting, government granted protected licensing agreements to radio and television entrepreneurs.[6]

The whole of this tension, however, cannot be understood by focusing solely on specific technologies. Rather, it should be viewed as the dynamic outcome of the long-standing conflict between two powerful values with roots traceable to the Founders' philosophical commitment to Enlightenment principles.

On the one hand, there is faith in the free market as a means of allocating goods and distrust of government, especially as regards control over information. More than in any other developed nation there is a view in the U.S. that any objective that can be attained by the free market should be left to the market. As applied to information and communication services, this sentiment is based partly on the preference for market economics but also on the classical liberal fear of abuse of authority by government.

On the other hand, there is a quasi-egalitarian sense that both representative democracy and capitalism require equal access to information, in order for citizens to experience equal opportunity when making political and economic choices. This point of view is not grounded in any explicit legislative act; instead, it has off-and-on been expressed as a necessary precedent to political equality and meaningful democracy. That citizens need information has been felt so strongly that government has developed four sets of institutions through which it provides information and communication services: the post office; public education; public libraries; and, the provision of data collected by the Census Bureau, Bureau of Labor Statistics, the Agricultural Extension Service, along with other arms of government.

Though always competing with private alternatives, these four information-oriented institutions have built their legitimacy upon two widely accepted axioms. First, most Americans agree that all participants in public discourse must have the data upon which to base judgments. Second, if the market is to function efficiently most Americans, as consumers, feel that they must have information relevant to their choices. So, out of a belief in the importance of rationality, fairness, and efficiency, Americans deduce the need for equality of opportunity and, therefore, equality of access. It is this logic which frames public policy issues regarding information and communication. Thus, the fundamental policy tension for the information society may be restated as follows: because information and communication are essential to the fairness and efficiency of social organization, government ought to have the responsibility for guaranteeing that citizens have access to the information they need, as well as to appropriate channels of communication; however, because government's intrusion into the flow of information in society is inherently suspect, permitting abuse and inefficiency, it seems appropriate for these functions to take place in the market, with as little intrusion by government as possible.

For 150 years, the cross-currents of this tension put tolerable strain on American institutions. However, since the 1950s a series of changes have upset the balance. Larger enterprises have required the allocation of more resources devoted to communication and information in order to accomplish the demanding task of coordination. Markets themselves have gotten bigger, pulling together regional markets from around the world into integrated global markets, and requiring more information to manage demand and to coordinate supply. As information itself has become a product in demand, the information sector of the global economy has grown tremendously. In response, there has been a dramatic increase in the commercial value of information and communication services; which, in turn, have intensified the contradictions inherent in a tension whose stresses are rooted in the incompatibility between the requirements of democracy and the motivations of capitalism. The ensuing traction has reopened an old debate over the proper allocation of information—whether to exploit it as a commodity in the market, or to disseminate it widely as a public resource—and has driven up the stakes for public policy decision making.

In the 1990s, the policy battle is certainly not an equal contest. On one side is corporate capital and the momentum of deregulatory ideology. Those who provide information services in the private sector maintain that their markets ought to be expanded. At the extreme are those who are ideologically committed to the market as the best source of all decision-making in society; they have supported every reduction in the production and distribution of information by government. However, moderate Republicans and Democrats alike—given impetus by the confounding factor of inflation which dramatically increased the price of all services—were behind the pressure to privatize government provision of information in the late 1970s and 1980s.[7] In particular, privatization arguments reshaped numerous information and communication industries, e.g., telephony, data services, R&D, and government publishing.

On the other side stands an array that includes librarians, information scientists, public educators, interest groups supporting the idea of "public" networking, liberals, and a heterogeneous collection of those who oppose the advance of big business. Librarians and some information professionals figure prominently, because of their new found status at the core of the information society. In addition, educators seeking to reform their system increasingly link education to the heart of an economy which will grow in its demand for a highly skilled and literate information labor force. Groups like these defend an active role for the public sector and support an interpretation of information as a public resource.

To date, the advantage has decidedly gone—as it has historically—to the advocates of increasing allocation of information and communication to the market. But this is not a finite contest. Rather it is a tension; and, since it is one of the information society's essential tensions, advocates of both positions will continue to raise the issues and the values at stake—values that have been the keys to the debate since the founding of the republic.

Therefore, the continued and heated discussions that bring this tension to the surface will reappear again and again on three fronts. In an infinite number of variations on the primary issue, Americans will clash over which kinds of information ought to be exchanged as exploitable commodities in the marketplace, and which ought to be distributed as a public resource. Since modern democracies are founded on the premise that citizens must be informed in order to execute their civic obligations, a derivative issue will emerge that focuses on the dangers of social fragmentation, uninformed political choices, and trivialization of governance in the media, as consequences of the commercial bias in information and communication services. And, because the question of equity must be reinterpreted when a democracy evolves into an information society, thoughtful citizens will debate whether the growing, marketplace-induced imbalance in access to information between the information rich and the information poor poses a threat to social cohesion and a just society. The intractable nature of the tension means that its repercussions will be felt across the information society, but in two areas especially—privacy and the need to be informed.

Privacy

We traditionally think of privacy—at least in the policy sense—as security against intrusion by government; now, however, the commoditization of information has made it necessary to consider the invasion of privacy by corporations.

The sale of databases containing information on individuals adds a dimension of social control that is new to the marketplace. Since large databases create both economies of scale and the raw material from which customized information can be extracted, there is a real incentive for corporations to collect as much information as possible for packaging. Just as in markets for physical goods, competition impels information sellers to try to attract customers, either by offering the lowest price on commoditized information or by serving a niche market with very specialized information. Seen in this light, information markets operate as does the market for any product. So, although corporations gather information for purposes of informing their own decision making, once that information exists in a database there is great incentive to retail it.

There is little question that organizations—business and public sector—need information about people in order to conduct operations. They need credit information on individuals in order to protect themselves from bad risks. They conduct analyses of consumer behavior for purposes of market planning. They fund studies of values, attitudes and lifestyles, which lead to the construction of consumer profiles to aid executives in choosing marketing strategies. And, they survey opinions in order to take the measure of the public's sentiments toward decisions affecting public policy. However, the presence of this information, often gathered passively without the subject's knowledge, may also constitute a threat to privacy.

Still, even when the gathering of information is a legitimate function of management in the private sector and of administration in the public sector, ethical questions arise. Should there be limits on who may gather this information? Should there be limits on what kind of information may be gathered? Should subjects be informed of information gathering; and, if so, should they be informed after the fact or before?

It is inevitable that individuals will be wrongfully harmed by errors and inappropriate decisions. For example, credit information is routinely gathered for sale to businesses. However, in the process of entering the data, mistakes occur which create the possibility that an individual may suffer a bad credit rating due to a keypunch error or an improperly merged file. Once the error is made, the tendency is to perpetuate it. That is, the cost of correcting a false entry is a cost against profits, whereas the cost of entering data in the first place is an investment in pursuit of profits. So the tendency is to allocate a low priority to the correction task. For that matter, if the problem ended with an eventual correction, an equilibrium might set in as errors came to be offset by corrections. But the continual movement of data from one database to another means that each copy contains errors of the original at the time of duplication; and, since each copy may be duplicated in turn, the possible number of errors in circulation is without limit, even if the original is corrected. In this case, the forces of the marketplace act against a corrective equilibrium.[8]

Another example. Corporations may legitimately gather information on delinquent renters and sell it to landlords who wish to protect themselves from bad risks in the process of doing business. Yet, in a market where rental space is scarce, individuals may be excluded from renting because they fit an undesirable profile. Landlords experience a disincentive to take a chance on a person labeled a potential risk in a credit report, whether proven or not, when other renters are available. So, apart from the truly delinquent—and there is no guarantee that they will even show up in a database—other groups may suffer. By employing database-generated profiles, unscrupulous landlords may systematically exclude minorities, the elderly, or low-income families, sight unseen.

In markets characterized by large organized vendors and individual consumers, e.g., the rental market in New York City, the extensive collection of data on individual consumers greatly swings the balance of power toward the large vendors; and, consequently, opens the door to abuses. Therefore, unlike the old version of this tension, where privacy is threatened by malicious government à la *1984*, in the new version those who gather information do so in order to turn the wheels of commerce. Information is gathered so that the economy can support its participants. What could be more beneficial? Yet the implicit threat lingers because, once gathered, information in databases can take on a life of its own.

Privacy may also be threatened by intelligent marketing. Marketing executives gather information on profiles of customers, along with more general information on segments of the market, in order to maximize the efficiency of targeted selling. Corporations invest in extensive surveys, ask customers to fill out marketing questionnaires as part of warranty cards, and reanalyze data generated by the government. Ironically, much of the erosion of individual privacy that results from audience targeting and market segmentation occurs with the consent of the individual. For example, in credit applications and in direct mail address lists compiled from requests for catalogs, there is an exchange of information for service in the interest of mutually perceived economic advantage. When confronted with requests for information of value to marketers, most people surrender their privacy in pursuit of the economic rewards of efficiency. How freely this occurs is unclear since they often have no choice. Therefore, since information constitutes an item of exchange in the marketplace, how much control over this valuable commodity does an individual deserve?

A version of this issue has already been dealt with in regard to Customer Proprietary Network Information (CPNI), i.e., information about a business customer's use of a network. The precedent is an intriguing one because the current policy expectation is that the customer cannot negotiate an agreement over what information will be available to the exchange carrier for use in targeted marketing. The customer must instead choose between allowing no use of his or her personal information or making it available to anyone who wants it for marketing purposes. Therefore, as telecommunication carriers get into providing video services, the question arises as to whether the CPNI principle should be extended to give individual customers a yes-or-no choice between full disclosure of their viewing habits or no disclosure. This question is especially timely because new interactive services are now approaching the marketplace. If the carrier can neither claim nor negotiate—with its customers—a property right in information about their viewing habits, can interactive video transmission prices be set in such a way as to allow the carrier to capture enough of the revenue potential to justify the costs of capitalizing the network? In any case, unless video viewing habits become an issue in intelligence gathering or in criminal justice surveillance, privacy as an issue for new video applications seems likely to evolve as a contractual issue. To the extent that it does, the policy objective should be fairness in the negotiation of the exchange of personal information—and, therefore, privacy—for economic advantage, with the goal of establishing a body of individual information privacy rights.

If the detailed facts of one's identity are to be treated as a commodity which is part of an exchange, then perhaps consent should be expressed and not implied. In an information society, data about a person constitute a potent form of identity; therefore, there is a basis for arguing that the collection and use of personal information should be conditioned on a person's explicit consent. No use of information collected from or about viewers, subscribers, renters, borrowers, customers, etc., should be permitted other than for the uses to which they have agreed; and, as always, fraud on the part of either party would vitiate consent.

Americans entered the information age sensitive to the question of privacy, whether as defined by the writers of the Constitution or translated by George Orwell. As each new information or communication technology appeared on the scene, Americans asked themselves, "How much should government know about us?" Now, the collection of credit and marketing information without the subject's permission represents a threat to privacy that reaches out to every individual in society. So pervasive are these activities that they suggest the addition of a new question, "How much should private sector organizations know about us?"

Interestingly, the ubiquity of the problem is cause for optimism that solutions will be worked out. The very blindness that causes computers to distribute errors at random means that the influential and the powerless alike will suffer mistaken credit ratings, inappropriate marketing profiles, and other violations. When the wrath of professionals and the upper middle class is aroused, regulatory solutions are much more likely to be found than they would be if computer errors singled out the poor.

Information Needs

Where lies the best path to an informed public, and who bears responsibility? The question of information needs demands attention because it pulls across the ideological as well as the economic fabric of society. Pressures within capitalism encourage individuals to seek wealth by selling information, but other pressures of similar energy demand that government seek to maximize the informed participation of its citizens. That is, in order to protect the democratic process, government must insure the availability of information, since information is the means by which the citizenry can achieve the informed status necessary for them to make democracy work. Thus, the tension over information needs pendulates between the right of business to profit from the sale of information, and the obligation of government to insure that all citizens, regardless of income, have the means to inform themselves. For while this is a perennial controversy in American public life, the rising importance of information-oriented activities intensifies the stress.

Even if the public's information needs posed only a question of private sector versus public sector paradigms, they would certainly deserve recognition as a matter of public policy. But the issue carries additional dimensions because of the theories that originated the concept of the information economy. A basic assumption underlying the work of Machlup, Bell, and Porat is that information can and should be treated as a commodity. Their collective accomplishment was to lay the foundation for the idea of an information society, and to focus attention on information as an economic good.

As other scholars probed the dimensions of society from this new perspective, they quickly concentrated on the mechanics of market entry. Schiller identified the processes through which information is removed from the sphere of public resources and converted into private property for resale as a commodity.[9] Demac, in *Keeping America Uninformed*, outlined the areas where this process is most rapidly occurring and specifically criticized the Reagan administration for allowing valuable public information to fall into the hands of private companies, under the aegis of a policy of deregulation.[10] Mosco described how promising technologies like videotex and interactive video become tools for market domination in the hands of large corporations.[11]

Others, like Entman, Kern, Lowi, and Oettinger, examined the relationship between information and politics; Entman, and Kern in particular, focused on the role of the commercial media in elections.[12] When taken together, they validated the theories that described the social shift to an information-oriented society; but more significantly, they revealed the primary tension of the new society at a time when fundamental changes were taking place. Conducted mostly during the Reagan administration, when the federal government pursued a policy of transferring to private vendors the publication and distribution of data gathered at the expense of the federal government, these studies described the transfer, which continues today, and which forms one of the bases for the rapidly growing database industry.

These criticisms have found a strong voice among librarians and information scientists; and, over the last ten years, a policy position has emerged from within the profession condemning the loss of public information into the private sector as contrary to the ideal of a well informed public in a democratic society. Librarians argue that information, previously available from government at low cost, must now be purchased from private vendors at much higher prices. For example, to electronically access the Library of Congress catalogue, the complete source of all publications available in the U.S., individuals must pay for access through private vendors who charge for time spent connected online; the same is true for many databases collected by the federal government. This means that while the Library of Congress catalog continues to be maintained by Congressional librarians, the provision of electronic access to the database is a private fee-based service. In the face of rising costs for these and other services, many individuals find that they can no longer afford to access the latest information, information that might affect one's understanding of the law, campaign issues, or of local government—information that would facilitate active participation in public life. To make matters worse, public libraries, once temples of learning for those unable to pay for an education or for access to society's stock of knowledge, also find themselves unable to keep up with soaring costs. Consequently, a gap is emerging between the information "haves", and the information "have-nots". The haves, mostly corporations and individuals with access to corporate resources, enjoy the full bounty of the information age by virtue of their ability to pay for entry, while the have-nots, mostly individuals from the middle class on down, experience marginalization as more and more critical information is effectively denied them.[13]

To make their point, librarians often define information as a public good and use the lighthouse analogy. No one is charged specifically when they benefit from the beam of the lighthouse; nor is anyone else deprived of light by use. If anyone chooses to forego the lighthouse, it is still there for others; therefore, all benefit. The lighthouse is the optimum structure for guaranteeing that all may benefit; because when all benefit, all are better off. Also, lighthouses are absolutely necessary for the collective safety of mariners. Thus, their presence benefits all mariners, even those who did not need to use the lighthouse. When used as a metaphor for the distribution of information, the lighthouse presents a powerful image, because a lighthouse can be compared to information via the bridge concept of "enlightenment".

By arguing for the indispensability of easily available information to the democratic process, and by envisioning information as a public good, librarians and information scientists have positioned themselves as the critical profession of the information society. In so doing, they have taken the position that democracy is threatened by the wholesale privatization of government information. Without their collective voice, there would be no debate.[14]

Yet the fact that information professionals have become aware of the transference of information from the public to the private sector—at just the time when the idea of an information society has gained popularity—has resulted in equating the tension with the concept. Since the information society is generally thought of as a recent phenomenon—post-industrial theory still holds sway—the tension between private and public information is easily interpreted as a new development. In a sense, this is due to the deterministic role which information technologies are thought to play in the information society. This view sees new technologies as driving forces behind the emergence of the information society; and, also, as the creators of new markets that convert public information into private information. Because the information commodities in greatest demand are databases that can only be assembled and accessed electronically, the implication is that the tension results from these recent technological developments.

However, such *post hoc ergo propter hoc* logic leads to several misinterpretations.[15] Considering the tension between public and private information as a recent development reinforces the view that the information society is a new social development, and a successor to industrial society—with theoretical implications beyond the scope of this chapter; it, therefore, follows that the commoditization of information must be an event without precedent in history, denying the value of historical experience to those concerned with information policy.

As a result, the entire debate is couched solely in terms of present circumstances. This is both heady and frightening—heady because the discussion is heavily sprinkled with terms invoking a high tech future, and frightening because the discussion contains few options for consideration. Plus, any lessons from previous episodes involving the tug between private and public, such as the development of the postal service, the telegraph, or the telephone, remain unexplored due to the impression that the present debate entails an all new society brought about by revolutionary technologies. In reality, the exclusion of history from the controversy creates invalid theory and makes for near-sighted public policy.

So, while those opposed to the transfer of information from the public to the private sector assume that the government give-away undermines the openness of democratic society, it may not be so; under certain conditions, the delivery of information as a commodity may further the realization of the ideal of democratic society. For example, the growth of the penny press in the 1830s illustrates how the sale of cheap newspapers, as information commodities, broadened the base of information available to the public and encouraged political participation.[16] On the other hand, the establishment of publicly subsidized free libraries in eastern cities, at a time when those cities were experiencing the flood of immigrants from Europe, clearly performed an important function in the education and assimilation of those multitudes.[17] In other words, awareness of the past contributes to better reasoned choices for the future.

To frame the policy debate solely in terms of the present also misrepresents the nature of the tension. While librarians, information scientists, and others correctly claim that the tension lies at the core of the information society, they sometimes deduce wrongly that the emergence of the information society brought about the tension. In fact, this tension is a basic condition encountered in all states that simultaneously embrace private ownership of property and government by the people. When seen from this perspective, the current policy discussion takes on greater significance; for the participants are actually redefining the means for meeting one of the conditions fundamental to any functioning democracy.

The tension public and private information can never be resolved conclusively because changes in society will always provoke reinterpretation. Those who speak out in this public policy discussion should maintain their awareness of the larger stage upon which they also act. After all, the search to profit from the sale of information represents the frontier of capitalism today. Whatever equilibrium emerges will reflect the national commitment to the ideals of capitalism as a social form. On the other hand, this is one case in which the sum of the players' economic self interests will not necessarily further the cause of democracy. Instead, the participants should turn a critical eye to the changing conditions of the information economy, in order to determine how those changes modify the promise of an informed citizenry. The public policy question should not be phrased in an either/or context, i.e., whether it is better for information to be treated as a private commodity or as a public resource. Rather, the question should seek to identify the appropriate balance, given the needs of American society today. For like the poor, the basic tension of an informed democracy will always be with us, because it is built right into the fabric of the republic.

The Infrastructure of the Political Process

Throughout the 20th century, the American economic system has evolved away from the production and distribution of material goods. The information economy and workforce, which replaced the old arrangement, set in motion new tendencies visible across all areas of social life, from private to public, from personal to political. Of these, two, in particular, hold consequences for the practice of political life: the progressive integration of political communication into the commoditized and commercialized provision of information; and, the fragmentation of the electorate by means of its segmentation as an audience.

Integration

Beginning with the telegraph, telecommunications technologies allowed newspapers to pioneer the integration of national markets for news and launch the era of big media. By mid 20th century, a few newspaper chains concentrated ownership of most of the significant newspapers and relied on three news agencies—the Associated Press, United Press International and Reuters—to gather news stories from around the globe. In broadcasting, the power of a single newscaster to reach the entire nation encouraged the integration of disparate news markets into national networks. The household penetration of television resulted in a true national market for news, with coverage of the events surrounding the assassination of President Kennedy providing television's first market test.[18] As a result, the recognition that mass audiences for news attracted profitable advertising led to adoption of the economics of large scale news production.

In order to generate profits, the networks currently minimize costs by maintaining news crews in the largest U.S. cities where, they reason, news stories are most likely to occur. As a result, a crime or fire in New York or Los Angeles is more likely to gain air time than a similar occurrence in Cincinnati or San Antonio. In addition, network news producers seek out scheduled events that can be planned into the day's production decisions. In response, government has learned to schedule media events, such as press conferences, at convenient times. So, in a deepening recession, President Bush announced his acceptance of a bill extending unemployment benefits for workers laid off during the recession on a midsummer Friday, when other news activity is typically low, thus insuring prominent placement on the nation's news shows and front pages. In addition, he made his announcement while on vacation in Kennebunkport, Maine, since the press was already assembled to cover his vacation.[19] By relying on events whose sole purpose is to attract media attention, big media and big government have turned press conferences and presidential ceremonies into the premier news stories of the public agenda.[20] The commercial/competitive nature of the mass media encourages reliance on politically managed news events and attention paid to political personalities, so that in the end, the news, like entertainment programming, is made attractive to the largest possible number of viewers.[21]

However, there are counter currents. The mass communication of political news seems to be changing in response to the proliferation of cable systems throughout the United States. Pressure to supply programming to the many channels offered by cable systems has resulted in some departures from network news practice. In order to fill its day-long program schedule, Cable News Network (CNN) offers foreign news organizations the opportunity to present news stories to U.S. audiences. For the first time, Americans can see a steady fare of foreign produced and edited news stories. The availability of political news produced according to different cultural assumptions is significant because it challenges some of the programming conventions created by the networks. Moreover, due to its reciprocation policy, CNN reaches viewers in numerous countries including Russia, raising the possibility that CNN might become the dominant network for the global dissemination of news. There are signs that this global market for international news is attracting other entrants, such as Rupert Murdoch's media empire and the Reuters news service. Regardless of who is successful, the trend indicates the integration of the world news market into an information system dominated by a few giant suppliers, with CNN taking an early lead. It seems likely that the new providers will replace the national networks as the arbiters of political news values.[22]

CNN's current successes also highlight the fact that television continues to serve as the primary source of political information for the bulk of the public. With newspapers in decline, most political information available to the public consists of sound bites, headlines, and photo opportunities enforced by the calculus of commercial TV news production. Such in-depth programming that does get air time draws small audiences. The result is that most Americans receive political news that is shallow, emphasizes personalities, and is often limited by the visuals available.

So tightly do the networks' algorithms determine content, that a symbiosis exists between TV news and government. Whereas presidents once met the press as adversaries, today presidential public relations staffs manage the information fed to the networks by packaging it in such a way that it is hard for a producer to alter the spin already put on it. By manipulating the rules of the

supply news items made to fit the networks' formu-
e influence over the public's political agenda. Thus
national television has been matched by big govern-
ublic relations presidency. Together they dominate

erican politics has also been affected by point-to-
technologies. Telephone and direct mail appeals
ve than the old mass rally. The image of the can-
lag draped stage and passing the hat has given
is telemarketing solicitors managed by a central
ally itself survives mainly as a nostalgic back-
televise the image of the candidate to the audi-
applications of technologies allow campaign
managers to direct national campaigns from a central location, and to bypass local political organizations. The result has been a flow of power
from the grass roots to the center, comparable to the integration that led to
a few dominant TV networks.[23]

Ultimately, it is the convergence of big media and consumer culture that
has brought about the tendency to treat political campaigning as marketing.
Consumer culture encourages individuals to meet their needs by purchasing
products. It does not advocate community values, nor does it foster the culti-
vation of public discourse with other members of the community. Instead, it
promotes individualistic purchasing of products and the consumption of commu-
mercial media. In effect, consumer culture creates its own symbols for communicating its primary theme; and because these values permeate culture
through advertising, they dominate the symbolism of public discourse, so that
the form, rhetoric, assumptions and taboos of public political discussion and
political messages have gradually taken on the forms of commercial media.
Not surprisingly, political messages look and feel like commercial ads, because ad-oriented political strategists encourage candidates to market themselves, rather than present their ideas to the electorate.

The tendency of political candidates is to adapt the patterns of consumer
culture to their political ends, with the result that politicians tend to be mar-
keted like commercial products. Today, political hopefuls at all levels routinely expect their campaign strategies to include a large dose of media
packaging, with an emphasis on image. The more professional the campaign,
the more the candidate's ads resemble those for consumer products. The integration of consumer culture is so advanced, that political candidates either
conform or lose contact with voters—and those who challenge the prevailing
norms jeopardize their elections. Though the goal of getting elected has remained the same for the past 200 years, candidates of the 1990s face a system
of news production which limits the depth of political discussion, as well as a
culture of consumption that shapes the symbolism of political language. The

integration of markets, set in motion by the impulse of 19th century industrialization, has wrapped American national politics in a strait jacket.

Fragmentation

Marketing theory dictates that successful vendors identify discrete market segments, so that they may package and advertise their product to appeal to the characteristics of one or more segments. Consequently, the media environment contains a host of programmers, advertisers, publishers, actors, announcers—along with a few politicians—competing for the attention of the segmented audience. Contrary to the nation-as-community image depicted during election years, the audience actually presents a highly fragmented appearance to the message producer; while from the perception of the audience, the media environment appears as a rush of discrete messages aimed at eliciting decisions to purchase discrete products.

Such is the power of commercial media as a genre that they shape the language of politics. As a result, television advertising styles used for selling cars dominate political communication as well. On a typical TV evening, the viewer absorbs one ad after another—laundry soap, kitty litter, make-up, car, deodorant, cereal, shampoo, dating services, toilet paper—with no apparent order or context, but with familiar styles and plots. Thus, the context and form of nearly all media encourage individuals to approach the political agenda as they would the products advertised on prime time TV; in other words, a lineup of unconnected, unrelated issues.

Political messages framed within this genre focus on image through the use of over-simplified emotional appeals, while they ignore complex interrelationships such as the intricate give and take of each party's legislative agenda. In addition, the pervasiveness of messages delivered by big media establishes an environment in which individuals experience information overload on a daily basis. Not only must citizens be alert to the occasional political message, but they must also contend with the obstacle of sheer volume should they choose to participate in public political discourse. Given these conditions, and with the exception of the influential citizen, active political discourse never takes center stage. So, not surprisingly, when voters turn out, they enter the voting booth with a view of politics limited to one or two issues.

When individuals apply patterns of consumer behavior to political behavior, they bring the context of the fragmented audience to the political experience. Because fragmentation results from the experience of receiving messages as discrete bits of content, voters find it easy to develop a tunnel-vision conceptualization of the political agenda that encourages single issue voting. Also, the disconnectedness of fragmentation masks the importance of political organizations by picturing candidates as free floating individuals, not unlike the fictional characters seen on TV. Cynicism with regard to political parties and low appreciation for party platforms are among the results. So, as consumerism and fragmentation replace participation, political and consumer choices acquire equal significance. Consequently, individuals may be inclined to dismiss the significance of government and consider political activities trivial, thus contributing to a spiral which devalues participation in political life.

When citizens choose politicians and groceries according to the same consumer paradigm, they force political candidates to rely more heavily on the marketing approach; and so, further debase political discourse. Therefore, given the struggle of political communicators to be heard from within the blizzard of commercial messages, it is easy to imagine a fragmented electorate leading to a fragmented democracy; or, at least, a condition where the governed have voluntarily alienated themselves from those in power. Ironically, James Madison's fear of factionalism appears as likely in the information society, the epitome of interconnectedness, as it did when he wrote Federalist paper No. 10. As always, erosion at the base leaves the democratic process vulnerable.

Americans' high involvement with media demonstrates their acceptance of the behavior patterns that go with consumer culture, while continued low rates of voting indicate disinterest in the electoral process. In fact, between 1960 and 1988, the percent of voting age population that actually voted dropped from 62.8% to 50.2%. Given the long-term decline in voter participation, it is not clear whether the increased turnout for the Bush-Clinton election signifies a new trend.[24] Given these figures, it is tempting to deplore the decline in voter participation during the elections of the last thirty years on the basis of an earlier era of virtuous American voters. But Americans have never gone to the polls in the numbers typical of elections in many European countries. The most heavily attended presidential election of all ended the race between William Henry Harrison and Martin Van Buren (1840); 80.2% of the eligible voters cast a ballot and Harrison won. In 1896, William McKinley narrowly defeated William Jennings Bryant in a hotly contested election that drew a 79.3% turnout; whereas, the election with the lowest rate of voter participation (26.9%) resulted in Andrew Jackson's defeat by John Quincy Adams. In general, elections during the 19th century drew voter participation percentages in the 70s; while, in the 20th century, participation has hovered in the 60s and 50s, although In 1920 and 1924, voter participation was 49.2% and 48.9% respectively.[25] Too much can be made of television's enervating effect on voters. In addition to television, alienation from the election process probably reflects a sense of powerlessness that is not of recent origin.

The mass media are not the only media, and political activism is not entirely a thing of the past. Some local issues—usually issues rather than candidates—draw intense voter responses. Moreover, communication technologies responsive to individual uses play an important role in the local expression of political power by reinforcing a kind of community. In Santa Monica, California, landlords circulated videotapes showing pro rent control members of the city council in an unfavorable light and won the next election on a wave of voter indignation. In New Jersey, opponents of a tax hike used a local call-in radio station to air grievances, draw attention to a growing tax revolt, and promote membership in their organization, "Hands Across New Jersey." These and other examples indicate that individuals numbed by the unresponsiveness of national politics sometimes still feel effective within the scale of local issues. What's more, small technologies, e.g., video and audio cassettes, telephone banks, local mailings, files organized on personal computers, fax machines, etc. appear well suited to activism at this level, and not only in the United States. In eastern Europe, Poles, Czechs, and Hungarians, defied their governments' control over television content by using homemade satellite dishes to receive foreign programming. In particular, *Solidarity* kept its movement alive in Poland by producing video documentaries distributed for viewing on videocassette recorders.[26] It appears that micro participation can coexist with macro disengagement.

Individuals who live fragmented lives continue to experience the desire for community and for dialogue. As social, family, and political attachments weaken, individuals recreate interconnectedness through the use of communication technologies. Increasingly, Americans live in communities structured by communication networks. These communities exist as connections without the geographic boundaries of village or town. In a highly mobile population friends and even the nuclear family stay "together" through frequent telephone calls, shared audio and videocassettes, and a few letters. Their actual physical contact sometimes only occurs between long intervals of separation. These communities constitute both a response to fragmentation and a reification of fragmentation. In effect, they are virtual communities.

Among the first of these new communities to be studied, computer bulletin boards have drawn considerable attention to the patterns of association generated when members of the community interact solely through typed messages. Made up of computer programmers and users, and known as network communities, they emphasize the special attachments formed by individuals who are not in physical contact.[27] In terms of activism, users of computer bulletin boards often urge members to take positions on political issues and offer information on how to make oneself heard. Their potential for challenging centralized elites—both governmental and corporate—sometimes leads to networks—not all electronic—that generate political cohesiveness through identification with the values shared by other members of the network. With their latent political muscle, it may even be that bulletin board communities constitute the basis for new political agendas. Possibly, they may even be the source of a new political force within the information society.[28]

Yet though new technologies appear to contribute to new social forms, the fragmentation that Americans experience poses a challenge to any lasting sense of community, by suggesting the possibility of permanent alienation, and resurrecting that part of the classical debate of political philosophy which concerns itself with the proper size of the political community. Plato's recommendation of a population of about 40,000 was based on the necessity that citizens be able to communicate directly with each other in order to maintain a shared sense of community. Of course, among his 40,000 people only 5,000 were citizens and, lacking communication media, 5,000 represents the probable limit of personal interconnectedness. Reflecting on Plato, Aristotle thought even this number too large, saying that the limit should be no more than "can be taken in at a single view,"[29] in other words, the number of citizens capable of meeting in one place and making decisions. By this, he suggested that the nature of the community must be understandable to its members and that they must share a definition of themselves as a group.

In modern society the mass media are the means by which we share that definition. The face-to-face discussion of political issues idealized in the New England town meeting has been replaced by television styles of news portrayal combined with controversial issues like child abuse that form the core of the plots of dramatic programs. Media theorists have long posited that mediated messages serve to connect diverse publics to a common agenda, but that community constitutes the arena where the agenda is digested.[30] If the balance in video programming were to swing toward individually targeted programs such that themes appear in different terms and emphasize different values for each segment of the market, then Americans stand to lose one of the most important means by which they share a definition of themselves as a group, no matter how superficially the media have constructed that definition in the past. If targeted programming succeeds in establishing distinct virtual communities, then the principal place for an individual to experience the interpersonal dynamics of community will be among one's fellow workers, and then the workplace will replace the family as the primary group. Indeed, for the 22 million Americans who live alone and comprise 24% of all households, that reality is now.[31]

If the information society conjures up images of computer assisted communities, then one variant is the computer interactive network. Imagine, if you will, the households depicted in the opening quotes of chapter 4. In an interactive environment, households such as these will be able to assemble the evening's viewing schedule by choosing from a video library of programs. Moreover, individual members will shop according to their own individually constructed marketing profiles, and vote from their homes. But at the other end of the network, statisticians will record and analyze choices communicated via the video screen, so as to maintain a marketing profile for each individual. Any clusterings of taste, styles, or political preferences will appear to network executives as statistical summaries based on each person's profile.

In contrast to the virtual communities of computer bulletin board users, in this setting, the average person may have no clue as to the existence of like-minded individuals. Indeed, if individuals seek feelings of community by supporting entertainment and information video programming through individualized subscription and targeted marketing in an interactive network, then video may become the most powerful source of social stratification and alienation in society. There are those who predict an epoch of immediate computer democracy with every citizen connected to a terminal capable of registering every vote no matter how trivial. But even the most optimistic futurists admit that such a setup is an ideal marketing device providing personalized commercial messages and instantly recording consumer decisions.[32] The attraction of individualized lifestyles grounded in an interactive media environment may result in fragmented lives isolated from meaningful human contact. In any case, few if any suggest that coherent public discourse can exist within a highly fragmented audience; for under such circumstances, interactive video may stretch alienation to its limits.

The tendency toward big news organizations and integrated information markets dominated by a few corporations continues to coalesce; and along with it, national political media campaigns. Yet individuals find themselves increasingly caught in fragmented media environments. In response they gravitate to segregated—perhaps even isolated—virtual communities, while sometimes exploiting small media for local political purposes.

The resulting incongruity has changed the old political mix of bases connected to national agendas, and jeopardizes the classical principles of democracy. As long as Americans disengage from national politics and turn their backs on the process of legitimation, the claim to democratic representation rings hollow. Perhaps surprisingly, the political role of the television networks and cable news services may have increasing value. Surely it will seem peculiar, after so many have commented on the negative impact of network television programming aimed at the "least common denominator," to look to television as a factor in ensuring political discourse in American culture. But since national (possibly international) television news sets the common agenda, that potential is there. Of course, the media focus on image rather than substance, but there is, in the national media at least, the potential for calling nationwide attention to emerging issues. Whatever laurels the three networks may deserve for their past performances in this regard, they are likely to have the only clear opportunity to serve this function well into the future. Should television evolve into a medium for increasingly individualized programming and advertising, the prospects for healthy political discourse become gloomy indeed.

It seems fairly clear that the tension between integration and fragmentation of political communication will increase. At this point there are no coherent indications as to whether it will result in the re-emergence of a common public agenda, or virtual communities, or merely a nation of television viewing couch potatoes.

Distributional Justice

New times require fresh conventional wisdoms to offer guidance in the face of altered circumstances. In the information society, the reigning conventional wisdom holds that information is power. Among aphorisms, this one has attracted exceptional attention because it suggests that a redistribution of information might lead to a reordering of society. Thus, given the new sensibilities with which people have come to regard information, the relationship between information and power bears consideration.

Information Poverty

The nexus joining information to power and wealth is so strong that the phrase information poverty is now commonly used in policy circles to refer to an emergent social problem. As Thomas Childers described it in his pioneering analysis, "a closed system harboring an inordinate amount of unawareness and misinformation [myth, rumor, folk lore]."[33] The title of his book, *The Information Poor in America*, elicits images that tie in with those underlying beliefs which Americans hold for information policy in general. At the most obvious level, the premise that a portion of the population can be thought of as information poor connotes that an important gap exists between the information poor and some other group logically construed as the information rich. Moreover, the gap appears to threaten negative consequences, for if information is a major resource in modern society, then to be without it signifies powerlessness, isolation, deprivation, and misfortune—the same conditions that blight the lives of the materially poor.

This, in turn, raises an association between information poverty and equity, and thereby introduces familiar questions into a new vocabulary: Should society accept conditions of information poverty? How much and what kinds of information do people need to better their lot in life? What's fair? Such questions imply, correctly, that any focus on the information poor should be a part of a broader focus on the social distribution of information. In other words, poverty and wealth are not independent conditions. It follows that the information poor and the information rich must be studied as two parts of the same relationship, if one wishes to understand this important dimension of the information society. In the background, Americans have gradually adopted the view that individuals with access to more information will experience a higher quality of life than those with access to less information. Thus, notions of information poverty and wealth nearly always come attached to notions of material poverty and wealth. Consequently, when Americans say that information is power, they mean that information holds the key to a better standard of living.

Not surprisingly, anyone aware of the dynamics of the information society can sense that information poverty should be taken seriously. After all, in an economy that demands more and more highly educated workers, lack of education—a form of information poverty—spells underemployability at best. Plus, to anyone familiar with negotiating public and private bureaucracies, a lack of understanding of their inner workings—another form of information poverty—means wasted time, money, and, ultimately, failure. In this case, popular sentiments are backed by more rigorous analysis. The lack of information, and the lack of access to information, does seem to make a difference in one's success, and the literature is unanimous in its concern for the consequences of information gaps.[34]

Yet if the lack of information seems to be a problem, it also seems a problem capable of solution. For unlike material poverty—where policy solutions often founder on the zero sum consequences of cross subsidization, and against which the direct application of funds has little long term effect—information poverty appears susceptible to the direct distribution of information, with the added benefit that no one is denied information once it has been distributed to someone else. In principle, the economies of scale of most kinds of information are so enormous that the information society is often thought of as an age of plenty, where the information poor, unlike the economic poor, need not always be with us.

Here, then, is the promise: if information can be cheaply duplicated, distributed, and made accessible so that individuals benefit from its availability, then any positive correlation with standard of living or material quality of life amounts to a very low cost social benefit. Furthermore, the rich need not be deprived by the distribution of information to the poor. It sounds like the perfect policy solution, but it doesn't work that way in real life.

In real life, information resources and economic resources sometimes confound each other. For example, when properly interpreted, information can increase the productivity of capital; but that same information, applied erroneously, can lead to losses. In addition, information alone does not guarantee any advantage in the marketplace. Capital must be brought to bear. Recognizing this, inventors and other creative individuals who wish to exploit their ideas for profit seek out financial backers, and it is in this arena that venture capitalists operate. When individuals value information as a commodity, they may suffer negative consequences as a result of its wide distribution; software writers make this argument when they lament the widespread unauthorized copying of their programs.

The complexities inherent in the value of information are further illustrated when one compares the information rich with the economically rich. Indeed, the information rich are not always economically rich. University professors and librarians present cases in point. Professors stand at the top of the education scale, and, so, generally speaking, qualify as among the richest in information. But since university professors average $41,000 income (for 1989), they still fall below 17% of the working population.[35] Similarly, librarians, having the highest information search skills and capable of accessing the greatest amount of information, average around \$18,000, and so fall well below professors.[36] Antithetically, the wealthiest tenth of the population are not the best educated. Yet when one looks at the opposite end of the income scale, one sees that those who suffer economically also tend to lack education. The relationship between economic wealth and information wealth exhibits no symmetry.

Nor is it so easy to determine who is information rich and who is information poor. Because information is subjectively acquired and subjectively valued, different groups can be information rich in ways that are appropriate to their own needs, yet have no connection to each others' needs. Maine lobstermen and women know a great deal about the interaction between lobster movements and the tides. By contrast, New York office workers possess considerable knowledge of commuting patterns and the ways to minimize time in transit. But neither body of knowledge is of particular use to the other group. In fact, each group is simultaneously information rich and information poor. If we choose cases that are not mutually exclusive, it becomes harder to delineate information rich from information poor. For instance, blue collar factory workers may possess significant knowledge of home maintenance, since they are more likely to bear responsibility for their own repairs. On the other hand, upper middle class professionals may know little about any aspect of home repair but they have the income to hire a contractor. To argue that upper middle class professionals are information rich because they know how to purchase services confuses information wealth with economic wealth. Still, there is a connection. At least in this example, economic wealth translates into access to information resources.

From this jumble of examples, it should be clear that information comes in many forms, and that there is no clear-cut relationship between information wealth and economic wealth. People need the information that is right for them, regardless of the total stock available. Therefore, no quantitative scale can adequately judge the full value of information. The fact is we know little about the multiple dimensions of how people value information. Without a doubt, the coming of the information society raises the ante for information as a stake in public, private, economic, and political life. But we can't know how every hand will be played. For these reasons, the question of who is information rich and who is information poor turns out to be complicated in the extreme. Nevertheless, the point remains that information poverty is relative to the information available to the society as a whole at any given time; so that, as the information orientation in a society increases, so too does the desirability of making information available to all of its members.

Policymakers should be lauded when they take the position that society is better off when all sectors of the public can access the information they need to better themselves economically, or to discharge their civic obligations. But policymakers should be cautioned that there is much more to information poverty than meets the eye. If there is a lesson from this discussion, it is that people are better off when they know how to access the information they want. In an information society, just as in a hunting and gathering society, it is better to teach people to fish than to give them fish. This is not to say that efforts to provide information are misguided—they can help redress past inequalities—it is only to say that without information seeking skills, people remain at the mercy of their circumstances.

Literacy

Recognition of the importance of information seeking skills to full fledged participation in the information society has generated pressure to identify a body of basic skills. Observers note that changes in the economy, coupled with new technological developments, require new skills from individuals. The continued expansion of the production and distribution of information in the economy requires an increase in the information workforce, with a resulting demand for computer programming, word processing, copy writing, and other office-related skills. Similarly, the introduction of computers into the workplace creates a need for workers with the capabilities of operating them and exploiting their potential. In the home, consumers have had to learn to program videocassette recorders, thermostats, and telephone answering machines. Although these various proficiencies seem to call on a wide variety of skills, they all build on a single intellectual technique—literacy.

It may seem anachronistic to focus on literacy in the era of the global village, since, as McLuhan put it, "In the electronic age which succeeds the typographic and mechanical era of the past five hundred years, we encounter new shapes and structures of human interdependence and of expression which are 'oral' in form...."[37] Like other futurists, he posited that the new age would reemphasize oral culture at the expense of the culture of print; and, if one takes a casual glance around, McLuhan seems vindicated by the visual-oral nature of most of the information technologies which have arrived in the home and workplace over the last 40 years. But in fact, the production of entertainment, scripts, ad copy, instructions, programming, calibrations, along with the interconnection of enterprises and services, depend entirely on the written word and constitute most of the information economy employing the bulk of the information workforce. As to the observation that the information society is a "visual-oral" culture, it persists as conventional wisdom because, in the words of Ong, "...with telephone, radio, television and various kinds of sound tape, electronic technology has brought us into the age of 'secondary orality'."[38] That is, we confuse the oral-visual environment in which we consume leisure information for the literacy-based edifice from which that information is produced. So, in ways that are not always readily apparent, literacy is more important today than ever before.

Yet literacy would not even be an issue worth mentioning were it not for ominous indications that illiteracy is on the rise in the United States. Not counting speakers of foreign languages, surveys indicate that roughly 6% of all adults in the U.S. are illiterate.[39] Furthermore, illiteracy may be just the tip of the iceberg. For some years now, university professors have complained that undergraduates demonstrate poor grammar, small vocabularies, and can't spell. If these students represent the educated elite of the nation—presumably, students who elect not to attend college are generally less accomplished than those who go on—then the skills base of the information society rests on a vulnerable foundation. Just how vulnerable is hard to judge because illiteracy is such a volatile issue. Americans who want to believe that they live in the world's foremost industrial nation find it hard to accept that their country ranks on a par with the illiteracy rates of Uruguay or Tonga, and below Cuba.[40] The possibility that a significant number of American adults can't read is so embarrassing that the federal government failed to report any statistics on literacy in either the 1990 *Statistical Abstract of the United States*, or *World Statistics in Brief*.

A more familiar issue, because it conforms nicely with popular thinking about the information society, concerns the need for skills to cope with new information technologies. Typically, demands for this new literacy, more often called computer literacy, challenge educators to teach children skills in preparation for using computers in the workaday world. Parents send their kids off to computer camps, and donate PCs to neighborhood schools, where computer literacy has become orthodoxy. Yet computer literacy requires knowledge of traditional literacy as much as the oral-visual proficiencies envisioned by McLuhan. In fact, some might argue that really understanding what computers do requires an understanding of programming, and therefore of formal language theory.

If a student is to learn more about computer use than keypunching, the ability to find and evaluate information must be taught as well. Some activists in educational policy have pressed for the expansion of educational curricula to include information seeking skills. They stress that the older skills of reading and writing must be augmented to include skills for manipulating information now appearing in new forms. These "'Rithms of the Future," as William Paisley calls them, demand competencies to maneuver through complex information environments; while, "…it cannot be said that a person who can read and write is illiterate…, such a person may be illiterate if he or she lacks other skills that must also be performed in *applying* literacy."[41] For Paisley and others with similar concerns, the new literacy means knowing how to access the information now stored in electronic databases. That is, in addition to reading and writing, one must learn the various techniques necessary to access and manipulate electronically stored forms of information, e.g., Boolean search strategies. Recognizing the validity of Paisley's views, some universities offer library orientation courses. Others offer an entire "learning to learn" curriculum. But these initiatives, though worth noting, are not widely adopted; and, in any case, they are inaccessible to those outside the university.

The problem, perhaps typical of any age of rapid change, revolves around the difficulties faced when deciding which skills to emphasize. That is, once beyond the 3 R's, the necessary minima of education become less certain. If it seems anachronistic to be concerned with literacy in the information age, it is because the legacy of the push for popular literacy is left over from the industrial times of the 19th century. Today, although everyone agrees that the kind of literacy appropriate for factory work may not be sufficient for producing software, there is no consensus on the new configuration of necessary skills; nevertheless, agreement exists on the main questions. What kind of literacy is needed for full-fledged participation in the information society? Also, what steps can the nation take to insure that all have access to these keys to participation?

Here is where the policy debate heats up, and properly so. Although the personal value of a given unit of information is hard to determine and presents obstacles to analysis, there should be little doubt that reading and writing are the basic building blocks of access. Policy objectives that seek to provide specific information to individuals or groups run up against the complexities of information economics and the difficulties of determining what information is appropriate to any group. A policy objective seeking to ensure that individuals have access to the information they define as appropriate for themselves seems more achievable. To achieve full participation in the information society, a combination of literacy and information seeking skills is needed. The challenge is to identify how best to provide it.

Universal Service

In a utopian information society all individuals would be literate and possess the skills necessary to use information technologies. The technologies themselves would be so user-friendly as to be transparent to the user, and the information necessary for full political and economic participation would be accessible to all through the use of these technologies. But for anyone who has patched together a personal computer network, or sought to customize multimedia communications services, the distance between utopia and reality is shocking. Of course, to compare any social reality with a utopian vision is unfair. Nevertheless, the utopian vision of the information society exerts great pull on the popular imagination, because we so frequently hear its promises of a better life; and, so derived, some version of that same vision lurks within the policy imagination as well. Put in practical policy terms, the question of how to get from here to there asks, "What underlying policy foundation must be institutionalized in order to enable participation by all in the information age?" The foundation in question is universal service.

In its simplest terms, universal service is the concept which holds that everyone should have the opportunity to communicate with whomever they wish at a reasonable cost. In principle, this has traditionally meant access to a telephone. For most of the 20th century, the idea that no one in America should be unable to get moderately priced telephone service has defined both the telecommunications environment and the citizen's rights within it. So powerful is this belief, that its essence permeates information policy thinking. Yet no explicit definition exists in any law. The language closest to a definition comes from the Communications Act of 1934, the *Magna Carta* of telecommunications, in which it is stated, "...so as to make available, so far as possible, to all the people of the United States a rapid, efficient, nationwide, and worldwide...communication service with adequate facilities at reasonable charges...."[42] Its predecessors, the Interstate Commerce Act of 1887, and the Radio Act of 1927, merely established the conditions for regulating communications as the "...public convenience, interest, or necessity...", and in so doing, created assumptions further developed in the Act of 1934.[43] In the Constitution, where lie the deepest roots, the connection is fainter still, "The Congress shall have the power...To establish Post Offices and Post Roads;" nonetheless, the notion of universal service can be discerned in the idea of a service to facilitate communication at a distance.[44] Even Theodore Vail, the energy behind the growth of AT&T, and the architect of telephonic universal service, came no closer than this statement from the AT&T *Annual Report of 1910:* "The position of the Bell system is well known... The telephone system should be universal, interdependent and intercommunicating, affording opportunity for any subscriber of an exchange to communicate with any other subscriber of any other exchange...annihilating time or distance by use of electrical transmission." Today it is routinely assumed that the telephone system of the United States was built on the premise of universal service, but the historical fact is that the idea was never thoroughly articulated. And it appears that the policy direction of the information society depends on this still ambiguous idea.

Universal service derives its significance from two promises and a bargain. In the first promise, all Americans are assured equal access to basic channels of communication. In other words, the citizens of a republic need to be able to communicate, in order to avail themselves of the information necessary to make reasoned political choices. Given the communication orientation embedded in the conception of participation which the founding fathers held, the pledge of equal access is not only logical, but absolutely necessary to the conduct of a free and open society. Within this framework, the establishment of the U.S. Post Office (1789), the authorization of the Post Road from New York to Philadelphia (1789), and the digging of the Erie canal (1817), represent commitments to this vision.

However, lest one misinterpret the construction of the vast infrastructure of the United States as an effort in pursuit of equality, the focus of this commitment is clearly on access, rather than outcomes. That is, while citizens are guaranteed the opportunity to avail themselves of existing communication channels, there is no promise that all will receive the same information.[45] So, in the tradition of the founders, maximum freedom is attained when individuals exercise free choice; thus, to the merchants and land owners who gathered to write the Constitution, equal opportunity and access represented the only reasonable obligation of society.[46]

The second promise reaches out to that aspect of the American character which de Tocqueville called, "the love of physical gratification."[47] That is, if the capitalist urge is to be satisfied, then government must bear the responsibility of laying a foundation that facilitates economic activities. To that end, Vail, the telephone, and universal service, contributed to a transformation of the conduct of business. By allowing individuals to send information as well as to receive it, the spread of telephone service enhanced interconnectedness— 35 million average daily conversations in 1910 to 1.7 billion in 1988[48]—thereby quickening the distribution of information necessary to coordinate the flow of commerce. The telephone increased the flexibility of the labor force—35% household penetration in 1920 to 93% in 1989[49]—so that, by mid century, there emerged a national market for labor. The telephone opened the door to a consumer oriented marketplace without geographic boundaries. The telephone led the way to the technological cornucopia built on the exploitation of electrical energy.

Finally, the concept of universal service is a bargain that conceded a monopoly on long interexchange business and most of the local exchange business to the company with the responsibility to make service universal. Thus, in its 1910 configuration, universal service became the indispensable policy of the information society. No wonder that the public's heightened attention to prophecies of the information age has led to calls for a new universal service. New technologies always suggest new potentials; and, as new applications have transformed the telephone, it makes perfect sense to reconsider the original idea. With a concept like universal service, which has always been technologically dependent, the inventions of the last 30 years clearly invite speculation as to what it ought to mean today, especially in light of the catalytic role played by the computer. Now, with the coming of the "intelligent network," a new meaning of universal service seems almost inevitable.

Perhaps with equal inevitability, the debate to define the new universal service has involved groups with numerous, sometimes conflicting, expectations. As arguments have emerged and evolved, shifts in the debate prevent any one group from being identified with a single position. So, for purposes of brevity, we lay out the debate and the actors in abstract form. Foremost— and loudest—is the demand for a universal service that will spur the rebirth of the American economy. Frustrated by declining productivity and competitiveness, business leaders and policymakers are unanimous in arguing for an information infrastructure that will do for the 21st century what the telephone did for the 20th. A computer enriched universal service seems to fit the bill.

For the technologically deterministic, the very existence of new technologies requires a response. In this view, technology drives history. Therefore, the discussion over universal service should not bog itself down considering questions of economic growth or social welfare. Instead, the technologies themselves will point the way to their own implementation for creating a new universal service.

Overlapping the interests of the first two groups, there are those who subscribe to a laissez-faire approach to policy. For them, the goal of society is to benefit the largest number of members; therefore, they accept conditions whereby some members of society are worse off, as long as the largest number are better off. Information serves—as does any other resource—to benefit the majority, or plurality, so that they tend to de-emphasize the "universal" in universal service, leaving it to the marketplace to set the price where the greatest number can afford the service. Any questions of justice are left to the invisible hand.

By contrast, for the proponents of participatory democracy, universal service is about inclusion and participation, and therefore, fundamentally about the mechanisms of democracy. For some, universal service is a kind of human right because it is necessary for individuals to exercise free speech in the information society. For this group questions of technology, though present, take a back seat to the goal of democratic participation. Proponents of universal service-as-democracy want to know how the lack of a telephone in a household affects participation in society. They ask whether interactive computer experiments in communities—such as the QUBE interactive cable system in Columbus, Ohio, or the PEN computer network system in Santa Monica, California—can enhance political dialogue. They look to developments in other countries for lessons relevant to the American experience. To them, the role of universal service is to further democratic participation, not as a concept but as the give and take of everyday life.

One last group participates in this debate. Their argument is that access to information through universal service is necessary if society hopes to diminish the information gap between rich and poor. Above and beyond guaranteed equal opportunity to access a standard communication technology, they see information as the key social component of the new infrastructure. Universal service, for them, is really access *and* information. This view sees universal service as a link in the basic safety net necessary for a just society and as a clause in society's definition of basic welfare. In other words, just as no citizen should experience barriers to full participation in society due to race, political beliefs, sex, or religion, so also should no citizen experience barriers due to inaccessible fundamental information. This position stems from the belief that no society acts morally when it knowingly pushes any portion of the population to the margins, where they are unable to participate in the political and economic life of the nation. Thus, a just and fair society accepts disparities of distributed resources only when they result in an improved condition for all of the members. Accordingly, citizens must possess information in order to make the choices that are in society's interest. Information, then, is a fundamental resource which must be made broadly available, in order to insure justice. The underpinnings for this perspective can be found in the writings of John Rawls, especially in *Justice as Fairness*.[50] Nevertheless, there is little agreement, in this group, as to exactly what information should be part of any universal service. Because they reject sole reliance on the marketplace as an effective distribution mechanism for information, they lack an explicit distribution mechanism outside of government, unlike their opponents who support a laissez-faire market.

Though the image presented by this review is of opposing groups jockeying for advantages in the arena of public debate, the reality contains fuzzy boundaries. Whereas participants in the debate do hold to distinct views, there is considerable groping for a new definition that still maintains continuity with what has gone before. Though the debate elicits genuine diversity of views, some agreement can be discerned. There is broad consensus that the development of a new technological environment merits a reconsideration of universal service. No one is proposing a universal service that does not contribute positively to the economic development of the nation. Nor is there any proposal that ignores some obligation to equal access. Also, even laissez-faire supporters acknowledge that the more people link into some de facto information technology infrastructure such as telephone, cable, PCs, online services, the more deprived will be those who are left out of the loop.[51] Among those not solely committed to the marketplace, there is general agreement that a measure of equity can be determined by asking how many and who are at the margins. Finally, and interestingly, the concept of bargaining a monopoly in return for universal service seems to have left the debate altogether. While it was a key element in AT&T's proposals in the early part of the century, and was recognized and endorsed by the 1934 Communications Act as necessary and appropriate, the idea of a regulated monopoly carrier serving the public interest where competition could not be sustained was gradually disavowed during the '70s and 80's, leaving a commitment to a competitive market in its place. (Note that it remains unclear what this says about the funding of universal service in the future. If subsidies are necessary to ensure affordability, where will those subsidies come from in a competitive market?) Whatever specific regulatory regime and industry structure shape the new universal service, it will almost assuredly emerge out of these premises.

To start with, since the idea of information access has always depended on a technological frame of reference, it is appropriate to begin with the technological constraints. Universal service, as imagined by Vail, depended on a pair of copper wires as the basis of the network. Today, the network integrates cable, optical fiber, microwave, and satellite technologies. While still capable of transmitting voice, the system can also transmit images and digital computer codes in analog form. Furthermore, as digital switches have been introduced to the network, these switches, which are actually dedicated computers, convert analog signals into digital sequences that can be read by other computers. With this advance, digital networks can manage voice and data traffic more efficiently, while at the same time generating signaling information necessary for enhanced services. Once fully implemented, the digital network will be capable of exchanging video, data, fax, and/or voice signals in the same transmission, without the intervention of a modem.[52] Here, then, is the stimulant for reconsidering universal service. The "intelligent network" is inherently capable of bringing any recorded information to any user—whether a fax, a television program, a neighbor's call, or the encyclopedia. In addition, the network's management capabilities extend to automated services, such as standby emergency alarms, or stored messages and phone numbers. With such potential, there is a compelling opportunity to reconsider the promises of universal service. Since old conceptualizations addressed access alone, the "intelligent network" clearly opens the door to the inclusion of information as well.

Three differing policy positions can be distilled from the debate seeking to redefine universal service.[53] The first position adheres to Vail's original vision. It asserts that the monopoly model best delivers universal service. In this view, the government's role is to preserve connectivity for all, and its heart is the cross-subsidizing rate structure that averages tolls, so that those connecting in sparsely populated areas can still benefit from reasonable rates. However, this proposal runs up against the American dislike for monopolies; to attempt to return to the "one monopoly, one regulator" approach would turn back the clock after a decade of popular support for competition. A policy enacting this view is likely to meet with resistance from the public, as well as the phone companies who wish to continue to exploit the possibilities of deregulation. Popular in the 1970s, in the 1990s there is little support for this position in its pure form.

The second position holds that unfettered competition results in the greatest good for the greatest number. From this perspective, the telephone companies should be allowed to maximize their profits, as they see fit, and government should stay as far away as possible. This position follows from the laissez-faire view and combines with the American penchant for competition and the least amount of government involvement. While this view conforms to deeply seated American beliefs, it is based on the assumptions of deregulation, rather than the reality. For, although deregulation certainly acts as a spur to competitiveness, in and of itself competitiveness provides no guarantee that everyone will be served at a particular level of service. Therefore, if past performance serves as a guide, deregulated telephone service is likely to lead to gaps between those who can afford enhanced services and those who cannot. Those living in remote areas are likely to experience reluctance to upgrade, on the part of telephone companies. So, while it may be argued that as advances trickle down, disparities will eventually disappear, the social cost paid by individuals who experience these gaps can never be made up. Therefore, a policy derived from the second position will support the goal of economic expansion, but at the expense of equitable distribution of access to information.

In the third position, flexible regulation is sought as a means to achieve the benefits of competition, while still maintaining the focus of universal service. To encourage upgrading the network to new standards, regulators in some states have provided incentive plans that allow phone companies to keep extra earnings, provided they plow them back into capital expenditures. As they have developed this view, some of its supporters accept utility type controls at the state level as the appropriate arena for working out a new universal service. In other words, this is a kind of middle path pioneered by the states, in the face of federal government disengagement. But if the states are to lead the way, then no national definition of universal service is probable. More likely the result will mirror the condition of roads and highways, with some states enjoying an excellent highway system while others suffer dismal conditions. One need only drive across the border from New Jersey to Pennsylvania to experience such disparities. In effect, from whatever position it is approached, the debate has tended to focus on regulatory forms and their consequences for existing universal service.

What is mostly overlooked is that, in the information society, one must be informed in order to function successfully. For, though interconnectedness oiled the spread of the first industrial society, by itself it cannot deliver the promise of the information society. If fragmentation is to be checked, then citizens need the answers to their questions, and they must have access to information in digestible form. If citizens are to avoid a surveillance state, or a surveillance economy, then limits must be placed on government's and business's access to information about individuals, while individuals need access to information gathered about themselves. Also, if they are to participate fully in the information economy as both consumers and producers, Americans must have the opportunity to avail themselves of lifelong learning. In short, though the impetus for redefining universal service may have come from a desire to keep up with technological advances, the rationale should stem from an obligation to seek the goals of democratic participation and economic growth, no matter how contradictory they might be in any given instance.

But if a redefined universal service is to stress information as well as interconnectedness, then which information needs should be met? On its surface, this is an unanswerable question, because each person's information needs are idiosyncratic and subjective. So any solution found should not attempt a direct answer. It must keep in mind that citizens are active information seek-ers. One approach is to specify spheres of obligation, by differentiating public needs from personal needs. A universal service oriented in this way obligates government to meet the demands of the public sphere, while facilitating the opportunities inherent in the private sphere. For example, in the public sphere, citizens need access to, and the knowledge of how to use, government ser-vices, and they should have access to channels of communication which pro-vide a public voice. In the private sphere, individuals should enjoy the opportunity to benefit from the wealth of the economy, to make intelligent economic decisions, and to maintain their privacy. More broadly stated, an informed and participating citizenry is the necessary condition for a participa-tory democracy, and an informed and economically capable public is a neces-sary condition for meeting the goal of a fair and efficient market.

That said, a concept of universal service derived from these considerations is not without difficulties. First of all, conceptual boundaries are never clear in real life. After all, in America the boundary between the public and private spheres constitutes contested terrain. But that may be an advantage, since the territory is well known and a socio-legal tradition already exists to show the way. Secondly, there is still no answer to the question of which information needs are to be met. However, there needn't be; the individualistic nature of the question guarantees that this will be a continuing issue for public discus-sion. In other words, given the predisposition of Americans to fear govern-ment when it is intrusive and the market when it fails, no codified compendium of necessary information resources will last for long.

The danger lies more in imbalances of power and influence. That is, be-cause the stakes are high, the information resources available through univer-sal service, at any given time, are likely to reflect a combination of special interests. If the public's voice is to be heard, it will probably emerge as citi-zens' groups become aware of the importance of information to their con-stituencies. A leading indicator of this trend can be observed in legislative proposals to promote truth in labeling, truth in lending, and truth in advertis-ing. Once the issue of information as a part of universal service information is understood, the role of citizens' groups can be seen as growing in importance. Without them, universal service will still take on an information obligation, but only through the interests of business and government.

Finally, which regulatory form will maximize the potential of universal service, as the information society unfolds? Perhaps a more realistic state-ment of the question is to ask, which regulatory forms do Americans find acceptable? Seen from this angle, no regulatory arrangement which bars com-petition will achieve sustained loyalty from the public. The public's underly-ing belief in the virtues of competition is primary. Likewise, the public will reject unfettered competition because the negative consequences of sole reli-ance on the market are too painful. Therefore the long-term prognosis is for an oscillating zone between these two poles. This is not so surprising, since regulation is an American tension that cyclically comes up for re-discussion. The question, as always, is what is fair and just?

If that question is to find an answer, then the redefinition of universal service must find a place on the public agenda. In addition, its fundamental importance to the progress of the information society must be recognized. So important is universal service to the shape of the information society, that it might better be understood as a bill of information rights. In pursuit of a democratic society, we might ultimately ask ourselves, what rights to information, and protections from information, belong to all Americans, regardless of their wealth, position, or language? If we direct our energies to answering that question, it should become evident that universal service is not really a single policy to be written by a government agency. Rather it is the guiding principle of the information society, and, as such, also a tension—always debated, always tested, always pursued.

Underlying Assumptions

Information policies, principles, regulations and tensions rest on a set of assumptions that often go unnoticed. For this reason, no public policy debate, of which universal service is an apt example, entertains all possibilities. In effect, Americans choose one policy direction over another within a set of beliefs, which, though sometimes contradictory, often not articulated, and never fully accepted, establish the norms against which choices appear more, or less, reasonable. For the most part, Americans expect information policies to reflect one or more of the following assumptions.[54]

First, and surely preeminent at the end of the 20th century, there is the proposition that the public's needs as consumers should dominate policy choices, so that any successful proposal must argue that it will satisfy the public's consumer needs best. From this perspective, Americans are not thought of so much as citizens of the republic, but as consumers in the marketplace. For example, supporters of the initiative to transfer government information to private vendors took the position that, as consumers, Americans would maximize their access to information if it were provided through the marketplace.[55]

Second, and closely related to the first assumption, most Americans believe that private enterprise is superior to public enterprise, which leads to the expectation that government interventions into the affairs of the marketplace should only occur as an exception, or as a last resort. Thus, while most countries located telephone and broadcast services in the public sector, Americans chose to rely on private enterprise in the belief that the profit motive results in the greatest benefit for the greatest number. The break up of AT&T, with its substitution of competition for monopoly, was supported by the view that government should stay as far away from the doings of the private sector as possible.

Third, the marketplace is thought to provide the greatest welfare under conditions of maximum competition; therefore, the goal of government regulation should be to promote competition. Again, the breakup of AT&T partially reflects this assumption.[56] In transportation, supporters of airline deregulation in the 1980s assumed that an unregulated market would lead to lower fares at no cost to safety.

But when there is a question of necessary regulation, a fourth assumption is invoked—especially for businesses subject to public interest considerations. In those industries where the vagaries of the market are deemed to be too unpredictable, utility-type controls are assumed to work best, so that in practice, Americans have opted for oversight functions conducted by supervisory boards, such as the Federal Communications Commission or the states' public utility commissions. Nevertheless, though Americans view such arrangements as superior to other types of controls such as direct government, management they persistently regard them with suspicion, due to an even more deeply rooted distrust of government.

Since the meeting of the private sector and the public sector often generates conflict, Americans further assume that the judicial process will guarantee fair policy and regulation. In other words, though Americans distrust government in general, they have great faith in the judicial system, and, therefore, look to the courts as the proper arena for resolving differences of interpretation between business and government. As a result, the courts hold great power for defining information policy, as in *Federal Communications Commission v. Pottsville Broadcasting Co.,* where the Supreme Court decided in favor of the FCC, endorsing the Commission's authority over radio station licensing, and upheld the standard of the "public convenience, interest, or necessity."[57]

Finally, because Americans always resent taxation, they tend to view government intervention from a cost-benefit perspective. They expect that the benefits of government should always outweigh the expense, even if government meets the goals set for it. Even though the Government Printing Office successfully disseminated information at subsidized prices for over a century, the Reagan administration held that the total cost of the GPO was excessive, when compared to the theoretical cost of providing the same information through private vendors. As a result, the ensuing policy debate turned on the perception that government is inherently less efficient than the private sector.

Taken together, the cumulative effect of these assumptions is to limit the range of the possible. Policy proposals that contradict one or more of the assumptions are not likely to be considered valid when introduced into public discussion, while those proposals that intentionally challenge the assumptions rarely gain long term support. Yet, as with any set of beliefs, these six underlying assumptions lack consistency. After all, excessive faith in the courts results in policy by judicial decree, rather than by representative government; likewise, extreme reliance on the marketplace does not guarantee consumer protection. Certainly, when analyzed one by one, each assumption reveals contradictions, and it is in the interstices that policy discussions often become heated. In fact, to explore the history of information policy in the United States is to discover heated debates revolving around contradictions embedded in underlying assumptions. Perhaps, since Americans rarely express the hidden assumptions, it seems to many that the lack of an explicit national information policy means that there are no policy axioms. Yet, were Americans to pay more attention to their own underlying beliefs, they would see the lack of a coherent national information policy as neither arbitrary nor directionless. The beliefs upon which Americans rely exhibit remarkable consistency; and, though rarely voiced or enunciated, they have been noticed by visitors as far back as de Tocqueville.[58]

As for the tensions explored in this chapter, they represent patterns that now dominate the information society and have become central in American life. Also, by reason of their place at the core of the information society, they cannot be "solved." That is, they are not problems. Instead, they constitute necessary constants which will be present throughout the information age. These tensions directly stem from the tendencies described in the preceding chapters. The connection between them is so fundamental that no enlightened policy dialogue can take place without an understanding of this critical relationship. Therefore, the tensions challenge Americans to continuously seek the balance which most closely meets the needs and protects the rights of every citizen. Consequently, that point—the balance prevailing at any given time—puts forth a measure of what society accepts as just. Seen from this perspective, the purpose of policy dialogue, at its most general, is to understand the nature and consequences of the tensions in order to propose specific remedies. Finally, it is important to note that the tensions do not erase the importance of gender, class, race, family, or poverty, as questions confronting thoughtful citizens. The social, political and economic reconfigurations brought on by the information society have not resulted, nor will they, in a new world where the ills of the past are vanquished.

Notes

1. Milton, J. (1644/1963). Areopagitica. In M. Davis (Ed.), *Areopagitica and Of Education*. London, UK: MacMillan, p. 25.
2. Eliot, T. S. (1920/1961). Gerontion. In T. S. Eliot (Ed.), *Selected poems*, (pp. 31-33). London, UK: Faber and Faber Limited, p. 32.
3. In this chapter, we use the phrase "information policy" to describe all policies relating to the allocation of resources for purposes of institutionalizing information and for providing access to channels of communication. We recognize that

information policies and communication policies denote different but overlapping sets of choices. But due to the more common use of the modifier information in the literature, we have chosen the phrase information policy to describe both.

4. Tocqueville, A. d. (1835/1964). *Democracy in America* (Reeve, Henry, Trans.). New York: Washington Square Press, p. 150.

5. Thompson, R. L. (1947). *Wiring a continent: The history of the telegraph industry in the United States 1832–1866.* Princeton, NJ: Princeton University Press (pp. 26, 27, 34).

6. Schiller, D. (1981). *Objectivity and the news: The public and the rise of commercial journalism.* Philadelphia, PA: University of Pennsylvania Press. Singleton, L. A. (1989). *Global impact: The new telecommunication technologies.* New York: Harper & Row (pp. 23–30).

7. Demac, D. A. (1984). *Keeping America uninformed.* New York: Pilgrim Press. Horwitz, R. B. (1989). *The irony of regulatory reform.* New York: Oxford University Press. Intner, S. S., & Schement, J. R. (1987). The ethic of free service. *Library Journal* (1 October), 5–-52. Schiller, H. I. (1981). *Who knows: Information in the age of the Fortune 500.* Norwood, NJ: Ablex. Schiller, H. I. (1983). Information for what kind of society? In J. L. Salvaggio (Ed.) (1989), *Telecommunications: Issues and choices for society,* (pp. 24–33). New York: Longman. Schiller, H. I. (1985). Privatizing the public sector: The information connection. In B. D. Ruben (Ed.), *Information and behavior: Volume 1* (pp. 387–405). New Brunswick, NJ: Transaction.

8. Under immense public pressure and negative publicity, two of the largest credit bureaus, TRW and Equifax, began to open up their files to individuals during 1991. However, their track records for correcting mistakes were spotty at best, while their charges for examining credit records were considered exorbitant by industry experts. Real and imagined abuses led to the initiation of legislation, in the Congress and in several states, seeking to impose regulations on credit bureaus' practices. Sloane, L. (1992, January 4). Credit reports: The overhaul rolls on. *The New York Times,* p. 48.

9. Schiller, H.I. (1981); Schiller, H.I. (1983); Schiller, H.I. (1985); Schiller, H. I. (1988). Old foundations for a new (information) age. In J. R. Schement & L. Lievrouw (Eds.), *Competing visions, complex realities: Social aspects of the information society* (pp. 23–31). Norwood, NJ: Ablex.

10. Demac, D. A. (1984).

11. Mosco, V. (1982). *Push button fantasies.* Norwood, NJ: Ablex. Mosco, V. (1989). *The pay-per-view society: Computers and communication in the information age.* Norwood, NJ: Ablex.

12. Entman, R. M. (1989). *Democracy without citizens: Media and the decay of American politics.* New York: Oxford Press. Kern, M. (1989). *30-second politics: Political advertising in the eighties.* New York: Praeger. Lowi, T. J. (1981). The political impact of information technology. In T. Forester (Ed.), *The microelectronics revolution,* (pp. 453–472). Cambridge, MA: MIT Press. Oettinger, A. G., Bergman, P., & Read, W. (1977). *High and low politics: Information resources for the '80s.* Cambridge, MA: Ballinger.

13. For versions of this argument, see e.g.: Childers, T. (1975). *The information-poor in America.* Metuchen, NJ: The Scarecrow Press. Hayes, R. M. (Ed.). (1985). *Libraries and the Information Economy of California: A conference sponsored by the California State Library.* Los Angeles, CA: GSLIS/UCLA. Intner, S. S., & Schement, J. R. (1987). The ethic of free service. *Library Journal* (1 October),

50–52. Turock, B. (1983). The public library in the age of electronic information. *Public Library Quarterly, 4*(2), 3–11.

14. See also, Bates, B. J. (1990). Information as an economic good: a reevaluation of theoretical approaches. In B. D. Ruben & L. A. Lievrouw (Eds.), Information and behavior, (pp. 379–394). New Brunswick, NJ: Transaction. Curtis, T. (1990). The information society: A computer-generated caste system? In V. Mosco (Ed.), *The political economy of information* (pp. 95–107). Madison, WI: University of Wisconsin. Kibirige, H. M. (1983). *The information dilemma: A critical analysis of information pricing and the fees controversy.* Westport, CT: Greenwood Press.

15. *post hoc ergo propter hoc* : "after the fact therefore because of the fact".

16. Brown, R. D. (1989). *Knowledge is power: The diffusion of information in early America, 1700–1865.* New York: Oxford. Schiller, D. (1981). *Objectivity and the news: The public and the rise of commercial journalism.* Philadelphia, PA: University of Pennsylvania Press. Thompson, R. L. (1947). *Wiring a continent: The history of the telegraph industry in the United States 1832–1866.* Princeton, NJ: Princeton University Press.

17. Johnson, E. D. (1970). *History of libraries in the western world.* Metuchen, NJ: Scarecrow Press (pp. 351–381).

18. Kennedy's assassination did not generate the first large TV audience for a news event. Previously, sizable audiences had assembled to watch General MacArthur's New York parade in honor of his return from Korea, the Army-McCarthy hearings, and Kennedy's own inauguration. But the death of the most popular president since Roosevelt produced the first national audience for television news.

19. Although the president agreed to sign the bill, he refused to allocate any money, effectively killing the possibility of real benefits for the three million Americans out of work more than six months. These later actions were not scheduled for prime time. Clymer, A. (1991, 17 August 1991). President to sign jobless measure but block money. *The New York Times,* p. 1, 7.

20. These orchestrated events are now commonly called media events. Dayan, D., & Katz, E. (1992). *Media events: The live broadcasting of history.* Cambridge, MA: Harvard University Press. But see Boorstin for the antecedent concept, the pseudo-event. Boorstin, D. J. (1961). *The image: A guide to pseudo-events in America.* New York: Atheneum.

21. Entman, R. M. (1989); Kern, M. (1989).

22. The Gulf War between Iraq and a loose alliance of nations led by the United States enhanced CNN's status as a world leader. Because of its coalition-based organization, the network emerged as the primary news source for hard-to-get stories, such as coverage of bombing raids in the middle of Baghdad. But more significantly, CNN became a truly international network in reception, so much so, that the leaders of Iraq, Kuwait, Israel, Saudi Arabia, Britain, France, and the United States, all tuned in to CNN for the latest news.

23. Altheide, D. L., & Snow, R. P. (1979). *Media logic.* Beverly Hills, CA: Sage. Bagdikian, B. (1987). *The media monopoly.* Boston, MA: Beacon Press. Boorstin, D. J. (1961). *The image: A guide to pseudo-events in America.* New York: Atheneum. Compaine, B. M. (Ed.). (1979). *Who owns the media?: Concentration of ownership in the mass communications industry.* New York: Harmony Books. DeFleur, M. L., & Dennis, E. E. (1988). *Understanding mass communication.* Boston: Houghton Mifflin. Deutsch, K. W. (1963). *The nerves of government: Models of political communication and control.* New York: Free Press. Entman, R. M. (1989). *Democracy without citizens: Media and the decay of American politics.* New York: Oxford Press. Epstein, E. J. (1975). *Between fact and fiction:*

The problem of journalism. New York: Vintage. Kern, M. (1989). *30-second politics: Political advertising in the eighties.* New York: Praeger. Neustadt, R. M. (1985). Electronic politics. In T. Forestor (Ed.), *The information technology revolution* Cambridge, MA: MIT Press.

24. Table 443 (1990). *Statistical abstract of the United States: 1990.* Washington DC: Bureau of the Census.

25. Tables Y 27-28, Y 79-83 (1975). *Historical statistics of the United States, colonial times to 1970* (Bicentennial Ed.). Washington DC: GPO.

26. Rosenstiel, T. B. (18 January 1990). TV, VCRs fan fire of revolution. *Los Angeles Times,* p. A1.

27. Hiltz, S. R., & Turoff, M. (1978). *The network nation: Human communication via computer.* Reeding, MA: Addison-Wesley. Rice, R. E. (1987). New patterns of social structure in an information society. In J. R. Schement & L. Lievrouw (Eds.) (1988), *Competing visions, complex realities: Social aspects of the information society* (pp. 107-120). Norwood, NJ: Ablex. Rogers, E. M. (1986). *Communication technology: the new media in society.* New York: Free Press. Turkle, S. (1984). *The second self: Computers and the human spirit.* New York: Simon and Schuster.

28. Broad, W. J. (26 August 1983). Rising use of computer networks raises issues of security and law. *New York Times,* p. A1(L). Chesebro, J. W. (1985). Computer mediated interpersonal communication. In B. D. Ruben (Ed.), *Information and Behavior: Volume 1* (pp. 202-222). New Brunswick, NJ: Transaction. Turkle, S. (1984).

29. Aristotle (350 B.C./1927). *Aristotle: Selections.* New York: Charles Scribner's Sons.

30. Bauer, R. A. (1964). The obstinate audience: The influence process from the point of view of social communication. *American Psychologist, 19,* 319-328. DeFleur, M. L. (1970). *Theories of mass communication.* New York: David McKay. Katz, E., & Lazarsfeld, P. F. (1955). *Personal influence: The part played by people in the flow of mass communication.* New York: Free Press. Klapper, J. T. (1960). *The effects of mass communications.* Glencoe, IL: The Free Press. Lang, K., & Lang, G. E. (1971). The unique perspective of television and its effect: A pilot study. In W. Schramm & D. F. Roberts (Eds.), *The process and effects of mass communication* (pp. 169-188). Urbana, IL: University of Illinois. Lippmann, W. (1921). *Public opinion.* New York: Free Press. Schramm, W., & Roberts, D. F. (Eds.). (1971). *The process and effects of mass communication.* Urbana, IL.: University of Illinois Press. Steiner, G. A. (1963). *The people look at television: A study of audience attitudes.* New York: Knopf.

31. Tables 55, 58, 61 (1990). *Statistical abstract of the United States: 1990.* Washington DC: Bureau of the Census.

32. Feather, F. (1989). *G-forces: Re-inventing the World.* Toronto. Masuda, Y. (1981). *The information society as post-industrial society.* Bethesda, MD: World Future Society. Neustadt, R. M. (1985). Electronic politics. In T. Forestor (Ed.), *The information technology revolution* Cambridge, MA: MIT Press. Pool, I. d. S. (1983). *Technologies of freedom.* Cambridge, MA: Belknap. Sussman, L. R. (1989). *Power, the press & the technology of freedom: The coming age of ISDN.* Boston, MA.

33. Childers, T. (1975). *The information-poor in America.* Metuchen, NJ: The Scarecrow Press, p. 32.

34. For discussions of information poverty, access to information, the consequences of a lack of information, and the importance of the delivery of information to the

public, see: Childers, T. (1975). *The information-poor in America.* Metuchen, NJ: The Scarecrow Press. Curtis, T. (1990). The information society: A computer-generated caste system? In V. Mosco & J. Wasko (Eds.), *The political economy of information* (pp. 95–107). Madison, WI: University of Wisconsin. Demac, D. A. (1984). *Keeping America uninformed.* New York: Pilgrim Press. Hepworth, M., & Robins, K. (1988). Whose information society?: A view from the periphery. *Media, Culture and Society, 10,* 323–343. Hixson, R. F. (1985). Whose life is it anyway? Information as property. In B. D. Ruben (Ed.), *Information and behavior: Volume 1* (pp. 76–92). New Brunswick, NJ: Transaction. Intner, S. S., & Schement, J. R. (1987). The ethic of free service. *Library Journal* (1 October), 50–52. Lyon, D. (1988). *The information society: Issues and illusions.* Cambridge, UK: Polity Press. Meehan, E. R. (1988). Technical capability versus corporate imperatives: Toward a political economy of cable television and information diversity. In V. Mosco & J. Wasko (Eds.), *The political economy of information.* Madison, WI: University of Wisconsin. Mosco, V. (1989). *The pay-per-view society: Computers and communication in the information age.* Norwood, NJ: Ablex. Rose, E. D. (1983). Moral and ethical dilemmas inherent in an information society. In J. L. Salvaggio (Ed.) (1989), *Telecommunications: Issues and choices for society* (pp. 9–23). New York: Longman. Schement, J. R. (1990). An information theorist looks at technology and global sustainability. In J. Opie (Ed.), *Technology and Global Sustainability* (pp. 13–17). New Jersey Institute of Technology: NJIT Press. Schement, J. R., Curtis, T., & Lievrouw, L. A. (1986). Information policy issues for latinos. In A. Valdez (Eds.), *Hispanics and telecommunications policy* (pp. 119–127). Stanford, CA: Stanford. Schiller, H. I. (1983). Information for what kind of society? In J. L. Salvaggio (Ed.) (1989), *Telecommunications: Issues and choices for society* (pp. 24–33). New York: Longman. Schiller, H. I. (1985). Privatizing the public sector: The information connection. In B. D. Ruben (Ed.), *Information and behavior: Volume 1* (pp. 387–405). New Brunswick, NJ: Transaction. Turock, B. (1983). The public library in the age of electronic information. *Public Library Quarterly, 4*(2), 3–11.
35. Compiled from Table 271 (1990). *Statistical abstract of the United States: 1990.* Washington DC: Bureau of the Census, and Rose, E. D. (1983).
36. Compiled from Table 495 (1990). *Statistical abstract of the United States: 1990.* Washington DC: Bureau of the Census.
37. McLuhan, M. (1962). *The Gutenberg Galaxy: The making of typographic man.* New York: New American Library, p. 11.
38. Ong, W. J. (1982). *Orality and literacy: The technologizing of the word.* London, UK: Methuen, p. 136.
39. Harris, S., & Harris, L. (Ed.). (1986). *The teacher's almanac 1986–1987.* New York: Harper, p. 239.
40. (1988). *World statistics in brief* (Department of International Economic and Social Affairs Statistical Office Statistical Papers—Series V, No. 12 ed.). New York: United Nations Publication.
41. His italics. Paisley, W. (1985). 'Rithms of the future: Learning and working in an age of information. In R. M. Hayes (Ed.), *Libraries and the Information Economy of California: A conference sponsored by the California State Library* (pp. 160–227). Los Angeles, CA: GSLIS/UCLA, p. 172.
42. Communications Act of 1934, Title I.
43. Interstate Commerce Act of 1887. Radio Act of 1927, section 4.
44. The Constitution of the United States of America, Article I, Section B.
45. Only the idea of mass public education represents a departure from this principle; and, even there, the premise is that all citizens should be offered the opportunity to learn.

46. For a description of the economic backgrounds of the members of the Constitutional convention, see Beard, C. A. (1913/1965). *An economic interpretation of the constitution of the United States.* New York: Free Press (pp. 73–151).

47. Tocqueville, A. de (1835/1964). *Democracy in America* (Reeve, Henry, Trans.). New York: Washington Square Press, p. 202.

48. Series R 1-12 (1975) *Historical statistics of the United States, colonial times to 1970* (Bicentennial Ed. ed.). Washington DC: GPO. Table 918 (1990). *Statistical abstract of the United States: 1990.* Washington DC: Bureau of the Census.

49. Series R 1-12 (1975) *Historical statistics of the United States, colonial times to 1970* (Bicentennial Ed.). Washington DC: GPO. Table 918 (1990). *Statistical abstract of the United States: 1990.* Washington DC: Bureau of the Census.

50. Rawls, J. (1971). *A theory of justice.* Cambridge, MA: Harvard. Rawls, J. (1985). Justice as fairness: Political not metaphysical. *Philosophy and Public Affairs, 14*(3), 223–251.

51. Pressler, L., & Schieffer, K. V. (1990). A proposal for universal telecommunications service. *Federal Communications Law Journal, 40*(3), 351–375.

52. Williams, F., & Hadden, S. (1992). On the prospects for redefining universal service: From connectivity to content. *Information and Behavior, 4*, 49–63.

53. We are indebted to Susan Hadden and Frederick Williams, of the University of Texas at Austin, for clarifying this issue with us. For a more extensive analysis, see their excellent article, Williams, F., & Hadden, S. (1992). On the prospects for redefining universal service: From connectivity to content. *Information and Behavior, 4*, 49–63.

54. Here we follow in the tradition of the perspective first articulated by Emmett Redford. Redford, E. (1969). *The regulatory process.* Austin, TX: University of Texas.

55. For reviews of this debate, see: Demac, D. A. (1984). *Keeping America uninformed.* New York: Pilgrim Press. Hayes, R. M. (Ed.). (1985). *Libraries and the Information Economy of California: A conference sponsored by the California State Library.* Los Angeles, CA: GSLIS/UCLA. Intner, S. S., & Schement, J. R. (1987). The ethic of free service. *Library Journal*(1 October). Schiller, H. I. (1981). *Who knows: Information in the age of the Fortune 500.* Norwood, NJ: Ablex. Schiller, H. I. (1985). Privatizing the public sector: The information connection. In B. D. Ruben (Ed.), *Information and behavior: Volume 1* (pp. 387–405). New Brunswick, NJ: Transaction.

56. Coll, S. (1986). *The deal of the century: The breakup of AT&T.* New York: Touchstone.

57. Hixson, R. F. (1989). *Mass media and the constitution: An encyclopedia of supreme court decisions.* New York: Garland.

58. Tocqueville, A. de (1835/1964). *Democracy in America* (Reeve, Henry, Trans.). New York: Washington Square Press, pp. 33–36, 115–125, 133–135, 263–267, 313–318.

6

Technological Visions

The unwillingness to accept the natural environment as a fixed and final condition of man's existence had always contributed both to his art and his technics: but from the seventeenth century, the attitude became compulsive, and it was to technics that he turned for fulfillmment.—Lewis Mumford[1]

Today, the solitary inventor, tinkering in his shop, has been overshadowed by task forces of scientists in laboratories and testing fields. In the same fashion, the free university, historically the fountainhead of free ideas and scientific discovery, has experienced a revolution in the conduct of research. Partly because of the huge costs involved, a government contract becomes virtually a substitute for intellectual curiosity. For every old blackboard there are now hundreds of electronic computers.—Dwight D. Eisenhower[2]

But lo! Men have become the tools of their tools.—Henry David Thoreau[3]

Few of the many observers of the first mechanically driven textile mills saw a social transformation that would eventually reach out to the most remote corners of the globe. In fact, only after the industrial revolution reached full force did intellectuals go beyond reaction to attempt to understand the inventions whose power promised so many benefits and threatened so much misery. They asked, "What is a machine?" and answered with an emphasis on movement and interdependence, as in Franz Reuleaux's 1876 definition. Even today, the popular notion of technology stays close to Reuleaux's.:

A machine is a combination of resistant bodies so arranged that by their means the mechanical forces of nature can be compelled to do work accomplished by certain determined motions....[4]

To which Lewis Mumford added:

The essential distinction between a machine and a tool lies in the degree of independence in the operation from the skill and motive power of the operator: the tool lends itself to manipulation, the machine to automatic action....[5]

Though Reuleaux's and Mumford's definitions may be updated by introducing electrical forces alongside mechanical ones, the images they evoke are of material objects. For that matter, when we speak of technology in everyday talk, we usually mean machines: computers, typewriters, television sets, or telephones. On occasion, we may extend our usage to include the way in which a particular machine is employed, as for example when the computer is applied to word processing. But for the most part, since anyone can see the ubiquitous place of machines in everyday life, individuals freely substitute "technology" for "machine," so that blending the two concepts does not seem unreasonable.

Yet this equation does not stand up to closer scrutiny. For one thing, technology encompasses more than the machinery itself. It is a direct result of the social relations which make the applications of technology possible. The great sociologist Harold Lasswell defined these particular social relations as *technique*, or

> The ensemble of practices by which one uses available resources to achieve values.[6]

His colleague, Robert Merton, refined Lasswell's definition by emphasizing systematization, in order to clarify the significance of organized human behaviors as part of the concept of technology:

> Technique refers to any complex of standardized means for attaining a predetermined end. Thus, it converts spontaneous and unreflective behavior into behavior that is deliberate and rationalized.[7]

Jacques Ellul pushed Merton even farther:

> Technique is that totality of methods rationally arrived at and having absolute efficiency....[8]

But Ellul sought to include every possible situation, so that by extending the idea of technique as far as possible, he arrived at a definition too extreme to be useful. Nevertheless, by conceptualizing technology to include skilled behaviors, Lasswell, Merton, and Ellul demonstrated that writing, administrative management, and the scientific method are clearly technological, and that, as techniques, they are as influential as machines in affecting the development of the information society. Indeed, by the middle decades of the 20th century, most social observers recognized technology as resulting from specific behaviors, as well as machines. But such a mélange of definitions poses a problem. What is the common denominator between machines like the postage meter, and behaviors like regular staff meetings? What about implements like the memo, which are neither behavior nor machine; might the memo also qualify as a technology? In the early '60s, A. Svorikine, a member of the USSR Academy of Sciences, reviewed the literature and synthesized three typical definitions of technology,

...the aggregate of techniques directed toward the attainment of some purpose; specifically the aggregate of techniques directed against the forces of nature and towards the modification of materials.

...the aggregate of skills, abilities, techniques, and knowledge enabling man to utilize, for desired goals, the huge resources of raw material and energy existing in nature.

...activities directed to the satisfaction of human needs which produce alterations in the material world.

and found them guilty of insufficiently stressing the centrality of the means of production, an oversight corrected in his own definition:

Technology may be defined as the means of work, the means of human activity developing within a system of social production and social life.[9]

Svorikine understood the importance of stressing the human element and that machines are a product of human activities. But the common denominator was still missing.

If students from Russia traveled to the U.S. to study engineering, does their return to Russia constitute a transfer of technology? Likewise, if the U.S. sells computers to Russia, what else will the Russians need to make effective use of them? In the first question, knowledge gained in U.S. schools meets the conditions in Svorikine's first three definitions as well as those of Lasswell and Merton. In the second question, the Russians might learn a great deal regarding the construction of U.S. computers by dissecting one of the imports, but they will need software, manuals, and instructions to exploit the computers' potential. Both the returning engineers and the computers contain information, that, when added to the information provides by the software, manuals, and instructions, makes possible all of the technological capabilities. By visualizing information as a thing, machines and techniques can be seen as containing an essential ingredient; and, by visualizing information as an organizing principle, machines and techniques are seen as two faces of the same whole. Thus, the common denominator stems, not from human behaviors per se, nor from the machines themselves, but in the idea of information.

To discover the idea of information as an explanation of technology in the 1990s is not so surprising. After all, information has become so obvious that its presence is expected in most phenomena. But in the '60s, though increasingly aware of the information orientation of society, theorists were just becoming aware of the linkages. Emmanuel Mesthene was one of the first to enter this ferment and propose a synthesis that centered on information— expressed as knowledge—

we define technology as the organization of knowledge for the achievement of practical purposes.[10]

Mesthene observed that, as the United States became a major exporter of technology in the '50s, it shipped information as often as it shipped the machines themselves, and he grasped the significance of this development. By the '70s, most technology theorists recognized that the actual machine was not necessary for the technology to be present. What was necessary was the information for making and operating the machines. Therefore, technology transfers could also be seen as information exchanges.

At the same time, organizational behaviorists observed that the essence of an organization resides, neither in its products nor in its physical plant, but in the system that organizes the behaviors of its members.[11] That system, of course, emerged from the ideas of managers who saw information as the key element in technologies made up of human behaviors. Daniel McCallum had saved the New York and Erie Railroad by piling an abstraction upon an abstraction; his design of the organization chart constituted information for the purpose of regulating the transmission of other information.

The realization that information is the essence of all technologies now forms the main premise for our understanding of the complex relationship between humans, technology, and society. For example, in his review of the new media in society, Everett Rogers incorporated an information centered view by stressing design as the essence of technology.[12]

> …a design for instrumental action that reduces the uncertainty in the cause-effect relationships involved in achieving a desired outcome.[13]

By emphasizing instrumental action, Rogers described technology as a linear relationship. In other words, technology is what it takes to get from here to there, literally or metaphorically.

However, the road from concrete machines to ephemeral information is also the road to extreme generalization. When writing his massive history of civilization and capitalism, Fernand Braudel nearly explained the entire sweep of civilization as technology.

> In a way, everything is technology: not only man's most strenuous endeavors but also his patient and monotonous efforts to make a mark on the external world; not only the rapid changes we are a little too ready to label revolutions (gunpowder, long-distance navigation, the printing press, windmills and watermills, the first machines) but also the slow improvements in processes and tools, and those innumerable actions which may have no immediate innovating significance but which are the fruit of accumulated knowledge: the sailor rigging his boat, the miner digging a gallery, the peasant behind the plough or the smith at the anvil.[14]

Perhaps a definition of this scope was inevitable in a book encompassing the micro, middle, and macro development of capitalism in Europe. Nevertheless, Braudel drew an important distinction between "material technology" and "social technology," or what Marx referred to as the machine forces of production and the social relations of production. The computer, the television set, the clock, telecommunications networks, and the printing press are material technologies. The alphabet, the laboratory, administrative management, interpersonal networks, and the corporation are social technologies. In addition, Braudel understood that all technologies harbor elements of the society that produces them.[15] For example, labor is embodied within technology—and is one basis for productivity comparisons. Correspondingly, the information necessary to create and to apply a technology is embodied within it and is technology's essence—although information to reproduce a complex social technology may be difficult to communicate. Embodied information underlies the rationale for reverse engineering. Not only does each technology contain the information necessary for its creation, but that information also stands alone, available for trade and transmission. Finally, the values of the society that originate the technology are also embodied within it. Technology results from a set of historical circumstances, and carries its creators' original needs and values. As a result, not all cultures can assimilate a social or material technology with equal success.[16] Braudel's description of the variety of human inventions, their applications, and cross-cultural adaptations underscores the difficulties involved in defining this pervasive human endeavor. With his all encompassing vision, he argues convincingly against a decisive definition of technology.

Yet though we may never arrive at a final decision on the question of technology, it is equally true that we can not achieve a deep understanding of the information age without a grasp of its technologies and their influences on our thinking. Definitions are useful, as we have seen, and one that centers on those technologies characteristic of the information society offers a more focused glimpse into this difficult phenomenon. The challenge is compelling and, in that spirit, we attempt one more definition.

Information technologies, that is, the material and social technologies of information, are socially evolved designs of hardware, software, and organizational structures through which information is recorded, stored, processed, transmitted, and/or communicated.[17]

In this sense, information technology is used as the overall term and communication technology is taken as a subset. The debt to Lasswell, Merton, Mesthenes, Rogers, and Braudel is apparent, since information technology represents more than mechanical and electronic devices. By stressing the primacy of ideas and by emphasizing the catalytic role of human behavior, we firmly embed information technology within the fabric of society and reject any notions of it as an independent force. For example, a social technology such as the decimal system contributed to so many later inventions that it is easy to overlook the contribution of those early mathematicians who developed it. Like the decimal system, many earlier technologies are represented in later inventions. Thus, the development of the camera depended on the synthesis of at least two earlier information technologies, the decimal system as applied to calibration, and lenses. Most new technologies build in part on old discoveries and interpret them in new ways. To ignore either social technologies or the influence of previous inventions imposes a false image of the history of information technology, giving the impression that one invention follows neatly after its predecessor, or that each device sprang full blown from the head of its inventor.

Thus, at a very general level, this whole book can be read as an analysis of information technologies. But to do so would overemphasize the intentional and miss the happenstance. After all, both our purposeful efforts and our unplanned cumulative activities brought us to this juncture in history. Besides, since neither the idea of information nor the beliefs which privilege information in modern society constitute technologies, to overlook them is to produce an exceedingly shallow interpretation of the information age.[18]

The Dialectics of Information Technology and the Prisms of Popular Perception

From Prometheus' gift of fire—an early technology myth—to our own widely held belief in the superiority of the computer, all cultures have developed explanations for the mysterious, and the important. In the United States, as in all industrial countries, people encounter information technology as machines in every nook of their daily lives. At home, they switch on televisions, radios, record players, video and audio-cassette recorders, compact disk players, video cameras, photographic slide projectors, burglar alarms, smoke detectors, personal computers, telephone answering machines, and telephones. At work, they operate computer mainframes, personal computers, copy machines, typewriters, intercoms, and the transmission or production side of most of the appliances they use at home. In fact, so pervasively have the motifs of technology penetrated daily life, that Americans have evolved specific myths to aid them in making sense of the role of technology in society. For example, in one narrative—the most prevalent—Americans accept technology as a fact of life, "Just the way things are." In another theme, commonly accepted in those professions associated with the development of material technologies, technology is regarded as an ideal to be pursued. When its naked power looms visible, as it did during the Cold War or at Chernobyl, many of these same Americans shrink from technology and fear it as Damocles feared the sword above his head. Finally, when they describe other aspects of their lives, Americans often employ technology as a metaphor to explain themselves and their lives. It is not surprising that Americans portray themselves as living in a machine age or culture. After all, the existence of so many technology myths provides a rich language with which to interpret modern society; and as with any language, each myth becomes a prism through which the world can be viewed.

Yet the commonplace acceptance of all of these myths suggests contradictions in the relationship between Americans and their technologies. In the following sections, we explore the connection between myth and contradiction.

Information Technology as a Fact of Life

The late 20th century landscape is dotted with artifacts of the information and communication systems that interconnect institutions and facilitate industrial life. A casual tour through urban or rural America will pass telephone poles, radio and TV transmission towers, cables, and parabolic satellite dish antennas. A tourist is likely to see old information devices, like traffic lights and pay telephones, sharing the scenery with more recent automatic teller machines and surveillance cameras. In some cities, the visitor might seek information from a video tourist kiosk.

These examples are just a few, but they suggest that the presence of information technology is a fact of life for most Americans—as it is for all peoples in advanced industrial societies. Once a person learns to operate the automatic teller machine, the credit card phone, or the digital watch, the behavior becomes part of the round of daily activities which facilitate more purposeful pursuits and fades into the invisible background. If only death and taxes were inevitable in Ben Franklin's day—"In this world, nothing can be said to be certain, except death and taxes"—then modern day Americans may add the continual introduction of new devices for processing information as a third constant.[19]

From the point of view of the individual, the emergence of the information society appears as a tide of waves of inevitable technological changes. For example, it is an image that holds for the movies, first confined to movie houses, then expanded to include drive-in theaters, and then the home itself. It also holds for the telephone, from a box on the wall, to an alcove in the hall, to the bedroom, to the car, to call waiting, and call forwarding. That is, as new technologies, or fresh variants of old technologies, enter the marketplace, the total picture is one of a society perpetually absorbing the new and novel. In this image, technology emerges as the engine which drives social change and the information age appears as a time of never-ending technological revolution. Such an interpretation creates a vision of America as a technological nation, and conveys the feeling of technology as an inevitable fact of life in that technological nation.

Almost without exception, the public expects new information technologies to make life easier, increase convenience and enhance leisure. Videocassette recorders and compact disks are welcomed because of their potential to enhance leisure. Business executives look forward to innovations because they present opportunities for greater productivity and profits—the more obvious the business advantage, the more rapid the diffusion of any information technology. Military staffs continually seek information technologies to add to an already impressive lineup which allows commanders to coordinate the complicated systems necessary to wage war. Information technology means progress. Americans are most comfortable with this image of information technology, as it best captures the popular view of the information society. Nowhere are the values of St. Simone and the technocrats of the Enlightenment more alive than in the United States, where the new and "high tech" are, by definition, valuable, and where information technologies are the newest and highest of high tech.

A belief in progress also plays an important role in making sense of the course of the information society. In 1930 an American received an average of 1.5 pieces of daily mail per person and used the telephone less than once per day. By 1990, he or she received nearly two pieces of daily mail per person, and spoke on the phone over seven times each day.[20] Only a few Americans owned a radio, a phonograph, and a telephone in 1930. The 1990 homeowner possesses audio equipment capable of merging the functions of radio and phonograph, adds to it equally diverse video equipment, and uses a phone system with only minor similarities to the 1930 model. From 1930 to 1990, the population grew by 200% but per capita advertising expenditures increased by over 2,200%, a less visible but highly important contribution to changes in daily life.[21] For anyone reflecting on the flow of 60 years,—even for anyone too young to remember black and white television—the readiest image of the passage of time is one which strongly reinforces a sense of technology and progress.[22]

Not surprisingly, Americans burden most new information technologies with a demanding set of expectations. Some telephone forecasters predicted that a world telephone system would necessitate the global adoption of a common language—presumably English. Others saw the telephone as the solution to crime in America's cities. Still others saw it as the cause.[23] Americans hoped television—and we hoped—would improve the education of their children.[24] Business observers projected that computers would produce a paperless office, and management specialists have estimated that personal computers will reverse the trend toward centralization in corporations.[25]

For the most part, these predictions propose far-reaching advances from the introduction of a single device, and project broad improvements in society as the result of a single technological innovation. What they have in common is a logic which sees the application of a particular technology as predestined to lead to a better world. Technology equals progress. In order to maintain this faith, Americans take their belief in progress through technology and wrap it in the social institution they believe most likely to ensure positive outcomes— the marketplace.

Connecting a belief in technology-as-progress to a belief in the virtues of the marketplace serves several purposes. First of all, by linking the technological side of life to the activities of the marketplace, the consumption of information technologies takes place in a safe setting. Americans encounter technologies most visibly as goods to be consumed; the fact that information technologies are acquired in the marketplace confers a kind of timelessness, since the act of buying is a constant in American life. Secondly, association with the marketplace ties technology to the web of beliefs represented by free enterprise and individualism, thereby reinforcing a belief in technology as part of the national mythology. Thus, linking information technology to the marketplace fosters a sense of security that, despite each new wave of information technology, things remain the same.

In this view, the history of information technologies is explained as a series of inventions—each one better than its forerunner—an additive function, as it were—and science is allocated the role of bringing better products to the marketplace. The main characters are rugged individuals and lone inventors—sometimes confused with scientists—who create masterpieces against all odds. The litany of saints includes Alexander Graham Bell, Thomas Edison, Guglielmo Marconi, Steven Jobs and Steven Wozniak, and some scientists like Albert Einstein—who, after his first visit to the United States, criticized this aspect of popular culture, "The cult of individualism is always, in my view, unjustified.... It strikes me as unfair, and even in bad taste, to select a few of them for boundless admiration, attributing superhuman powers of mind and character to them."[26] In this scenario, the inventor, distrustful of big government, brings his creations to the marketplace where business can take over. The inventor gets rich and the general welfare improves.

Yet beneath the belief in marketplace virtues lies the reality of big science and government investment. For one thing, new technological developments rarely emerge from individuals working alone, especially in the 20th century. The vast majority of the more than 4.6 million scientists and engineers in the U.S. are employed in big science and big engineering projects.[27] In fact, collaborative research is the norm across the board, even in the university, once thought of as the last holdout of the solitary scholar.[28] Furthermore, ever since the establishment of the post roads in the 18th century, the U.S. government has been involved in the development of nearly every material information technology. In 1988, for example, R&D expenditures amounted to $513.00 for every man, woman, and child in the United States [126.1 billion], and the federal government contributed about 50% of that total. The other half came from industry, practicing its version of big science.[29] Technological developments such as radar, sonar, microwave broadcasting, the computer, television, lasers, and satellite communications owe much of their success to the support of the federal government, especially the military. The government has consistently subsidized the development of technologies which were later made available to entrepreneurs for sale in the marketplace by accepting the part of risk absorber and catalytic agent. Thus, technology is a fact of life precisely because a large institutional infrastructure has been created to stimulate it. Nevertheless, the fictions of free enterprise and individualism, part and parcel of the mythology of the marketplace, make the technology myth seem a fitting fact of life.

Individuals holding this outlook go about pursuing their activities and pay scant attention to the technology that facilitates their daily lives. People take most information devices for granted, knowing little of their underlying workings. Unlike automobiles, locomotives, airplanes, or ships—which Americans of an earlier generation anthropomorphized with names—telephones, automated teller machines, televisions, and computers remain largely anonymous, regardless of their importance. New devices are encountered, their use mastered, and their visibility fades into the commonplace. To say that they are experienced as a fact of life is almost to say that they escape notice.

Americans take their technological landscape as a matter-of-fact because American culture predisposes them toward the technological. Yet matter-of-factness breeds complacency and even fatalism. To view the technological face of the information society as a fact of life dims the vision of the information age as a threshold potent with active choices. Ultimately, for a people who see the conquest of nature as their God given right, and who despise history, to take such a philosophical position is supremely ironic.

Information Technology as the Pursuit of an Ideal

If the general public regards information technology as a fact of life, for certain elite groups it holds a far more compelling attraction. They are the scientists, engineers, and others directly involved in the development of new technologies, both material and social. Many commit their lives to creating a technological future and, in so doing, become part of one of the oldest traditions in western culture. As Mumford observes in the opening quote to this chapter, the desire to live independently of climate, and to win release from the strait jacket of nature, eventually turned into a long conquest of the environment. Technology, reinforced by science, ultimately came to lead the assault, so that now it seems that it is nature that can not escape man.

Today, technology is sometimes saddled with responsibility for a damaged earth. Though this view has only won general acceptance since the 1960s, for most of the last 500 years, the creators of new technologies pursued a higher vision through which they attempted to fashion a better world. Lipershey invented the telescope and Laënnec the stethoscope in order to overcome the physiological limits of sight and hearing. Gutenberg's printing press and Babbage's analytic engine extended the abilities of hand and brain. All of the countless contributors to information and communication technologies have attempted to compensate for the physical limits of senses and brain, and that tendency is observable even before the technological explosion that accompanied the industrial revolution. The timeline illustrates the four intertwining paths of the developmental process: speed and distance; storage and capacity. Each path has advanced at a different rate, as scientists, engineers, inventors, and lone tinkers focused on some information machine or some aspect of the technology and contributed a spurt in that direction; yet the drive exhibits remarkable consistency.

From the earliest attempts to communicate at a distance, humans looked for faster alternatives, but all were constrained by the physiological limits of the senses. When Roman legions built Hadrian's wall, they constructed "mile castles" at intervals of one Roman mile and then inserted two watch towers in between. The towers raised the speed of communication to the maximum, but required simple messages and were forced to stay within the range of the human eye. Greater distance between the towers would have disrupted the connections. In effect, the towers functioned as switches and speed depended on coordinating all of the links in the chain. Yet, clearly, watch towers were extraordinary forms of communicating; for, in all other circumstances, the speed of a message coincided with the speed of physical transportation. Until the 1830s and the development of the steam locomotive—capable of 60 mph when recklessly driven—communication remained where it had always been, at the pace of hoof, foot, or sail.

The real communications revolution in speed took place with the invention of the telegraph. The day that Morse asked, "What has God wrought?" communication burst its shackles.[30] Morse's keystroke accelerated communication from the speed of a locomotive to the speed of light, and a new era commenced with information no longer dependent on transportation. By severing communication from transportation, Morse also disconnected it from the confines of human senses. Information now possessed a new pathway, under new laws of motion. Engineers expanded their thinking to include roads for messages as distinct from roads for people and, when combined with the extreme increase in potential speed, these new characteristics fundamentally transformed efforts to communicate. Since then, each advance in communications has refined this breakthrough. Thus—in the sense that a revolution constitutes a radical departure from the previous order of things—the invention of the telegraph, with its exploitation of digital data sequences and electronic energy, set in motion a true information revolution.

This explains why people previously found it so hard to distinguish information from the activities it supported. Messengers and letters crisscrossed the globe along roads and sea lanes as part of the flow of cargo. Communication was transportation, and information was in the messenger. In this context, killing the messenger may have made some sense. Information came along with everything else, so that to distinguish it as a thing apart required a great propensity for abstract thinking. Until Morse broke through the old relationship between time and distance, information was securely embedded in its physical container, whether it be a stone tablet, a book, or a messenger. After Morse, momentum grew as inventors, scientists, technicians, and entrepreneurs focused on increasing speed over every possible communication path, and, in the process, shrinking distance. Working out from the center, they sought to automate every possible node in the communication loop. Thus, the telegraph also served as a vehicle for a new paradigm. With it, communication could be conducted independently of transportation, thereby opening opportunities for information to be treated as a good with its own markets. As Neil Postman observes in *Amusing Ourselves to Death*, "The telegraph made information into a commodity, a 'thing' that could be bought and sold irrespective of its uses and meanings."[31] With the telegraph, one leg of the communication chain could travel at maximum speed to unprecedented distances. Perhaps more importantly, the idea of information became easier to imagine.

Like speed and distance, storage and capacity have been goals of information technologists since earliest recorded time. Sumerian clay tablets may be the first storage devices, and their catalogues the first attempts at increased capacity.[32] Their problem—how to increase the amount of information transmitted in a given medium—continues to confront developers 4,000 years later. In the case of the telegraph, the earliest lines handled one message at a time, like the Roman watch towers. Later cables increased capacity by accommodating multiple messages simultaneously. The quest for greater channel capacity has continued unabated for 150 years. Yet, from the earliest single-strand wires of the transcontinental railroad telegraphs, to the optical fiber trunk lines which speed messages to and from major telecommunications centers, the search for more capacity has persistently met growing demand.

Simultaneously, developers have sought additional memory, in order to allow more complex functions. In the quest for more applications, simple instructions, such as rotary dialing, led to complex instructions requiring more memory, i.e., capacity. A 150 year spiral of development of more and more capable systems ensued, with a pronounced spurt in the last half century. Computers, at the upper tip of the spiral, epitomize the ascendancy of complex functions. In order to increase their performance, they need the capacity to accommodate more extensive programs; thus, the quest for memory. Furthermore, since users realize the greatest advantages when they process large amounts of data, they too have consistently demanded additional memory, so that computer specialists adhere to the axiom that each new development demands more memory. So intensely has the search been conducted that completely new technologies for storage media are being added every few years.

Inventors and tinkers, scientists and engineers—all of the parties involved in the development of information technologies—have persistently sought increased speed and distance, along with greater storage and capacity. As a consequence, the technological environment for communicating has grown in density and variation. The 19th century saw the beginnings of convergence from simple information processing devices to more complex ones like the phonograph, the radio-telegraph, and the recording adding machine. In the 20th century, technologies for manipulating and transmitting information have proliferated to a marked degree, especially since World War II. So, though some devices, like the original telegraph, have been replaced, most have been integrated into more complex forms, capable of more complex functions.

A glance at the 19th century segment of the timeline reveals that the development of information technologies was intensified by capitalism and the commoditization of information. Capitalism legitimized the desire to sell information and its attendant technologies. It created a far more flexible role for the inquisitive tinker than the Renaissance system of captive patronage. If the Italian courts of the 16th century produced Leonardo and Galileo, then the American economy of the 19th century produced Bell and Edison.[33] Edison, a highly inquisitive man, pursued technology as an ideal but managed to nest his vision within the reward structure of capitalism.[34] His hand-to-hand grappling with the technologies of his day reflected a general attitude in a country of tinkers. For that his country lionized him, and his "idea factory" in Menlo Park, New Jersey, became a metaphor of the age. Though Edison shared the trait of inquisitiveness with every other human being, his combination of inquisitiveness with the willingness to tinker seems deeply rooted in Western culture. This is not to say that inquisitiveness exists only in the West; such a view is ethnocentric and false. This particular kind of inquisitiveness appears to be a privileged value in the West. Western style inquisitiveness is often held in opposition to tradition, where tradition and the traditional mentality are seen as obstacles to progress.[35] Linked to progress, inquisitiveness has become institutionalized. First it was channeled into the scientific mindset. Then, as capitalism industrialized, science was itself incorporated into the industrial system so that science-as-information became a commodity. Inquisitiveness became a tradition in the West with its own rituals and myths; and, as its value became apparent in the new industrial economy, it became institutionalized as science and engineering.

Science disciplined inquisitiveness. From the last decades of the 19th century the technological future has belonged to the scientists and engineers, with their belief in systematic analysis and theory construction. Making systematic use of previously gathered knowledge, the scientific approach directs the researcher to ask questions in light of previously established knowledge and to propose testable statements in the hope of ultimately disproving as many of them as possible. With science, the desire to achieve freedom from the limitations of nature received a powerful ally. Harnessed to the resources of the industrial system, science became the ideal approach for finding and developing innovations in profitable, or militarily successful, information technologies.

Unlike the intuitive tinkers of the 19th century who swamped the patent office with their ideas, the new technologists cultivated an attitude toward knowledge embodied in the scientific method, and, as they evolved professionally, they elevated this attitude into a calling every bit as captivating as the vocations of medieval monks. By devoting themselves to the pursuit of a technological ideal, scientists and engineers developed an occupational attitude which elevated work containing much tedium into an integrated activity capable of great fulfillment. Here is Einstein explaining the scientific ideal in a tribute to Max Planck.

> What has brought them to the temple[of science]?... A man tries to make for himself in the fashion that suits him best, a simplified and intelligible picture of the world; he then tries to some extent to substitute this cosmos of his for the world of experience, and thus to overcome it.... The longing to behold this pre-established harmony is the source of the inexhaustible patience and perseverance with which Planck has devoted himself, as we see, to the most general problems of our science, refusing to let himself be diverted to more grateful and more easily attainable ends.... There he sits, our beloved Planck, and smiles inside himself at my childish playing-about with the lantern of Diogenes.[36]

Einstein's tribute bears the eloquence of his personal commitment, but it would be misleading to extrapolate his reverence to all who have shared his profession. Scientists and engineers also suffer the darker side of humanity—some are greedy, others dishonest, still others manipulative of those around them. They experience alienation as does everyone else. But unlike many workers they possess a powerful ideal to fall back on. Its power can be glimpsed in its persistence through shifts in fundamental perspective. For even after the dismantling of logical positivism, with its literal concept of truth, the ideal persists, albeit as a commitment to the betterment of humanity.[37] However, it is manifest—either as the ideal of a higher calling, as a special role, a quest for knowledge, a commitment to the intellect, or even as a grail—it fuels the single mindedness with which the researcher seeks to create an "intelligible picture of the world." Yet it is this very single mindedness which makes the researcher vulnerable to manipulation by the larger forces of society.

In the Information Age, belief in the technological ideal—however disguised by professional rhetoric—co-exists with the industrial economy and the demands of capitalism. What Eisenhower lamented as the demise of the solitary scientist became known as "big science,"—the pursuit of scientific inquiry where the problems addressed are so multifaceted, and the necessary tools so expensive, that large research teams are required, with funding on a scale affordable only by big government or big business.[38] The military-industrial complex and the transnational corporations that dominate most sectors of the modern economy have generated a propensity for large scale R&D projects, so that the goals of these institutions have become the goals of applied science. Within this structure, the individual scientist experiences a predictable narrowness of scope. Still, the researcher can find fascination in an abstract problem, whether the research team develops a new nasal decongestant which alleviates Rhinitis, or a new hair spray which attacks the ozone layer. The same is true in engineering. Like the scientist, the engineer can be enticed by intellectual challenges, regardless of the consequences. Thus, even in circumstances far removed from those of Einstein or Planck, the joys of inquiry continue to beckon, and as long as they do, the practice of science and engineering will continue to respond to a higher calling, however ironic.

Information Technology as The Sword of Damocles

Technology also inspires fear. Just as most Americans take for granted the technologies which structure their environment, so too does technology in general evoke a threat. Because of the nature of the technological environment, individuals experience this fear at various levels of awareness.

The most easily understood occurs where humans meet threats posed by interactions with the artifacts that populate the technological landscape. Most television viewers know they might receive a jolt if they investigate the innards of the appliance, or incorrectly pull the plug. An earlier generation of parents feared that watching television might damage children's eyesight. Today, key punchers who look into cathode ray tubes for extended periods, may also fear damage to their eyes. In the home, ubiquity may not mean security. For instance, microwave ovens have diffused to most households, while critics express concern over possible exposure to radiation. The hazards are numerous, though mostly avoidable as individuals learn the proper cautions: VCRs can shock; paper cuts painfully; and the many cables surrounding a computer workstation should be traversed with caution. In all of these examples the threat can be identified with a particular device encountered in everyday life. And, as familiarity with the device grows, the threat abates.

Beyond these direct threats, people may fear threats to the balance of their lives. For example, information workers may fear displacement from their jobs; they may wonder if they will be replaced by a computer or a mechanical process. Since management introduces information machines in order to increase productivity, subsequent automation usually results in the loss of jobs. Or, management may monitor the actions of its employees through the very computers which workers use to enter data. What management sees as an issue of policies to increase profits, workers see as machines taking jobs, or spying. In circumstances such as these, information workers who are apprehensive about their employment may misdirect their anger onto the machines. But for the most part, information workers fear the effects of managerial decisions made to increase productivity. The fear is real and underlies the attitudes of unions toward mechanization, as well as the concern of labor sociologists for alienation among workers.[39]

Traditionally, what Americans have feared most is information gathered by government. So, in an age when the telescope, or spy glass, was the most powerful instrument of surveillance, the founding fathers grappled with the tension between government's legitimate need to gather information and citizens' right to lead private lives. So concerned were they that the newly ratified Constitution was judged to contain insufficient protections. They added an amendment, so as to further secure their fellow citizens from the eye of government: "The right of the people to be secure in their persons, houses, papers, and effects, against unreasonable searches and seizures, shall not be violated...."[40] Since then, the threat of a prying government sending its officials to search a citizen's home has been intensified by advances in surveillance and data storage.

In fact, it is the threat to privacy evoked by information technologies, such as surveillance cameras, phone taps, and computerized databases, which causes George Orwell's premise in *1984* to loom so menacingly. In other words, in the 20th century Americans fear the eye of government as much as the hand—perhaps more. So there exists a second level of awareness. Individuals also fear information technologies as components of a larger social technology with the power to withhold assets, cancel jobs, or deny rights.

At an even more ambiguous level of perception, information technologies are perceived as threats to the cultural landscape. For instance, older Americans sometimes blame television for a decline in public discourse, recalling when the living room served as a salon and center of neighborly conversation. Similarly, Americans periodically recycle a number of public questions aimed at the relationship between information technologies and the quality of life. Does television dull children's minds? Do sexually explicit films undermine moral values? Has the telephone destroyed the art of writing letters? Are we less literate because television and telephones discourage reading and writing? Does the computer create a more impersonal society?

What distinguishes these questions is their resilience. In one form or another, they have been part of public discourse since Americans became aware of the presence of information technologies. Before TV, parents wondered if time spent in the neighborhood movie theater was turning their children into illiterate delinquents with bad eyes.[41] Also, these questions contain a strong element of technological determinism. For example, television is thought to cause the decline in achievement test performance by American children, or films are seen as a cause of moral decay. Such causal statements are worth noting because, in general, Americans who expect their lives to be shaped by technology explain social changes accordingly. Yet these same questions also reflect the ambivalence with which Americans regard most information technologies. The public wants a rich information environment but fears an erosion of moral values. Even so, fear is too harsh a word for these feelings. More likely, they constitute an emotional awareness that the quality of life has changed in ways that are hard to articulate.[42]

Whether threat, or fear, or ambivalence, it is clear that people experience unease with information technologies at orders of magnitude ranging from the micro-personal to the macro-societal. As long as humans have pursued information technologies for the power they bring to the ability to communicate and to process information, they have experienced a level of threat from the technologies of their own invention. That this awareness occurs at multiple levels testifies to the fact that concerns raised by information technologies are part of the larger threat posed by all technologies. There is nothing new in that, Americans have pondered the consequences of technology for 200 years.[43]

What is new are the particular threats brought to the foreground by the information society. Unlike the perils emanating from the machines of the early industrial revolution, these new threats are more pervasive and diffuse. Yet even given the pervasiveness, Americans have not reconciled their conflicting attitudes toward information technologies, so that both allure *and* threat persist. The need to understand them is greater today, but so is the challenge. Should Damocles return to observe technology today, he would see no sword, but he would still sit uneasily.

Information Technology as Metaphor

The coming of the railroad shattered the Jeffersonian vision of a nation of yeomen farmers and captured the imagination of the new industrial age. Words which were shaped by the vocabulary of the locomotive, like piston, gear, emission, engine, combustion, and horsepower entered common speech and became symbols of the age of steam and steel. By the end of the century, Thomas Jefferson's ideal of the small farmer had given way to Theodore Roosevelt's gospel of progress. A handful of men commanded the new industries where new technologies were applied to the production of goods, to the organization of bureaucracies, and to the division of labor. But even a knowledgeable person could not actually see these developments. The amorphous character of many technologies, especially social technologies, made it difficult to directly observe industrialization. However, one could see the steam engine, larger than life, made of iron, black with soot, and hissing danger to those nearby. Because it progressively interconnected the country between 1850 and 1900, every hamlet felt its presence. As Nathaniel Hawthorne recorded in his notebook following an early encounter,

> But hark! there is the whistle of the locomotive—the long shriek, harsh, above all other harshness, for the space of a mile cannot mollify it into harmony. It tells a story of busy men, citizens from the hot street, who have come to spend a day in a country village, men of business; in short of all unquietness; and no wonder that it

gives such a startling shriek, since it brings the noisy world into the midst of our slumbrous peace.[44]

Hawthorne spoke for millions; for, when gazing on a locomotive in its full fury, it took little imagination to envision the essence of industrial society. Thus, the locomotive "explained" the industrial revolution.[45]

Today, there are still railroads, but they do not explain the end of the 20th century; and one must travel to museums to see steam engines. Instead, Americans rely on other technologies to explain a society even more incongruous than the one confronted by Hawthorne 150 years ago. In an age when most adults work close to a computer and take their leisure in front of a television set, these two machines are the successors to the locomotive; and, like the iron horse, both are highly visible. TV sets are present in every household, while the time spent watching them adds up to years of every person's life.

Television is truly ubiquitous; its programs contribute the substance of daily conversations, talk show personalities become household names, and personal schedules give way to program schedules. By contrast, computers are less immediately obvious. Nevertheless, their presence can be detected at work, at the bank, in the grocery checkout line, at school, and in every interaction with a large organization. Their detritus—forms, bills, printouts, junkmail, pay stubs, and little strips of paper with holes in them—is everywhere. Other technologies are equally felt with comparable impact, but none rank as high in projecting an image of the times. Americans feel comfortable describing their age as the age of television, or as the computer age.[46]

To begin with, these two machine systems have contributed jargon to common speech. We use television words like sitcom, ratings, and reruns, or VCR terms like fast forward, to express our ideas on non television topics. The same is true for computer terms like bit, data, database, and digital, although their use is more common in certain work settings.[47] Beyond single words, we say that we saw an event on TV, in order to give it validity—much as youngsters spoke of the movies in the 1930s and '40s. Or, we say that we saw a product on TV, to give it status. Similarly, we assign responsibility for record keeping in organizations to the computer. We say, "It's in the computer," to signify an accomplished task, or we say, "It's lost in the computer," to indicate a mistake. We trade terms, as when we assign descriptions of the brain to the computer, and descriptions of the computer to the brain—computers are discussed as having memory and intelligence, while the brain is termed a storage medium with circuitry. And, given the images elicited by the information society, it should come as no surprise that we equate the most significant machine of the period with what we believe to be the most significant organ in the body. What makes these word manipulations and meaning attachments significant is not their occurrence—for we routinely adapt words to new uses—but their pervasiveness. They are everywhere and make sense to nearly everyone.

One indication of the metaphorical power of television and the computer is that Americans invest them with both positive and negative values. For example, Americans tend to accept the youthful and athletic bodies projected on TV as ideal types; so much so that we spend billions of dollars on diets, toiletries, and cosmetic surgery, in order to come closer to what we see represented on television as the perfect body configuration.[48] This simplifies the argument a bit, since American culture has tended to idealize youth at least since the turn of the century. Television programming has become the method by which these values are taught. They are accepted wholeheartedly by most viewers. Because of the metaphorical status of the medium, it represents reality. At the same time, to work with computers is to achieve success. Whether among high school graduates vying for jobs as computer programmers, or among surgeons learning to use computer assisted techniques, involvement with the computer confers the power attributed to the technology onto its human associate; and, thereby, projects an image of achievement.

Yet Americans also imbue television and the computer with negative values. From time to time, TV is declared a wasteland, and its programs are accused of excessive sex, violence, and trivialization.[49] Similarly, the very cause for attraction to the computer, its power to manipulate vast quantities of information, is also cause for aversion. To many minds, computers are associated with a less than optimistic view of the future.[50] People see the positive and the negative in their own society through TV and the computer because they have elevated these machine systems to the status of primary symbols. The fact that people see these two technologies as representing both positive and negative aspects of our society indicates the metaphorical roles they play.

Television is a powerful metaphor because it is always there as part of one's consciousness with the same seamless quality as the rest of one's life. TV sets occupy every home yet seem harmless. They are accepted as members of the family and missed when absent.[51] Even more than radio, television functions as a window whose non random, highly stylized images represent life beyond the immediate knowledge of most citizens. It stands first among sources of information because it is immediate in an immediate society.[52] Television maximizes the speed of information transmission to the individual, who is aware that he or she lives in an era when information flows at its maximum speed. Television is instant ever-presence.

Computers, on the other hand, though their presence seems pervasive, are largely invisible. Personal computers are absent from over 60% of all business establishments, and 70% of homes.[53] In their role as hidden processors of streams of data, computers imply a highly rational social system in which huge anonymous organizations function at a level inaccessible to the individual. In this sense, the computer symbolizes the larger society, and the helplessness of the individual within it. Yet the computer also symbolizes the arrival of the future; and, because most Americans value the future over the past, this provides its positive connotation.

Taken together, television and the computer serve as comfortable metaphors because Americans value technologies, and the information society is quintessentially a technological society. When individuals refer to the computer age, or to the television age, as a way of explaining society, they invoke a shorthand for describing its most important characteristics. To label an entire historical period with the names of two technologies nominates them as the most important characteristics of the era. In our case, this means that TVs and computers rank above war, big government, or the decline of the nuclear family.

To name our era after the television and the computer is to invest two technologies with great potency. As metaphors they have great power precisely because they define the social experience. It says a great deal about Americans that they comfortably describe themselves as living in the age of television and the computer. When individuals treat a technology as the primary descriptive icon of their society, they structure their expectations accordingly. The problems of America are variously attributed to impersonal computers, or too much television, or both. Other competing explanations, such as over emphasis on the profit motive, ill prepared school systems, or declining economic opportunities, remain on the periphery because they are essentially non technological. In our time, unlike the one that Hawthorne described, there is no "long shriek, harsh, above all other harshness," to assault our senses; but, like Hawthorne's, our thinking bears the stamp of technological images.

A Comment on Technological Determinism

If most Americans share contradictory views of information technologies— celebrating them while fearing them—it is because they look to technology as a key metaphor with which to explain and represent a complex society.[54] What appear as contradictions on the surface are likely to have a common denominator at some deeper level. The common denominator can be found in texts describing the social role played by information technologies. In other words, the assumptions behind our thoughts may be hidden, but their reflections are discoverable in our statements, as they are in the following.

> If technology is indeed a main engine of social change, we might be curious as to what lies ahead.—Walter Baer on the subject of telecommunications technologies in the 1980s.[55]

> Any child can list the effects of the telephone or the radio or the motor car in shaping the life and work of his friends and his society.—Marshall McLuhan on the obvious impact of machines.[56]

> The entire texture of society will be changed by telecommunications and related products.—James Martin on changes occurring toward the end of the twentieth century.[57]

> Information technology from Silicon Valley is now impacting American society: office automation, home computers, video games, and microcomputers in the

schools.—Everett Rogers and Judith Larsen on the microelectronics industry in northern California.[58]

What these statements have in common is their logic. Each assumes that technology directly alters human behavior and social relations, at a level of power above other change agents.

These are forceful images. They place information technology at center stage; and, they imply that society changes because information machines cause change. In so doing, they impose a logic for understanding change: the machine is the cause, therefore, study the cause. McLuhan, and Martin, write of the future by analyzing the machines of the present. Rogers and Larsen explore the course of the information society by examining the social technology that produces a basic device, the microprocessor. Writing in the 1970s, Baer reviewed the development level of 55 communication devices and applications in order to predict the state of telecommunications in the 1980s.

Their assumption reveals the great power Americans ascribe to information technology—actually, all material technologies. In all circles, from the workshop to the seminar room, most Americans assume that technology determines social change. They observe and interpret information technology through this window, and to them it makes common sense. Based on this premise, labels such as the steam age, railroad age, automobile age, or computer age, touch a receptive nerve by conjuring a world molded by its most visible machines. If television and the computer appear as the newest influential gods in American mythology, it is because technology in general is one of the oldest and most durable.

However, analyses which solely focus on the technical characteristics of computers, or even on the larger system of television, do not necessarily reveal the consequences for society. The examples chosen throughout this chapter illustrate intimate interactions between human choices, human intent, and inanimate devices, which are not nearly as simple as McLuhan's flip observation. If these examples demonstrate a collective truth, it is that technology never stands alone. On the other hand, technology clearly makes a difference; and, in some instances, operates as a catalytic agent. So then, where lies reality? Do information technologies cause society, or does society cause information technologies? Do social groups adapt themselves to a new technology or do they adapt the technology? Do individuals experience choice and freedom, or constraint and coercion? One way out of this quandary is to examine these questions according to their levels of abstraction.

The Macro Level: Does Information Technology Determine Change in Society?

To argue that technology determines the course of change in society, and therefore history, is to argue that machines shape society. This logic forms the essence of technological determinism and is reflected in the statements quoted at the beginning of the chapter. Interpretations grounded in this logic contribute to histories that view the development of society through a sequence of improved machines, as if there were inherent and fixed laws of motion for technology. These interpretations sometimes imply that all nations must pass through a sequence of technological phases, each determined by a dominant technology. In this vein, the last 150 years is often described as a succession of technological "ages", from steam engine, to computer. That these "ages" last for only a few decades should raise eyebrows, but they appeal to a popular American notion that we live in times of rapid change. Technological histories often reveal a *post hoc ergo propter hoc* sequence of machines implying that one inevitably led to its successor.

As television and the computer captured the popular imagination, information machines became the focus of deterministic observations, prompting journalists and scholars to ask loaded questions, such as: What effect does television have on children?; Do computers cause unemployment?; Will interactive video systems increase political participation?; or, Can reconnaissance satellites create more open international relations?

Questions of this nature define an information device as the active variable in simple cause-and-effect relationships and ignore important social relationships. They ignore the human motivations that determine the initial implementation of any technology. They ignore values and the assumptions underlying the structure of the machines themselves. For example, the question of television effects on children assumes that television acts independently of the interests of those who created the commercial broadcast system, so that any differences between the implementation of American commercial television and European government systems remains hidden. Asking how computers affect unemployment implies that computers have will and that humans have none; but, more importantly, the question ignores the motivation of management to raise productivity by cutting labor costs. Likewise, futurists predicting increased political participation through interactive television fail to account for Americans' long-standing distrust of politicians and the political process.[59] Speculations as to the impact of reconnaissance satellites on international relations visualizes satellites as pro-active and nations as reactive. In fact, the reverse is true. Satellites respond to commands from the ground, and nations use them as tools to reach their political objectives. The existence of reconnaissance satellites says more about the state of international tension than it does about the future effects of information technology.

To examine a society's machines tells little of its culture. Should alien visitors drop in on industrial museums in the United States and Mexico, they would see many similar machines. But if they inferred cultures of equal similarity, they would be wrong. The point is that machines alone do not make a culture. The culture of the information society resulted from the growth of capitalism and the uses of industrialization to benefit capitalists. Its most important socioeconomic manifestations, the commoditization of information and information work, are the logical outgrowths of capitalism. Individuals invented new information machines, in order to profit from selling information. Industrialists increased demand for information workers, because of the need to make informed decisions. Add to this an aggressive attitude toward nature, as well as the scientist's affinity for technology, and the picture is one of a complex system of social relations with information technology as one particular element. The point is that, at the macro level—the level of society—information technology does not produce social relations; rather social relations produce information technology. In the words of medieval historian Lynn White, "As our understanding of history increases, it becomes clear that a new device merely opens a door, it does not command one to enter."[60] But for the door to stay open, changes may be necessary in the middle range.

The Middle Level: Do Social Groups Adapt to Information Technology?

"The hand-mill gives you society with the feudal lord; the steam-mill, society with the industrial capitalist."[61] Marx's famous dictum relates specific technologies to a distinct economic order. For the steam mill to operate, it needed an industrial infrastructure to support it. So, while technology is a result, rather than a cause, at the macro level, in the middle range, it plays a more active role.

Each development in technology places requirements on the surrounding social system. When typewriters dominated offices, managers sought services to keep them functioning—services which were of a mechanical nature, since typewriters consisted of rods, springs, wheels, and levers. A mechanical industry produced typewriters and mechanics repaired them. As the personal computer supplanted the typewriter, it required a change in the supporting infrastructure. Now, the electronics industry produces personal computers and those who repair them are versed in the nuances of microprocessors and cathode ray tubes. While old brand names like Olivetti and IBM remained to produce and maintain the new infrastructure, other names like Apple and Wang appeared which had not existed during the heyday of the typewriter. When managers chose to adopt personal computers, they sent ripples of change throughout the surrounding corporate and industrial systems. Thus, in the middle range, where institutions, organizations, and groups predominate, a new technology causes change by necessitating adaptations.

Once an information technology enters a particular system, e.g., the office or the home, the system must respond. In order to make use of the new technology, individuals in groups may have to adopt changes to suit its needs. To achieve maximum access to the TV set, families made changes in the organization of their living rooms. But the flow is not solely one way; people in the system also have an opportunity to affect the technology, molding its applications to their own uses. In the early winter of 1986, New York City police jammed police radios as part of a work slow down. They did so to thwart police management and to publicize the rank and file's dissatisfaction with City Hall's policies. By constantly depressing the transmitter buttons on their radios, they effectively severed communications between themselves and their supervisors.[62] What is of interest here is that such a use of police radios was probably not envisioned by communications planners or designers. The police overrode the intended use of the information technology, creating an unforeseen application.

New York City's police rebellion of the winter of '86 demonstrates that technology is not all powerful within any social system, but responds to social forces. Radio required technical skills from police officers, in order for them to exploit its potential for police work. Having acquired the necessary skills, police officers were able to use the radio as a tool for advancing their labor negotiations. Technology itself is a vehicle for people to get what they want, and to have an effect on others. Therefore, at the middle range where groups predominate, the direction of effects runs in both directions, from the information technology to the group and from the group to the technology.

The Micro Level: Does Information Technology Limit Individual Freedom?

The individual experiences limited power in modern society. At the very least, the great size of institutions, corporations, and government forces their constituents to conform to predetermined roles. So, it should not be surprising to find Americans projecting limited power onto their own experiences with information technologies. In addition, because most individuals live and work in environments structured to accommodate information machines, it is easy to conceptualize them as an independent force, and as direct agents of social change.

In the home, the individual confronts information appliances as fixtures. The television set appears as a box with options to turn the power on or off, and to change the channels. Television's potential as an educational medium, tool for political demagoguery, or force for cultural integration is less apparent. At work, the stenographer who encounters a computer as her replacement cannot see those who made the decision, and so she is likely to see the computer as the cause of her unemployment. When interactions of limited power constitute the norm for daily encounters, as they do for most people, seeing technologies as the causes of change is not unreasonable. Nevertheless, as the case of Mrs. Schement illustrates, human ingenuity always finds ways to manipulate technologies by introducing novel uses (see "When Television Came to West Houston Street," in the appendix.) Yet, all things being equal, Americans tend to see themselves as passive, and technology as active; or, as Thoreau laments, machines drive and men ride the current.

However, our point here is somewhat different. Whether television or the computer limits personal freedom depends on the power of the individual. For the powerless stenographer, who lacks control over her circumstances, the computer acts as an agent of constraint resulting from management's decision.[63]

As a way of looking at the world, technological determinism focuses on machines and de-emphasizes or ignores social elements of causation. If we believe that technology causes social change, then does it matter who owns or controls it or what their motivations are? Probably not, since the source of change has been assigned to the technology itself, rather than to the motives of those who control it. When tensions are thought to result from the force of technology, then there is little we can do but ride the wave. Were such a perspective true there would be little need to conduct public discourse, or to seek solutions and accommodations. But technology, like all aspects of society, results from human decisions and reactions.

Americans have a natural fascination with machines, a fascination that goes back as far as the industrial revolution when Alexis de Tocqueville observed, "These very Americans, who have not discovered one of the general laws of mechanics, have introduced into navigation an engine which changes the aspect of the world."[64] In the 20th century, this fascination continues; and, as Americans find themselves negotiating life in an environment dense with information technologies, they have developed attitudes which help them cope. Information technologies are so important to Americans that when they try to make sense of the information society, their explanations of social phenomena often rely on a machine system as the primary agent of change. Because Americans conceive of the information society as the age of information technology, they tend to over-emphasize the role of machines, and their interpretations are sometimes faulty.

Notes

1. Mumford, L. (1934/1962). *Technics and civilization.* New York: Harcourt, Brace, and World, p. 52.
2. Eisenhower, D. D. (1960). Farewell Radio and Television Address to the American People, January 17, 1961. In *Public Papers of the Presidents of the United States, Dwight D. Eisenhower, 1960–61* (pp. 1035–40). Washington D.C.
3. Thoreau, H. D. (1854/1942). *Walden; Or life in the woods.* New York: New American Library, p. 29].
4. As quoted by Mumford. Mumford, L. (1934/1962) p. 9.
5. Mumford, L. (1934/1962) p. 10.
6. As quoted in Ellul, J. (1964). *The technological society.* New York: Vintage Books, p. x.
7. Ellul, J. (1964) p. vi.
8. Ellul, J. (1964) p. xxv.

9. Stover, C. F. (Ed.). (1963). *The technological order: Proceedings of the Encyclopedia Britannica conference.* Detroit, MI: Wayne State University Press, p. 59.
10. Mesthene, E. G. (1970). *Technological change: Its impact on man and society .* New York: New American Library, p. 25.
11. Bittner, E. (1965). The concept of organization. *Social Research, 32,* 239–255. Chandler, A. D. J. (1962). *Strategy and structure.* Cambridge, MA: MIT Press. Perrow, C. (1972). *Complex organizations.* Glenview, IL: Scott, Foresman and Company.
12. Shannon, C. E., & Weaver, W. (1949). *The mathematical theory of communication.* Urbana, IL: University of Illinois Press.
13. Rogers, E. M. (1986). *Communication technology: the new media in society.* New York: Free Press, p. 1.
14. Braudel, F. (1979). *Civilization and capitalism 15th–18th century: The wheels of commerce.* New York: Harper & Row, p. 334.
15. Walter J. Ong, and Langdon Winner preceded Braudel and elaborated on this point. Ong, W. J. (1962). *The barbarian within.* New York: Macmillan. Ong, W. J. (1977). *Interfaces of the word.* Ithaca, NY: Cornell University Press. Ong, W. J. (1982). *Orality and literacy: The technologizing of the word.* London, UK: Methuen. Winner, L. (1977). *Autonomous technology: Technics-out-of-control as a theme in political thought.* Cambridge, MA: MIT Press. Winner, L. (1986). *The whale and the reactor: A search for limits in an age of high technology.* Chicago, IL: University of Chicago.
16. Goulet, D. (1977). *The uncertain promise: Value conflicts in technology transfer.* New York: IDOC. Lewis, A. O. J. (Ed.). (1963). *Of men and machines.* New York: E.P. Dutton. Mead, M. (Ed.). (1955). *Cultural patterns and technological change.* New York: New American Library. Mesthene, E. G. (1970). *Technological change: Its impact on man and society .* New York: New American Library. Rybczynski, W. (1983). *Taming the tiger: The struggle to control technology.* New York: Viking. White, L. J. (1962). *Medieval technology and social change.* London, UK: Oxford University Press.
17. A version of this definition appeared in Schement, J. R., & Stout, D. A. J. (1990). A time-line of information technology. In B. D. Ruben & L. A. Lievrouw (Eds.), *Information and Behavior* (pp. 395–424). New Brunswick, NJ: Transaction, and owes much to Rogers, E. M. (1986). *Communication technology: the new media in society.* New York: Free Press. We also gratefully acknowledge our valuable discussions with Dallas Smythe, of Simon Fraser University, and Daniél Dayán, of the University of Paris.
18. This chapter is not a review of information technologies per se. For an excellent overview of information technologies, see Singleton, L. A. (1989). *Global impact: The new telecommunication technologies.* New York: Harper & Row. For those interested in historical analyses that include information technologies, we recommend: Beniger, J. R. (1986). *The control revolution.* Cambridge, MA: Harvard University Press. Ellul, J. (1964). *The technological society.* New York: Vintage Books. Giedion, S. (1948). *Mechanization takes command: A contribution to anonymous history.* New York: W. W. Norton. Mumford, L. (1934/1962). *Technics and civilization.* New York: Harcourt, Brace, and World.
19. In a letter to Jean-Baptiste Le Roy, 13 Nov. 1789.
20. Since these are averages, they hide the unevenness of the distribution of services. Most Americans had no telephone in 1930. Tables R172-187, R1-12 (1975). *Historical Statistics of the United States, Colonial Times to 1970* (Bicentennial Ed.). Washington DC: GPO. Tables 911, 918 (1990). *Statistical Abstract of the United States: 1990.* Washington DC: Bureau of the Census.

21. Table T444-471 (1975). *Historical Statistics of the United States, Colonial Times to 1970* (Bicentennial Ed.). Washington DC: GPO. Tables 2, 932 (1990). *Statistical Abstract of the United States: 1990.* Washington DC: Bureau of the Census.

22. The expectation of progress, like the idea of information, has roots in the Enlightenment. For the origins of the notion of progress, see Bury, J. B. (1932). *The idea of progress: An inquiry into its growth and origin.* New York: MacMillan.

23. Pool, I. d. S., Decker, C., Dizard, S., Israel, K., Rubin, P., & Weinstein, B. (1977). Foresight and hindsight: The case of the telephone. In I. d. S. Pool (Ed.), *The social impact of the telephone* (pp. 127-157). Cambridge, MA: MIT Press.

24. Schramm, W., Lyle, J., & Parker, E. B. (1961). *Television in the lives of our children.* Stanford, CA: Stanford University. Steiner, G. A. (1963). *The people look at television: A study of audience attitudes.* New York: Knopf.

25. On the paperless office see, Masuda, Y. (1985). Parameters of the post-industrial society: Computopia. In T. Forester (Ed.), *The information technology revolution* (pp. 620-634). Cambridge, MA: MIT. Toffler, A. (1980). *The third wave.* New York: William Morrow. Vyssotsky, V. A. (1979). The use of computers for business functions. In M. L. Dertouzos & J. Moses (Eds.), *The computer age* (pp. 129-145). Cambridge, MA: MIT Press. On computers decentralizing organizations see, Hiltz, S. R., & Turoff, M. (1978). *The network nation: Human communication via computer.* Reeding, MA: Addison-Wesley. Masuda, Y. (1985). Naisbitt, J. (1982). *Megatrends.* New York: Warner Books. Vyssotsky, V. A. (1979).

26. Einstein, A. (1954). *Ideas and opinions.* New York: Bonanza Books, p. 4.

27. 4,627,000; includes social scientists since they contribute to the development of social technologies. Table 999 (1990). *Statistical Abstract of the United States: 1990.* Washington DC: Bureau of the Census.

28. Basalla, G. (Ed.). (1968). *The rise of modern science: External or internal factors?* Lexington, MA: D.C. Heath and Company. Dixon, B. (1988). Science and the information society. *Scholarly Publishing* (October), 3-12. Hall, A. R. (1954/ 1962). *The scientific revolution 1500–1800: The formation of the modern scientific attitude.* Boston: Beacon Press. Horowitz, I. L., & Curtis, M. E. (1982). The impact of new technology on scientific and scholarly publishing. *Journal of Information Science Principles & Practice, 4* 87-96. Kevles, D. J. (1979). *The Physicists: The history of a scientific community in modern America.* New York: Vintage. Noble, D. F. (1977). *America by Design: Science, Technology, and the Rise of Corporate Capitalism.* Oxford, UK: Oxford University Press. Price, D. J. d. S. (1963). *Little science big science.* New York: Columbia University Press. Ruskin, J. (1883). *The eagle's nest.* New York: John Wiley.

29. Compiled from tables 2, 985 (1990). *Statistical Abstract of the United States: 1990.* Washington DC: Bureau of the Census.

30. Thompson, R. L. (1947). *Wiring a continent: The history of the telegraph industry in the United States 1832–1866.* Princeton, NJ: Princeton University Press.

31. Postman, N. (1985). *Amusing ourselves to death: Public discourse in the age of show business.* New York: Penguin, p. 65.

32. Dalby, A. (1986). The sumerian catalogs. *Journal of Library History, 21*(3), 475-487.

33. The altruistic Morse did not really fit the temper of the times, and so was brushed aside as soon as the first telegraph syndicate was formed. On the other hand, in his history of weapons and war, Robert O'Connell describes the motivations of the 19th century founders of the military-industrial complex, and notes that the inventors were mostly tinkers attempting to mechanize or improve the weapons, while the organizers were entrepreneurs exploiting the potential of this particular market. In few cases, did they see the long-term consequences of their actions.

O'Connell, R. L. (1989). *Of arms and men: A history of war, weapons, and aggression.* New York: Oxford, pp. 190–196.

34. In this regard, inquisitiveness can be thought of as the tendency to ask questions and to examine what is of interest, so that it is really an attitude combined with a behavior.

35. To be sure, this oversimplifies a complex argument. Daniel Lerner's analysis of cultures in transition from traditional to modern, *The Passing of Traditional Society,* typifies the view that held sway in international development circles until the mid 1970s. In the view of the modernist school [sometimes referred to as the dominant paradigm in development studies], people in traditional agricultural societies have static views of the world around them and are unable to imagine themselves beyond their immediate circumstances [termed a lack of empathy by Lerner.]. Lerner further thought that this condition resulted in a lack of inquisitiveness and contributed to the sense of "backwardness" reported by visitors from industrial nations. On the other hand, members of modern industrial societies learn empathy, through the consumption of information from the mass media, which facilitates their ability to participate in the public discourses of the larger society. See Lerner, D. (1958). *The passing of traditional society: Modernizing the middle east.* New York: Free Press. Lerner, D., & Schramm, W. (Ed.). (1967). *Communication and change in developing countries.* Honolulu, HI: East-West Center. Schramm, W. (1964). *Mass media and national development.* Stanford, CA: Stanford University. Lerner and other social theorists of the mid 20th century believed socioeconomic evolution followed a linear path. They saw industrial society as the ultimate in social organization and concluded that all of the world's nations must become industrialized according to the Euro-American model or be left behind. For the clearest representation of this theory, see Rostow, W. W. (Ed.). (1963). *The economics of take-off into sustained growth.* New York: St. Martin's Press. Rostow, W. W. (1971). *The stages of economic growth* (2nd ed.). Cambridge, UK: Cambridge University Press. Rostow, W. W. (1978). *The world economy: History & Prospect.* Austin, TX: University of Texas Press. In the last fifteen years, Lerner's ideas have been debunked as these easy distinctions were shown to lack validity. For critiques, see Goulet, D. (1977). *The uncertain promise: Value conflicts in technology transfer.* New York: IDOC. Goulet, D. (1978). *The cruel choice: A new concept in the theory of development.* New York: Atheneum. MacBride, S. (Ed.). (1980). *Many voices one world.* London, UK: Kogan Page. Morris, M. D. (1979). *Measuring the condition of the world's poor: The physical quality of life index.* New York: Pergamon. Nevertheless, Lerner's theories illustrate the important value placed on inquisitiveness in Western intellectual circles.

36. From an address delivered in 1918 at a celebration of Max Planck's sixtieth birthday before the Physical Society in Berlin. Einstein's reference to Diogenes alludes to his search for an honest man [in this case, Planck], but perhaps also to Diogenes' advocation of a simple life emphasizing self-discipline and training of the mind. Einstein, A. (1954). *Ideas and opinions.* New York: Bonanza Books, pp. 22–227.

37. Kuhn, T. (1962). *The structure of scientific revolutions.* Chicago, IL: University of Chicago. Kuhn, T. (1977). Second thoughts on paradigms. In F. Suppe (Eds.), *The structure of scientific theories* Urbana, IL: University of Illinois Press.

38. Price, D. J. d. S. (1963). *Little science big science.* New York: Columbia University Press, pp. 2, 3, 4, 18.

39. Kraut, R. E. (1987). *Technology and the Transformation of White-Collar Work.* Hillsdale, NJ: Lawrence Erlbaum Associates, pp. 1–21.

40. *The Constitution of the United States of America,* Amendment IV.
41. For a sociological discussion of the transition from movie-oriented childhoods to those structured by television, see Schramm, W., Lyle, J., & Parker, E. B. (1961). *Television in the lives of our children.* Stanford, CA: Stanford University.
42. There are technology fears that operate across all levels; thus, making them difficult to categorize. For example, military weaponry, especially nuclear weapons, provoke alarm because of their inherent potential for wreaking death and havoc. For the more thoughtful, there is the realization that information systems which soldiers use to coordinate and direct the bombs and missiles increase the killing power of armies. Social technologies of coordination, along with the use of "smart bombs," allowed the U.S. military to devastate its Iraqi opponent. Most of the 100,000–150,000 Iraqi deaths can be attributed to air and sea bombardments dependent on sophisticated information technologies for their implementation. These, and other fears associated with the relationship between technology and war, are not fears of technology per se; rather, they are fears of capabilities with which technology abets human nature. See also Gellner, E. (1989). *Plough, sword, and book: The structure of human history.* Chicago, IL: University of Chicago. Innis, H. A. (1950). *Empire and communication.* Toronto, Canada: University of Toronto. O'Connell, R. L. (1989). *Of arms and men: A history of war, weapons, and aggression.* New York: Oxford. Rybczynski, W. (1983). *Taming the tiger: The struggle to control technology.* New York: Viking. White, L. J. (1962). *Medieval technology and social change.* London, UK: Oxford University Press. Winner, L. (1977). *Autonomous technology: Technics-out-of-control as a theme in political thought.* Cambridge, MA: MIT Press. Winner, L. (1986). *The whale and the reactor: A search for limits in an age of high technology.* Chicago, IL: University of Chicago.
43. For example, Marx, L. (1967). *The machine in the garden: Technology and the pastoral ideal in America.* New York: Oxford University Press. Mumford, L. (1934/ 1962). *Technics and civilization.* New York: Harcourt, Brace, and World. Pursell, C. W. (Ed.). (1969). *Readings in technology and American life.* London, UK: Oxford University Press.
44. Stewart, R. (Ed.). (1932). *The American notebooks.* Columbus, OH: Ohio State University. pp. 102–105. The theme of technology corrupting nature also appears in the work of other American 19th century romanticists, such as Wordsworth and Melville. For a fuller treatment of technology and the pastoral ideal in America, see Leo Marx's 1967 classic, *The Machine in the Garden.*
45. Marx, L. (1967) pp. 3–11.
46. There are other "ages" competing for attention. But neither the automobile age, nor the nuclear age, nor the age of plastics, nor the "me" era, seem to capture the feel of the times as popularly as do the television and the computer.
47. For an analysis of the language of computers among computer science students, see Turkle's, S. (1984). *The second self: computers and the human spirit.* New York: Simon and Schuster.
48. In 1988, TV and magazine advertising for toiletries alone amounted to 1.7 billion dollars in expenditures. This does not include direct consumer expenditures for products. Tables 936, 937 (1990). *Statistical Abstract of the United States: 1990.* Washington DC: Bureau of the Census.
49. For a discussion of the complexity of these charges, see Gerbner, G., & Gross, L. (1976). Living with television: The violence profile. *Journal of Communication, 26,* 173–179. Kubey, R., & Csikszentmihalyi, M. (1990). *Television and the quality of life: How viewing shapes everyday experiences.* Hillsdale, NJ: Lawrence Erlbaum. Postman, N. (1985). *Amusing ourselves to death: Public discourse in the age of show business.* New York: Penguin.

50. For a discussion of the down side of the diffusion of computers, see Brod, C. (1984). *Technostress: The human cost of the computer revolution.* Reading, MA: Addison-Wesley. Curtis, T. (1990). The information society: A computer-generated caste system? In V. Mosco J. Wasko (Eds.), *The political economy of information.* (pp. 95–107). Madison, WI: University of Wisconsin. Hartmann, H. I., Kraut, R. E., & Tilly, L. A. (Ed.). (1986). *Computer Chips and Paper Clips: Technology and Women's Employment.* Washington DC: National Academy Press. Kaltwasser, F. G. (1987). Dangers for the modern information society in the computer age. *IFLA Journal, 13*(2), 111–119. Mosco, V. (1989). *The pay-per-view society: Computers and communication in the information age.* Norwood, NJ: Ablex.

51. Kubey, R., & Csikszentmihalyi, M. (1990) pp. 190–191.

52. Postman, N. (1985) pp. 7–8].

53. (1990). *Statistical Abstract of the United States: 1990.* Washington DC: Bureau of the Census, p. 946, also table 1340.

54. In the following section, we refer to material technologies when using the term "technology", unless otherwise noted. For an excellent discussion of technological determinism as an idea in social theories, see Langdon Winner's *Autonomous Technology* (1977) pp. 73–88.

55. Baer, W. (1978). Telecommunications technology in the 1980s. In G. O. Robinson (Ed.), *Communications for tomorrow: Policy perspectives for the 1980s* (pp. 61–123). New York: Praeger, pp. 61–123.

56. McLuhan, M. (1964). *Understanding media: The extensions of man.* New York: New American Library, p. x.

57. Martin, J. (1981). *Telematic society: A challenge for tomorrow.* New York: Prentice-Hall, p. 3.

58. Rogers, E. M., & Larsen, J. K. (1984). *Silicon valley fever: Growth of high-technology culture.* New York: Basic Books, p. 203.

59. For predictions of this type, see Martin, J. (1981). *Telematic society: A challenge for tomorrow.* New York: Prentice-Hall, pp. 60–66, and Toffler, A. (1980). *The third wave.* New York: William Morrow, pp. 429–430.

60. White, L. J. (1962). *Medieval technology and social change.* London, UK: Oxford University Press, p. 28.

61. Marx, K. (1963). *Poverty of philosophy.* International Publishers, p. 10.

62. *New York Times,* 10 November 1986.

63. We have presented an approach to understanding the causality of information technologies in society. However, we did not address the question of whether laws exist governing technological development. In fact, a case can be made in support of the proposition that every technology carries within it the burden of prior decisions and historic events, which don't necessarily follow a rational path, but are, nevertheless, irrevocable and gradually reduce the degrees of freedom for further development of that technology. That is, technological development, as a product of history, must bear some regularities which govern the nature of change and time. So, when humans try to mitigate the path of technological development, they can never truly reverse it, though they always have the power, in the present, to create history. In this sense, assumptions of technological determinism do not stem from systematic observations of real world processes, because there is no iron law of technology; but there may be a cycle of development for technology as a historic event. For an example of changing degrees of freedom over time, in one case of technological development, see the case of the QWERTY arrangement of typewriter keys, and their persistence for 150 years, David, P. A. (1986). Understanding the economics of QWERTY: The necessity of

history. In W. N. Parker (Ed.), *Economic history and the modern economist* (pp. 30–49). Basil Blackwell Inc. Gould, S. J. (1987). The panda's thumb of technology. *Natural History*(1/87), 14–23.

64. Tocqueville, A. d. (1835/1964). *Democracy in America* (Reeve, Henry, Trans.). New York: Washington Square Press, Ch. 22.

7

The Information Society as a State of Mind

The hero was distinguished by his achievement; the celebrity by his image or trade-mark. The hero created himself; the celebrity is created by the media. The hero was a big man; the celebrity is a big name. Formerly, a public man needed a private secretary for a barrier between himself and the public. Nowadays he has a press secretary, to keep him properly in the public eye.—Daniel Boorstin[1]

We have reached a similar point of data gathering when each stick of chewing gum we reach for is acutely noted by some computer that translates our least gesture into a new probability curve or some parameter of social science. Our private and corporate lives have become information processes because we have put our central nervous systems outside us in electric technology. That is the key to Professor Boorstin's bewilderment in *The Image, or What Happened to the American Dream.*—Marshall McLuhan[2]

Broadly speaking, if industrial society is based on machine technology, post-industrial society is shaped by intellectual technology. And if capital and labor are the major structural features of industrial society, information and knowledge are the major structural features of industrial society. For this reason, the social organization of a post-industrial sector is vastly different from an industrial sector, and one can see this by contrasting the economic features of the two.—Daniel Bell[3]

In the 1960s, Daniel Boorstin and Marshall McLuhan constructed images of society that drew widespread attention and stimulated public discourse in America.[4] They are of interest to us here because each explored information and communication related phenomena, in order to explain changes in society. Their ideas inspired college students to reflect on the societal role of the mass media. But neither contributed a systematic macro theory explaining the significance of information structures and communication processes in American society. In their wake, scholars of communication and information studies retrenched and largely ignored the goal of explaining society.[5] Not until Daniel Bell, a sociologist, published *The Coming of Post-Industrial Society* did a macro theory take root.[6] Bell's theory, later refined by Porat and then elaborated by others, suggested that a new and fundamentally different social order had arisen in response to recent transformations in work, technology, and the economy. Like Boorstin and McLuhan, Bell took information and communication as central themes; and, as a triumvirate of must-read books, they shaped the popular images and scholarly interpretations which have come to dominate thinking about the information society.[7] Their ideas prompted us to write this book and to propose the macro theory which we describe in this chapter.[8]

Communication and information studies have enjoyed a rich tradition of theory explaining social behavior. Profound insights reward the reader of early contributors such as Raymond Bauer, Boorstin, Charles Cooley, Melvin DeFleur, Carl Hovland, Elihu Katz, Harold Innis, Harold Lasswell, Paul Lazarsfeld, Daniel Lerner, Walter Lippmann, Wilbur Schramm, McLuhan, and Raymond Williams.[9] However, only a handful attempted a communication and information centered macro theory; i.e., a coherent and verifiable explanation of contemporary society as organized around information structures, communication channels, and the mobilization of resources necessary to produce information as its major product. Of those, Boorstin and McLuhan came closest.[10]

Boorstin will long be known for his description of the pseudo-event. Perhaps as a result, his larger ideas stand hazy behind the brightness of his one famous phrase. Had he been solely concerned with the manufacture of news or the ephemeral nature of press conferences, as he is remembered, he would not qualify as a macro theorist. But Boorstin's analysis covered much more; he sought to explain a shift within modern American society, toward image and away from substance—a shift which, he argued, penetrated every nook of public life.

> The making of illusions which flood our experience has become the business of America, some of its most honest and most necessary and most respectful businesses. I am thinking not only of advertising and public relations and political rhetoric, but of all activities which purport to inform and comfort and improve and educate and elevate us.[11]

The acceptance of the artificial over the real, of image over actuality, suffused the individual's sense of identity and expectation, thus restructuring the conduct of one's inner life as well.[12]

A historian, Boorstin saw a new American society forming out of roots stretching back to the graphics revolution touched off by Gutenberg. Beginning in the 15th century, new image technologies gradually established the technological base for the development of the mass media. By the 20th century, the media's insatiable appetite for novelty encouraged the manufacture of events as artificial reality, thus the origins of the pseudo-event. Boorstin documents the resulting impact on society: the loss of heroes as role models of greatness, and their replacement by celebrities whose fame rests on managed images. He also situates his thesis among the forces set in motion by the industrial revolution. The new industrial society introduced the mass production of art and literature in forms that did not represent the context of the originals, and corrupted cultural ideals by subverting them into the themes of advertising. In public life, the attractiveness of image seduced politicians away from the riskiness of substance. He predicted a society increasingly trivialized by its dependence on images, and clearly foreshadowed the obsession with image of recent presidential campaigns. Boorstin's analysis encompasses far more than press conferences; working through his focus on images, he described changes reaching into every corner of the public sphere.

Boorstin saw the American descent into image consciousness as a result of the rise of advertising, and acknowledged the news media's commercial dependence as a cause and effect relationship, but he did not explore the workings of that relationship. Nor did he examine the media's tendency to select some images over others. Therefore, as his thesis develops, capitalism hovers in the background without much clarity. Boorstin also lacks a theory of technology. Pseudo events occur in the mass media and depend on the technologies of communication to reach their audiences, so much so, that the entire framework within which Boorstin constructed his argument depends on a technological interpretation. Yet Boorstin provides none. Ultimately, the supremacy of images in public life implies the dominance of the mass media over political and economic life; and, though Boorstin pays attention to the impact of image management on susceptible institutions, such as religion and politics, he limits himself to the forms and content of public discourse. The power of Boorstin's analysis is in part due to its restricted scope. He suggests, but does not elaborate, a theory of society.

His contemporary, McLuhan, also saw the mass media as shapers of society and molders of thought.

> The medium, or process, of our time—electric technology—is reshaping and restructuring patterns of social interdependence and every aspect of our personal life. It is forcing us to reconsider and re-evaluate practically every thought, every action, and every institution formerly taken for granted. Everything is changing—you, your family, your neighborhood, your education, your job, your government, your relation to "the others." And they're changing dramatically.[13]

He defined media in the broadest possible terms, developing the notion that, because the media function as extensions of the senses, they also determine the ways in which a society functions, thus profoundly affecting people's thought processes and their organization of social life.[14]

> Societies have always been shaped more by the nature of the media by which men communicate than by the content of the communication.[15]

> "The medium is the message" means, in terms of the electronic age, that a totally new environment has been created. The 'content' of this new environment is the old mechanized environment of the industrial age. The new environment reprocesses the old one as radically as TV is reprocessing the film.[16]

Given his predilection for contextual structures, McLuhan viewed media as technology, and technology as the shaper of society. He grounded his theory in a rather strict technological determinism. Once this is understood, some of his pronouncements can be seen to follow from an interior logic. For example, he argued that the predominance of particular media give a culture its unique identity. That is, since the technologies of media shape society, an observer need only examine differences in the relative distribution of media to deduce the variations among cultures. Likewise, given the primacy of technology in his thinking, any new wave of technological innovation carries with it the potential for a new social order. McLuhan saw modern civilization as breaking with its industrial past and now entering a new age whose main characteristic is information.[17]

> In this electric age we see ourselves being translated more and more into the form of information, moving toward the technological extension of consciousness.[18]

Information technology forms McLuhan's core concept and central dynamic; modern society—indeed, all human history—is driven by a succession of material inventions, each recasting the social crucible wherein people's attitudes, values, and relationships form.[19]

McLuhan intrigues readers because he dazzles them with visual images. He captures the essence of a medium in a single phrase, as he does by describing the clock as "the scent of time," the automobile as "the mechanical bride," and radio as "the tribal drum." His narratives captivate the reader and form lingering images. He intensifies the punch of his argument by making little effort to consider the social relations surrounding whichever medium he is explaining. In McLuhan's vision, society is an aggregation of individuals; therefore, media affect people individualistically. Media contain inherent technological characteristics of a hot or cool nature which place distinct demands on the user by invoking high participation, i.e., cool media, e.g., television, the telephone; or low participation, i.e., hot media, e.g., radio, the movies.[20] He describes radio as "offering a world of unspoken communication between writer-speaker and the listener.... A private experience.... charged with the resonating echoes of tribal horns and antique drums" and, then goes on to conclude that "This is inherent in the very nature of the medium."[21] In other words, every medium has distinct and intrinsic characteristics that directly and immutably affect the individual. There is no room for explanations invoking currents of history or the nuances of culture. Social relations, such as class, ethnicity, gender, regionalism, or capitalism, are pushed to the background, receiving scant attention. His technological determinism forms the keystone of his metaphorical arch. Consequently, McLuhan finds few impediments when he wonders if information and communication technologies might be pushing humanity toward a single consciousness, or global village.[22] In the end, his thesis, though strong in images, falters due to the weakness of its explanatory power. It works when he discusses a single medium and a hypothetical individual, but it fails when he faces the complexities of society. It is for this reason that he concentrates on technologically autonomous media, and then leaps over society to arrive at the global village. McLuhan stirs the imagination with insights into the characteristics of particular media, but fades when society intrudes.

Neither Boorstin nor McLuhan constructed theories. Their themes resist conversion into hypotheses or statements able to guide rigorous research, and few researchers have attempted to fill in the blanks by operationalizing their ideas into research agendas. As a result, scholars in the social sciences took notice, generated discussion, and moved on—though McLuhan has remained controversial much longer than Boorstin. Today the tendency is to see both as failed theorists. McLuhan's overall thesis has passed into the realm of anecdotal vignettes, while Boorstin stands reduced to his singular phrase.

Neither Boorstin nor McLuhan deserve a following of theorists. Yet their examination of the whole of society through the lens of information-communication phenomena distinguishes them from others who have simply studied the media or the social role of information. For though they fell short of constructing theories, they nevertheless moved communication and information studies to a new plane.

It is the theory proposed by Bell that deserves special consideration as the first in communication and information studies to present a systematic macro explanation of society.[23] Bell's core concept of post-industrialism revolves around 11 changes which he saw occurring in the middle decades of the century: 1) growing dependence on theoretical knowledge; 2) creation of a new intellectual technology derived from linear computer programming; 3) spread of a knowledge class of technocrats; 4) change in the labor force from the production of goods to the provision of services; 5) change in the character of work from actions performed on things to relations between people; 6) a new era of status for women as the rise of service work enhanced their opportunities in this traditionally woman-centered sector; 7) institutionalization of science within the interests of government and the military; 8) ascendance of new scientific, technological, and administrative estates to supersede older forms of class conflict; 9) institutionalization of meritocratic rewards and the decline of privilege resulting from inheritance and property; 10) new scarcities of information and time alongside old scarcities of material resources further complicating the problem of allocation; and, 11) new cooperative strategies to insure the optimal distribution of information in society.[24]

His litany of carefully articulated outcomes provides the opportunity for others to verify specific points and, thereby, judge aspects of the theory. In this sense, he represents a distinct advance beyond the writings of Boorstin and McLuhan. The success of Bell's approach can be seen in the large research literature which has followed his analysis and built upon the original post-industrial theme. Of special note, of course, is Porat.[25] His empirically-based findings buttressed Bell's argument and led many social scientists to equate post-industrial theory with information society theory in their writings.[26] In effect, Porat's description of the information economy and workforce transformed post-industrial theory and remade it into a theory of the information society. Nevertheless, if Bell's and Porat's post-industrial/information society theory seems to rest on solid ground, its three major assumptions have come under growing criticism.

Bell's primary assumption holds that the dominance of the service workforce, attended by new information technologies, products, industries, and a class of technocrats, signals a break with the past—a disjuncture so momentous that it required the phrase "post-industrial" to describe it. Within the logic of his theory, the discontinuity assumption forms the lynch pin, so that all other deductions derive from it. But a logical framework depending on a social disjuncture for its explanatory power requires a description of historical events on both sides of the divide; and Bell is sketchy about events prior to the break. As a result, his critics have accused him of being a selective historian.[27] Their concerns have gained support from subsequent analyses of the historical circumstances that contributed to the production and distribution of information in the 20th century. The evidence from these later studies indicates that strong continuities exist from the forces of early industrialization to those identified with the information society; with the result that, in light of these later findings, the discontinuity presupposition appears weak.[28]

Bell's second basic assumption stems from the first. Once he identified a discontinuity, he judged it to be a revolution of the same order as the boundary between agricultural society and industrial society. The root of assumption number two rests in the proposition that the rate of technological and social change increased so much, in the course of the 20th century, that it precipitated a genuine discontinuity.[29] Researchers who accept this assumption take the proliferation of informational activities and technologies as validation for the idea of an information society of revolutionary proportions.[30] However, the revolution assumption has also come under attack. As discussed in chapter 1, critics have charged that the argument for a revolution suffers from its own weak logic.[31] Plus, there is empirical evidence that the information workforce evolved more gradually than previously thought.[32] However, the greatest challenge has come from Beniger, whose historical analysis of the control revolution as a disjunctive shift in the rules for controlling processes and organizations challenges Bell's claim for a revolution resulting from a simple increase in the rate of change. Beniger's demonstration that the control revolution occurred much earlier than Bell's proposed discontinuity further weakens Bell's basic premise; and, by association, calls into question those ahistorical futuristic studies premised on the assumption that a revolution has taken place.[33]

A less obvious flaw in Bell's approach concerns the role of capitalism in the emergence of the information society. His emphasis on the organization of work and new knowledge relegates acquisitiveness and profit seeking to the shadows. Technocratic efficiency emerges as the prime mover instead of economic necessity. Capitalism is present in his theory, but with little exploration of its effect on the development of post-industrial/information society. As a result, Bell failed to anticipate the bitter controversy which developed in the '80s over the commoditization of government information—a controversy which has swelled the literature on the information society.[34] Though his book aims to inform policymakers, the absence of a discussion of capitalism prevents exploration of the dynamics by which profit seeking intensifies tensions revolving around privacy, information needs, information poverty, or universal service. Therefore, he misses the role which capitalism plays in motivating individuals and organizations to create new markets for information, and to shape patterns of distribution. His omissions underscore the importance of factoring capitalism into any macro theory of the information society. Bell deserves major credit for being the first to construct a macro theory of the information society; however, the theory's flaws invite new proposals.

A Theory of the Information Society

Without Bell's initial framework, the literature would undoubtedly exhibit less theoretical rigor, and a narrower construction of the questions. But now, the picture emerging is more complex than the tidy image presented in the 1970s, and the evidence accumulated suggests some new directions. In this section, we present the framework of a theory derived from the tendencies and tensions discussed in chapters 1 through 6.

The Underlying Framework

Capitalism and Industrialization: Capitalism and industrialization are the primary forces shaping the information society. In the United States, the motivation to profit from information markets converged with the drive to control growing enterprises, and set in motion economic and social forces which we now recognize as the tendencies and tensions of the information age. Capitalism and industrialization converged and caused a transformation in the production and distribution of information in technology, in the economy, and in the workforce.

Evolution and Continuity: The information society is one representation of industrial society. The processes of industrialization are processes for organizing production and distribution, whether the output is material, informational, or personal; therefore, evidence indicating that information occupations are organized along industrial lines supports continuity rather than discontinuity. Historical studies demonstrating that changes in information work, in media environments, and in technological innovation took place over a long period of time—occasionally punctuated by periods of rapid development—

further support continuity. Conversely, post-industrial theorists, having accepted Bell's premise that a steep increase in the rate of change denotes a social revolution, observed the explosion of computer-based technologies and then inferred a discontinuity between the information age and the industrial age. But they missed the persistence of an underlying social organization strongly rooted in the industrial system and in capitalist values. They mistook changes in the outputs of the system of production for changes in the system of production itself. And, they failed to understand that rapid changes took place in concert with the forms of organization of industrial capitalism, rather than in opposition. The information society reflects continuity with industrial society. More precisely, the information society should be thought of as a development in the evolution of industrial capitalism; i.e., an information-oriented industrial society.

Tendencies

The Idea of Information: The fundamental condition that makes the information age seem understandable is the ease with which people think of information as a thing. As a result, economic innovations—e.g., new markets for information and social perspectives derived from this attitude—e.g., judging a newspaper by the "amount" of information contained have become so common that they are taken for granted. But the idea of information, as a social construction, is so recent that we are just beginning to understand its cultural and historical roots. What is clear is that the idea of information stands as the base of the information society, because it directs thinking in such a way as to encourage the information economy, as well as the language with which we make sense of the information society.

The Information Economy: This book focuses on the social dimensions of the information society, yet a tendency described and referred to throughout these chapters is the increasing production and distribution of information in the economy. Information holds a leading role in American economic life as an item of production and consumption. Information also constitutes a major item of export. America's status within the world's economic system now depends on its ability to compete in markets for information and information technologies. The information economy serves as a point of departure because it developed out of a series of events which flag the changes discussed in this book. Though our purpose has been the elaboration of a social theory and not a model of an economic system, the growing importance of information in economic relations is among the most powerful causal and defining forces in the information society.

Information Work: The emergence of a new work sector in the course of the 20th century has altered both the reality and the popular perception of the work experience. The majority of adults now work in occupations whose primary tasks involve manipulating information in some form. Of those in this workforce, some have gained new freedoms by capitalizing on the communication-transportation trade-off, and have achieved new levels of personal productivity by exploiting computer-based technologies. Most, however, continue to experience constraints imposed by industrial forms of organization, such as segmented work, de-skilling, and automation; for, though the setting is more often the office cubicle than the factory floor, the bulk of the information labor force experiences information work as industrial work.

Predictions of the centrality of scientists and engineers have been realized. Yet neither they nor any other group of scientific experts has emerged as a new class of information elites with a distinct technocratic agenda. The nexus of power in public policy continues to depend on politicians and the interest groups that influence them, rather than on the experts. Similarly within the corporation, managers maintain control with divergent interests from those of technical staffs; and, above them stands the more subtle influence of the American upper class.[35] So, contrary to the expectations of some post-industrial scholars, the emergence of information elites has occurred within the dynamics of existing groups and classes.

Interconnectedness: Fragmentation radically increases the frequency of our interactions with strangers. To be sure, individuals continue to rely on relationships organized around family, neighbors, and fellow workers. But though people maintain a small number of primary personal relationships, the number of secondary anonymous relationships vastly increases as individuals seek to accomplish tasks by relying on information received from strangers. Consequently, Americans live daily life amidst impersonal interactions; and many—if not most—are mediated through some form of communication technology.

Over and above the level of the individual, communication media, plus the technologies of organization, create the basis for complex organizations where the need to cope with uncertainty leads to the establishment of information systems and communication channels. As organizations become even more complex, communication structures—such as lines and staffs, divisions, matrices, and liaison offices—come into play. Each effort to cope with uncertainty and complexity leads to a more elaborate pattern of communication channels within organizations. As the information age progresses, the business world appears less as a marketplace made up of autonomous firms and more as an interconnected system.

At the global level the sovereign nations of what may soon become the *ancien regime* must increasingly share the playing field with corporate and non-governmental contestants. The artifice that divided the international system into first, second, and third "worlds" no longer holds meaning. Some "third world nations" like Somalia or Angola, once capable of being treated as sovereign so that all geographic regions might be fit into the international regime, now defy all efforts to treat them as national or sovereign. The collapse of the Eastern Bloc—threatening lingering economic catastrophe, civil strife, ecological crises, and mass emigrations—amounts to a failure of those national systems responsible for ensuring social order for a large proportion of the world's population. The inadequacy of the existing frame of reference has become apparent and it has become clear that there is a need for a new paradigm enabling global economic interconnectedness. In this new climate, global relationships can be seen as more important than the particular array of resources contained within any one political unit. Beyond the nation-state, one may imagine collectives of nations, corporations, and non-governmental organizations grouped by interdependencies rather than by sovereignty and geography.

Media Environments: Throughout the 20th century, Americans have acquired a host of devices for communicating, receiving, and processing information. With them, they have furnished their homes and contrived environments capable of receiving huge quantities of messages. Today, these media environments constitute an indispensable part of life in the information society—so much so that they now typify American households.

Workers who manipulate information as labor and then manipulate information as leisure reflect a growing reality. In particular, professionals experience fuzzy boundaries when they utilize information technologies to establish work-home settings; and, in so doing, they risk the loss of the recuperative value of home and leisure. Nevertheless, the work-home environment contains the potential for approaching a more inner directed life by allowing workers to gain control of their working time and activities. Yet regardless of personal outcomes, fuzzy boundaries will become permanent features of the information society as the division between work and home undergoes renegotiation.

At work, at leisure, in the marketplace, and beyond, individuals consume information, often via several channels simultaneously. They cope with a barrage of messages by learning to ignore the bulk, in order to pay attention to a small subset. Understood implicitly, this new strategy appears to be a common adaptation in response to information overload. But whether it results in greater knowledge is unclear, since it is a strategy aimed at reducing the overload, rather than at finding the most relevant information. By adapting to their mediated environments, Americans have created a culture of information consumption; yet it cannot be claimed unequivocally that they are better informed. What is clear, in this complex picture of life in the information age, is that media environments are pervasive.

At the same time, the mass media industry has grown into a colossus delivering huge quantities of messages through diverse media, across multitudes of channels. Market segmentation contributes the dominant logic behind the use of media for marketing the goods and services of the information economy. In some media, such as magazines, radio, and direct mail catalog sales, the effects of targeted marketing and market segmentation are already apparent.

Cable and the new video dial-tone services are moving television in the same direction. Ironically, for all its vacuity, the old three network television oligopoly seems to have been an integrating force in society. Now, the development of targeted "narrowcast" media in pursuit of efficient marketing leads to a segmented and stratified society that is incapable of commonly appreciated interests, and perhaps even cohesion.

Information Technologies: They are to the flesh of the information society as capitalism and industrialism are to the spirit. So pervasive are they that numerous observers view the development of the information society as a study in technological growth. But as with any social phenomenon, the outlooks people bring with them are decisive since people's attitudes largely determine their behaviors.

Four perspectives guide the relationship between Americans and information technology. First, the technological landscape is taken as a given fact of life; and, as a result, critical analysis and choice are often overlooked. Second, among those elites most involved in the development of information technologies, science and technology meld as the pursuit of an ideal; the joys of inquiry give science a special quality which thrives, even as scientific knowledge becomes a prized commodity. Third, technological growth elicits fear as people associate new developments with threats to privacy, free speech, occupation, and culture. Fourth, technological images—especially television and the computer—have entered language, risen to dominance as metaphors, and now serve as terms by which we explain society.

The contradictions among these views are obvious, and ensure that the technological path taken will not be without conflict. Yet each perspective has a place in the culture of the information age.

Tensions

The Social Value of Information: The distribution of information will continue to be a tension in the United States because of the presence of conflicting traditions. Whether to rely on the forces of the market or to depend on government for the proper allocation of information is both the essential tension and the most basic question of information policy. Moreover, this tension was institutionalized at the very inception of the republic, thereby creating a contradiction woven into the fiber of the American system.

Privacy: In the 20th century, the construction of privacy, as the right to be left alone and protected from physical invasiveness, has expanded to include a concern for loss of control over personal information. Informational privacy is under stress as more institutions take on the functions of gathering information about individuals. But unlike earlier concerns with their focus on governments and their potential for totalitarianism, concerns today stem from the potential for invasion of privacy by private sector institutions armed with new surveillance, monitoring, recording, and matching technologies.

Political Campaigning: The predominance of big media and centralized politics leads to political campaigns controlled by a nucleus of politicians and consultants. The tendency toward big news organizations and integrated information markets dominated by a few corporations continues to coalesce, and along with it, political campaigns operating almost exclusively at the level of national media. At the same time, individuals find themselves increasingly adrift in fragmented media environments. In response, they either: abstain and become apathetic; narrow their focus to single issues and simplified images; or, in some cases, gravitate to virtual communities, even opting to exploit small media for local political purposes.

Information Poverty: The centrality of information as a primary resource sets up a new analysis of what it means to be rich or poor. Information poverty is a phenomenon first described in the 1970s that has gained attention in the 1980s and '90s. Most critics and policy makers see information poverty as a deficit condition relative to the information available to the members of society as a whole at any given time, and contend that as the information orientation of society increases so too does the moral responsibility for making information available to all of the members. However, information poverty is dialectically linked to information wealth and interwoven with impressions of economic indigence, as well as affluence. What seemed like a simple idea in the mid '70s now looks like a complex phenomenon.

Some policy remedies call for identifying a stock of information that should be distributed to everyone. There are clearly circumstances in which specific information should be provided to specific people—e.g., prenatal care practices to poor pregnant teenagers or safe sex practices to people at risk for HIV infection. But since information poverty is a relative condition, no standardized body of information will serve everyone. Instead, people are better off when they know how to access the information they want. That is, if people learn the skills of information seeking, they can choose to inform themselves.

Literacy. The question of literacy reintroduces itself in the information society. It seems anachronistic to be concerned with literacy in the information age because the legacy of popular literacy harkens back to the industrial times of the 19th century. However, the occurrence of a decline in literacy confers an unexpected urgency to one of the central questions of our time. What kind of literacy is needed for full-fledged participation in society? Everyone agrees that the kind of literacy appropriate for factory work is not sufficient for producing software, but there is no present consensus on the new configuration of skills, except perhaps for a commitment to computer literacy. That is, once beyond the 3 R's, the path becomes less certain. In other words, what policy initiatives can the nation take to insure that all possess the key to participation? The policy debate heats up on this issue, and properly so. Some argue that in the future we will have information technologies with natural language speech recognition and virtual reality user interfaces which will allow information work to be done without need of literacy or numeracy. But simple trend analysis suggests the opposite. Every new generation of information technology (except, perhaps, video games) comes with a larger and more complex—some would say less comprehensible—documentation and set of instructions. So, there should be little doubt that for the foreseeable future, reading and writing will continue as the basic building blocks of access to information.

Universal Service: In response to the emergence of a new information infrastructure, a debate has emerged around the need for a basic universal service available to all. However, despite the ongoing development of the information infrastructure, the fundamental importance of universal service to the progress of the information society has yet to be recognized beyond the policy elites. What the policy debate does reflect is that universal service is not really a single policy to be written by any one government agency. So important is universal service, that it might better be understood as an information bill of rights. That is, in pursuit of a democratic society, Americans must ultimately ask themselves, what rights to information, and protections from information, pertain to all, regardless of their wealth, position, or language? If that question is to find an answer, then the redefinition of universal service must find a place on the public agenda.

Women: Predictions that the growth of information occupations would diminish the gender gap by raising the status of jobs traditionally held by women have not been realized. For one thing, central institutions, like universities and banks, have been slow to open their doors to women and minority professionals. Expectations of equality failed to anticipate the establishment of glass ceilings and the injection of male competitiveness to information work cultures. Still, women *have* made advances in the workforce. The demand for literate well-educated workers seems to have outstripped the supply of men, thereby boosting opportunities for women; and, quite apart from the tendencies of the information society, changing views, combined with political pressure, have slowly opened economic territory.

In the information sector, women find some of "their" jobs rising in status, as organizations realign themselves around the production and distribution of information. Within this climate, the decreased physical strength demands of many information jobs opens them up more easily, so that women entering these occupations are not so likely to encounter barriers which set jobs aside as "men's" work. Those jobs that facilitate interconnectedness carry few preconceived associations with masculinity within their occupational cultures.

For the most part, there is reason to be optimistic that the information age will provide opportunities for women to advance in the workplace.

African-Americans and Latinos: These two ethnic minorities make up 20% of the population of the United States.[36] In a nation marked by rich ethnic diversity, African-Americans and Latinos will have significant impact on the information society, by virtue of their changing numbers in media markets. Media aimed at them will profit from increased advertising revenues because, as distinct segments of the total audience, they—especially Latinos—are growing faster than the rest of the population.[37] In numerous metropolitan areas, as marketers increasingly segment Anglo audiences, minority audiences remain as large, identifiable segments, with the result that advertising aimed at minorities becomes more visible.[38] In addition, minorities, particularly African-Americans, are increasing their numbers within the mainstream media. In television, African-American actors regularly appear in prime-time. In print media, African-Americans and Latinos figure in news genres from which they were omitted a decade ago. But though these advances convey the impression that minorities are entering communication industries in large numbers, major barriers still exist. Behind the screen, minorities have found the ranks of producers, directors, and technical staffs slow to open, and few have broken into newsrooms as reporters, editors, or publishers. An imbalance persists; for, though they are readily identifiable as media consumers, African-Americans and Latinos have yet to convert their new found visibility into success as media producers.

Latinos represent an important challenge to equity in the information society, because they contain a large percentage of Spanish-speakers. As information becomes the primary product of the information economy, language becomes a strategic resource far beyond its importance in the old industrial era. Latinos, motivated to improve their levels of economic development and political participation, will likely press for greater access to information resources in Spanish. The logic of an open democracy will encourage them to do so. Yet such efforts are sure to trigger deep seated resistance by other Americans who fear the institutionalization of any language other than English. This is sure to result in renewed conflict over a national language, with calls to enforce the use of English becoming more strident. As a result, the idea of guaranteeing information to all, while seeming simple enough, will reignite the issue of English as a badge of national identity. It is hard to imagine a harmonious resolution; instead, the language sensitive nature of the information society leads us to predict an enduring conflict.

So, while the place of minorities in the information society will be affected by external factors deeply rooted in racism, economics, and culture, the realignment of forces brought about by the information society will bring consumption, employment, and language to center stage.

The Logic of Images: Constrained by the vast scale of American society, individuals increasingly experience important realities through images they receive from the media. Americans depend on mediated images to learn about the people, institutions, and events which affect their lives—even within their own communities. Though written over thirty years ago, Boorstin's warning in *The Image* contains particular significance since, to a large extent, the information society is also an image society.

But, while much of this mediation is the predictable consequence of the conditions which brought about the information society, the concentration on image as a primary goal of public communication is cause for concern. Increasingly, institutions address the improvement of their images as the solution to problems of substantive performance. Likewise, public figures concentrate on image management, to maintain the esteem of the citizenry. The logic of this strategy holds that public relations campaigns offer greater payoffs than direct redressing of the problem itself. Ushered to its current level by Ronald Reagan and the Republicans in the 1980s, the logic of images has spread to corporations and other public institutions. In 1991, the U.S. Post Office spent over 100 million dollars on a public relations campaign to improve its image by associating the Post Office with the Olympic Games, at a time when patrons were complaining of slow mail delivery.

However, image manipulation inserts a barrier between the public and those who control the nation's institutions. It furthermore threatens to create a real malaise within the information society which is likely to grow over time. Because image manipulation is such a tempting response to intractable tensions, there is the threat that fewer and fewer solutions will be sought to real problems and more and more attempts will be made simply to doctor the spin on the story as it is told in the media. The irony is that technological advances in interconnectedness hold the potential for informing the public as never before, yet these very technologies have become tools for manipulating public opinion. In an age of media and interconnectedness, the public will find it ever harder to inform itself, and this will nourish cynicism and contempt. The theory of the information society that emerges from this analysis of tendencies and tensions stresses a long term evolution triggered by the relationship between capitalism and industrialization, and facilitated by the emergence of the idea of information. The resulting manifestations can be observed across the topography of society; yet their visibility is not the key to the information society. To find the key, one must understand how the idea of information, as developed in the context of industrial capitalism, has resulted in an accelerating evolution.

This theory we propose in this book will not find ready acceptance in the popular mind. It challenges a widely accepted image of the information society that derives its explanation from appearances. The appearances seem to suggest discontinuity—that America is in the grip of one of the greatest transformations in human history. The visible evidence comes from the spread of personal computers, fax machines, photocopiers, "smart" typewriters, multitask telephone systems, and electronic mail in the office environment, as well as

VCRs, portable radios and TVs, cable TV, video games, CD and CD-ROM players, and microwave ovens in the home. The fact that these devices are directly observable constitutes, for many people, all the evidence necessary to pronounce the existence of the information age. Since the basis for this evidence comes from material objects, rather than from patterns of human behavior, a strong sense of technological determinism permeates the popular view. Reflecting this assumption, one regularly finds simplistic statements in the trade press declaring that the computer caused the nature of work to change in the 1980s, or that the VCR revived the movie industry. In the popular press, journalists and commentators alert audiences to be on the lookout for the next great invention that will change everyone's lives. As a result, more complex social changes remain in the shadows. Not surprisingly, individuals draw the conclusion that society is driven by its material creations and that people are along for the ride. The thrust of this rendition holds that the sum of these obvious changes represents a profound break with history, and with the social forces that caused the past to be as it was.

Of course, this interpretation would not find adherents were it not so deeply rooted in the underlying beliefs of American culture. Belief in the power of technology, progress, and their special place in history leads Americans to accept theories based on superficial changes. In this sense, most popular interpretations of the information society are not irrational, but constructed within a materialistic and technologically deterministic logic. But it is a logic that overlooks the human motivations behind the changes that Americans observe so readily. Therefore, the application of assembly line methods in software companies goes unappreciated because the material environment of a software company does not resemble the environment of a garment factory. Similarly, managerial decisions to alter relationships in the office by replacing workers with machines are seen as inevitable, rather than as conscious choices. In the long run, shallow causal explanations mean that, for most people, the concept of the information society falls into the category of a fashionable idea. That is, because it is not grounded in any rigorous or disciplined analysis, the popular interpretation of the information society will wax or wane depending on the rhetoric in vogue.

Yet the popular view is itself a measure of the evolution of the information society. For one thing, the idea of information is transparent in the popular view; that is, Americans have so completely incorporated the idea of information into their daily lives, that an information-oriented perspective makes sense, even though the underlying social construction remains invisible. Ironically, the very invisibility of the idea of information provides evidence for its dynamic presence in American culture. If the idea of information were not fully assimilated by Americans, they would feel uncomfortable with information-based explanations, e.g., the recognition that directory assistance, executive head-hunting services, political campaigns, banking, credit, etc., can be grouped together under the rubric of information. Also, by ignoring the past and depending on discontinuity to explain the information age, Americans reveal the lack of importance they assign to history. Yet, though the majority of Americans might be comfortable with a technologically deterministic, ahistorical interpretation of the evolution of the information society, the fact that they can pin its emergence to a period in time—the postwar computer revolution—implies a historical explanation open to analysis and revision. Thus, the popular view contains hidden but important contradictions; and, it is from these that we derive the theory presented in this book.

We have attempted to look beneath the surface in order to uncover an invisible mindset, a misunderstood history, social changes too pervasive to be observed, and counter-intuitive consequences of human behavior. From these excavations, we have assembled a mosaic depicting Americans and their images of the information society.

Ultimately, a theory of the information society is a method for constructing reality; because, like McCallum's organization chart, Shannon's definition of information, or Boorstin's and McLuhan's near theories, it offers an explanation. Although aspects of the tendencies and tensions observed in this book are visible and experienced on a daily basis, their larger meanings are not obvious. Therefore, by moving beyond anecdote and conjecture, we have sought a stricter logic and a more rigorous standard of analysis, in order to gain a greater understanding of this intricate social transformation.

Once articulated, social theories always lead to more questions concerning the quality of people's lives. And so we are left with the most important questions facing all who seek to understand the information age—Will the information society be a just society? Will the quality of people's lives be improved? The answers will depend on how well all of us understand the real choices confronting us, and their consequences. To that end, we hope that the readers of this book have become better informed.

Notes

1. Boorstin, D. J. (1961). *The image: A guide to pseudo-events in America.* New York: Atheneum, p. 61.
2. McLuhan, M. (1964). *Understanding media: The extensions of man.* New York: New American Library, p. 60.
3. Bell, D. (1976). *The coming of post-industrial society.* New York: Basic Books, p. xiii.
4. Boorstin, D. J. (1961). McLuhan, M. (1964). McLuhan, M. (1962). *The Gutenberg Galaxy: The making of typographic man.* New York: New American Library. McLuhan, M., & Fiore, Q. (1967). *The medium is the massage.* New York: Bantam.
5. "Communication and information studies" serves as a collective label for fields which share common interests, including library studies, information science, journalism, mass media studies, mass communications studies, speech communi-

cation, organizational communication, health communication, political communication, and telecommunications. For discussions of the relationships among the subfields, see Borgman, C. L., & Schement, J. R. (1990). Information science and communication research. In J. M. Pemberton & A. E. Prentice (Eds.), *Information science: The interdisciplinary context* (pp. 42–59). New York: Neal-Schuman. Paisley, W. J. (1986). The convergence of communication and information science. In H. Edelman (Ed.), *Libraries and information science in the electronic age*. Philadelphia, PA: ISI Press. Paisley, W. J. (1990). *Communication science: The growth of a multidiscipline*. Norwood, NJ: Ablex. Reeves, B., & Borgman, C. L. (1983). A bibliometric evaluation of core journals in communication research. *Human Communication Research, 10*(1), 119–136. Rice, R. E. (1988). Citation networks of communication journals, 1977–1985: Cliques and positions, citations made and citations received. *Human Communication Research, 15*(2), 256–283.

6. Bell, D. (1976).

7. Dertouzos, M. L., & Moses, J. (Eds.). (1979). *The computer age*. Cambridge, MA: MIT Press. Dizard, W. P. J. (1982). *The coming information age: An overview of technology, economics, and politics*. New York: Longman. Dordick, H. S. (1988). The emerging information societies. In J. R. Schement & L. Lievrouw (Eds.), *Competing visions, complex realities: Social aspects of the information society* (pp. 13–22). Norwood, NJ: Ablex. Dordick, H. S., & Georgette, W. (1993). *The information society: A retrospective view*. Newbury Park, CA: Sage. Edelstein, A. S., Bowes, J. E., & Harsel, S. M. (1978). *Information societies: Comparing the Japanese and American experiences*. Seattle, WA: University of Washington. Katz, R. L. (1988). *The Information Society*. New York: Praeger. Martin, J. (1981). *Telematic society: A challenge for tomorrow*. New York: Prentice-Hall. Masuda, Y. (1981). *The information society as post-industrial society*. Bethesda, MD: World Future Society. Masuda, Y. (1985). Parameters of the post-industrial society: Computopia. In T. Forester (Ed.), *The information technology revolution* (pp. 620–634). Cambridge, MA: MIT. Naisbitt, J. (1982). *Megatrends*. New York: Warner Books. Nora, S., & Minc, A. (1980). *The computerization of society: A report to the president of France*. Cambridge, MA: MIT Press. Ochai, A. (1984). The emerging information society. *International Library Review, 16*(4), 367–372. Porat, M. U. (1977). *The information economy: Definition and measurement*. No. OT Special Publication 77-12 (1). Washington DC: Department of Commerce/Office of Telecommunications. Toffler, A. (1980). *The third wave*. New York: William Morrow. Williams, F. (1982). *The communications revolution*. Beverly Hills, CA: Sage. Williams, F. (1988). The information society as an object of study. In F. Williams (Ed.), *Measuring the information society* (pp. 13–31). Newbury Park, CA: Sage.

8. We use the term "macro theory" to refer to any theory which operates at the level of abstraction where the unit of analysis consists of aggregates of groups or organizations; in contrast to micro studies, where the unit of analysis is the individual; and, in contrast to middle range studies, where the unit of analysis is a single group or organization.

9. See, for example, Bauer, R. A. (1964). The obstinate audience: The influence process from the point of view of social communication. *American Psychologist, 19*, 319–328. Boorstin, D. J. (1961). *The image: A guide to pseudo-events in America*. New York: Atheneum. Boulding, K. (1953). *The organizational revolution*. New York: Harper & Row. Boulding, K. (1956). *The image*. Ann Arbor, MI: University of Michigan Press. Cooley, C. H. (1909). *Social Orga-*

nization. New York: Charles Scribner's Sons. DeFleur, M. (1966). *Theories of mass communication*. New York: David McKay. Hovland, C. I. (1959). Reconciling conflicting results derived from experimental and survey studies of attitude change. *American Psychologist, 14*, 8–17. Innis, H. A. (1950). *Empire and communication*. Toronto, Canada: University of Toronto. Innis, H. A. (1951). *The bias of communication*. Toronto, Canada: University of Toronto. Katz, E., & Lazarsfeld, P. F. (1955). *Personal influence: The part played by people in the flow of mass communication*. New York: Free Press. Lasswell, H. D. (1948). The structure and function of communication in society. In L. Bryson (Ed.), *The communication of ideas*. New York: Institute for Religious and Social Studies. Lazarsfeld, P. F., & Merton, R. K. (1948). Mass communication, popular taste, and organized social action. In L. Bryson (Ed.), *The communication of ideas*. New York: Institute for Religious and Social Studies. Lerner, D. (1958). *The passing of traditional society: Modernizing the Middle East*. New York: Free Press. Lippmann, W. (1921). *Public opinion*. New York: Free Press. McLuhan, M. (1958). Media alchemy in art and society. *Journal of Communication, 8*, 63–67. Schramm, W. (1948). *Communications in modern society*. Urbana, IL: University of Illinois. Schramm, W. (Ed.). (1955). *The process and effects of mass communication*. Urbana, IL: University of Illinois. Schramm, W., Lyle, J., & Parker, E. B. (1961). *Television in the lives of our children*. Stanford, CA: Stanford University. Williams, R. (1962). *Britain in the sixties: Communications*. Baltimore, MD: Penguin.

10. By proposing a theory that is "verifiable," we do not mean to imply that the social sciences can operate at the same level of replicability as the physical sciences; for, unlike biology or physics, in the social sciences, the investigator examines human behavior, so that the observer shares many qualities with the observed. Social scientists must adapt their modes of inquiry to this reality and still adhere to standards of clarity, logic, and empirical analysis, so that others may "verify" their research.

11. Boorstin, D. J. (1961), p. 5.

12. Boorstin, D. J. (1961), pp. 259–261.

13. McLuhan, M., & Fiore, Q. (1967).

14. Innis, H. A. (1950). Innis, H. A. (1951). Most scholars agree that McLuhan derived his ideas from those of his mentor, Harold Innis. Innis was a graduate of the University of Chicago where he studied under Robert Ezra Park and was influenced by the work of Siegfried Giedion. Park's and Giedion's views on technology strongly influenced Innis, contributing to the element of technological determinism in his writings, and later in McLuhan's. Giedion, S. (1948). *Mechanization takes command: A contribution to anonymous history*. New York: W. W. Norton. Park, R. E. (1916). The city: Suggestions for the investigation of human behavior in the urban environment. *American Journal of Sociology, 20*, 577–612.

15. McLuhan, M., & Fiore, Q. (1967).

16. McLuhan, M. (1964) p. ix.

17. McLuhan, M. (1962) p. 325.

18. McLuhan, M. (1964) p. 64.

19. In summarizing McLuhan's ideas, we have shortchanged his breadth and complexity. Furthermore, we have limited our discussion to McLuhan's writings prior to 1970. As a result, the new directions which he charted in the '70s remain outside of our focus.

20. McLuhan, M. (1964) p. 36.

21. McLuhan, M. (1964) p. 261.

22. McLuhan, M. (1964) p. 67. McLuhan, M. (1968). *War and peace in the global village*. New York: Bantam Books.
23. What's in a name? In the 1980s, after Porat published *The Information Economy*, Machlup's term "knowledge" came to be replaced by "information." However, the reader should be aware of continuing sources of confusion, because "information society" has gained greater acceptance in the communication and information studies literature; whereas, in sociology and history, "post-industrial" seems to hold wider currency. Moreover, the differing usages are meaningful. "Information society" expresses the central focus of communication and information studies, while "post-industrial" expresses the importance of the industrial experience in the literatures of sociology and history. Conscious of academic boundaries, Bell understandably rejected the label "information society" as a descriptor for his theory, when he first published *The Coming of Post-Industrial Society* [p. ix]. But, later, perhaps due to the popularity of the term, he reversed himself accepting "post-industrial society" and "information society" as equivalent. Bell, D. (1976). Bell, D. (1981). Porat, M. U. (1977).
24. Bell, D. (1976) pp. xvi-xix.
25. Porat, M. U. (1977).
26. See, for example, Cleveland, H. (1982). People lead their leaders in an information society. In H. F. J. Didsbury (Ed.), *Communications and the future: Prospects, promises, and problems* (pp. 167-173). Bethesda, MD: World Future Society. Crawford, S. (1983). The origin and development of a concept: The information society. *Bulletin of the Medical Library Association, 71*(4), 380-385. Cuilenburg, J. J. v. (1987). The information society: Some trends and implications. *European Journal of Communication, 2,* 105-121. Dizard, W. P. J. (1982). *The coming information age: An overview of technology, economics, and politics*. New York: Longman. Dordick, H. S. (1988). The emerging information societies. In J. R. Schement & L. Lievrouw (Eds.), *Competing visions, complex realities: Social aspects of the information society* (pp. 13-22). Norwood, NJ: Ablex. Edelstein, A. S., Bowes, J. E., & Harsel, S. M. (1978). *Information societies: Comparing the Japanese and American experiences*. Seattle, WA: University of Washington. Martin, J. (1981). *Telematic society: A challenge for tomorrow*. New York: Prentice-Hall. Masuda, Y. (1981). *The information society as post-industrial society*. Bethesda, MD: World Future Society. Nora, S., & Minc, A. (1980). *The computerization of society: A report to the president of France*. Cambridge, MA: MIT Press. Ochai, A. (1984). The emerging information society. *International Library Review, 16*(4), 367-372. Pelton, N. J. (1983). Life in the information society. In J. L. Salvaggio (Ed.), *Telecommunications: Issues and choices for society* New York: Longman. Williams, F. (1982). *The communications revolution*. Beverly Hills, CA: Sage.
27. Harrington, M. (1977). Post-Industrial society and the welfare state. In L. Estabrook (Ed.), *Libraries in post-industrial society* (pp. 19-29). Phoenix, AZ: Oryx Press. Stearns, P. N. (1984). The idea of post-industrial society: Some problems. *Journal of Social History, 17* (Summer), 685-694.
28. Badham, R. (1984). The sociology of industrial and post-industrial societies. *Current sociology: La sociologie contemporaine, 32*(1), 1-135. Beniger, J. R. (1986). *The control revolution*. Cambridge, MA: Harvard University Press. Rosenbrock, H. e. a. (1985). A new industrial revolution? In T. Forester (Ed.), *The information technology revolution*. (pp. 635-647). Cambridge, MA: MIT. Schement, J. R. (1989). The origins of the information society in the United States: Competing visions. In J. Salvaggio (Ed.), *The information society* (pp. 29-50).

New York: Lawrence Erlbaum. Schement, J. R., & Lievrouw, L. A. (1988). A third vision: Capitalism and the industrial origins of the information society. In J. R. Schement & L. Lievrouw (Eds.), *Competing visions, complex realities: Social aspects of the information society* (pp. 33-45). Norwood, NJ: Ablex.

29. Bell, D. (1976) pp. 345-346.
30. See, for example, Baer, W. (1978). Telecommunications technology in the 1980s. In G. O. Robinson (Ed.), *Communications for tomorrow: Policy perspectives for the 1980s* (pp. 61-123). New York: Praeger. Chen, D., & Novik, R. (1984). Scientific and technological education for an information society. *Science education, 68*(4), 421-426. Cleveland, H. (1982). People lead their leaders in an information society. In H. F. J. Didsbury (Ed.), *Communications and the future: Prospects, promises, and problems* (pp. 167-173). Bethesda, MD: World Future Society. Cuilenburg, J. J. v. (1987). The information society: Some trends and implications. *European Journal of Communication, 2*, 105-121. Dizard, W. P. J. (1982). *The coming information age: An overview of technology, economics, and politics.* New York: Longman. Dordick, H. S. (1988). The emerging information societies. In J. R. Schement & L. Lievrouw (Eds.), *Competing visions, complex realities: Social aspects of the information society* (pp. 13-22). Norwood, NJ: Ablex. Dordick, H. S., & Georgette, W. (1993). *The information society: A retrospective view.* Newbury Park, CA: Sage. Edelstein, A. S., Bowes, J. E., & Harsel, S. M. (1978). *Information societies: Comparing the Japanese and American experiences.* Seattle, WA: University of Washington. Martin, J. (1981). *Telematic society: A challenge for tomorrow.* New York: Prentice-Hall. Masuda, Y. (1981). *The information society as post-industrial society.* Bethesda, MD: World Future Society. Masuda, Y. (1985). Parameters of the post-industrial society: Computopia. In T. Forester (Eds.), *The information technology revolution* (pp. 620-634). Cambridge, MA: MIT. Naisbitt, J. (1982). *Megatrends.* New York: Warner Books. Nora, S., & Minc, A. (1980). *The computerization of society: A report to the president of France.* Cambridge, MA: MIT Press. Ochai, A. (1984). The emerging information society. *International Library Review, 16*(4), 367-372. Rogers, E. M., & Larsen, J. K. (1984). *Silicon valley fever: Growth of high-technology culture.* New York: Basic Books. Salvaggio, J. L. (1983). The telecommunications revolution: Are we up to the challenge? In J. L. Salvaggio (Ed.), *Telecommunications: Issues and choices for society.* New York: Longman. Toffler, A. (1980). *The third wave.* New York: William Morrow. Williams, F. (1979). Communication in the year 2000. In D. Nimmo (Ed.), *Communication yearbook 3* New Brunswick, NJ: Transaction-ICA. Williams, F. (1982). *The communications revolution.* Beverly Hills, CA: Sage.
31. Robins, K., & Webster, F. (1986). *Information technology: post-industrial society or capitalist control?* Norwood, NJ: Ablex. Rosenbrock, H. e. a. (1985). A new industrial revolution? In T. Forester (Ed.), *The information technology revolution* (pp. 635-647). Cambridge, MA: MIT. Schiller, H. I. (1983). Information for what kind of society? In J. L. Salvaggio (Ed.), *Telecommunications: Issues and choices for society* (pp. 24-33). New York: Longman. Schiller, H. I. (1988). Old foundations for a new (information) age. In J. R. Schement & L. Lievrouw (Eds.), *Competing visions, complex realities: Social aspects of the information society* (pp. 23-31). Norwood, NJ: Ablex. Slack, J., & Fejes, F. (1987). *The ideology of the information age.* Norwood, NJ: Ablex. Slack, J. D. (1984). The information revolution as ideology. *Media, Culture, and Society, 6*(July), 247. Stearns, P. N. (1984). The idea of post-industrial society: Some problems. *Journal of Social History, 17*(Summer), 685-694.

32. Schement, J. R. (1990). Porat, Bell, and the information society reconsidered: The growth of information work in the early twentieth century. *Information Processing and Management, 26*(4), 449–465.

33. Beniger, J. R. (1986). *The control revolution.* Cambridge, MA: Harvard University Press. For example, the following speculations depend on an acceptance of Bell's discontinuity for their focus. Cleveland, H. (1982). Dizard, W. P. J. (1982). Martin, J. (1981). Naisbitt, J. (1982). Nora, S., & Minc, A. (1980). Salvaggio, J. L. (1983). Toffler, A. (1980). Williams, F. (1982). And, Jennings, L. (1982). Utopia: Can we get there from here—by computer? In H. F. Didsbury Jr. (Ed.), *Communications and the future: Prospects, promises, and problems* (pp. 48–52). Bethesda, MD: World Future Society.

34. See, for example, Hayes, R. M. (Ed.). (1985). *Libraries and the Information Economy of California: A conference sponsored by the California State Library.* Los Angeles, CA: GSLIS/UCLA. Hepworth, M., & Robins, K. (1988). Whose information society?: A view from the periphery. *Media, Culture and Society, 10,* 323–343. Hixson, R. F. (1985). Whose life is it anyway? Information as property. In B. D. Ruben (Ed.), *Information and behavior: Volume 1* (pp. 76–92). New Brunswick, NJ: Transaction. Intner, S. S., & Schement, J. R. (1987). The ethic of free service. *Library Journal* (1 October), 50–52. Kibirige, H. M. (1983). *The information dilemma: A critical analysis of information pricing and the fees controversy.* Westport, CN: Greenwood Press. Mosco, V. (1989). *The pay-per-view society: Computers and communication in the information age.* Norwood, NJ: Ablex. Robins, K., & Webster, F. (1986). *Information technology: post-industrial society or capitalist control?* Norwood, NJ: Ablex. Schement, J. R., & Lievrouw, L. A. (Eds.) (1988). *Competing visions, complex realities: Social aspects of the information society.* Norwood, NJ: Ablex. Schiller, H. I. (1985). Privatizing the public sector: The information connection. In B. D. Ruben (Ed.), *Information and behavior: Volume 1* (pp. 387–405). New Brunswick, NJ: Transaction. Slack, J., & Fejes, F. (1987). *The ideology of the information age.* Norwood, NJ: Ablex. Wessel, A. E. (1976). *The social use of information: Ownership and access.* New York: John Wiley & Sons.

35. For a review of theories of class and class domination, see Baltzell, E. D. (1964). *The protestant establishment: Aristocracy and caste in America.* New York: Vintage Books. Bottomore, T. B. (1964). *Elites and society.* Harmondsworth, UK: Penguin Books. DeMott, B. (1990). *The imperial middle: Why americans can't think straight about class.* New Haven, CN: Yale University Press. Domhoff, G. W. (1967). *Who rules America?* Englewood Cliffs, NJ: Prentice-Hall.

Domhoff, G. W. (1970). *The higher circles: The governing class in america.* New York: Vintage. Domhoff, G. W. (1974). *The bohemian grove and other retreats: A study in ruling-class cohesiveness.* New York: Harper & Row. Domhoff, G. W. (1978). *The powers that be: Processes of ruling-class domination in america.* New York: Vintage. Ehrenreich, B. (1990). *Fear of falling: The inner life of the middle class.* New York: Harper Perennial. Giddens, A. (1973). *The class structure of advanced societies.* New York: Hutchinson, Anchor Press. Giddens, A., & Held, D. (Eds.). (1982). *Classes, power, and conflict: Classical and contemporary debates.* Berkeley, CA: University of California. Gilbert, D., & Kahl, J. A. (1982). *The American class structure.* Homewood, IL: Dorsey Press. Mills, C. W. (1956). *The power elite.* Oxford, UK: Oxford University Press. Moore, T. S. (1985). The class patterning of work orientation. *Social Science Journal, 22*(2), 61–76. Newman, K. S. (1989). *Falling from grace: The experience of downward mobility in the American middle class.* New York: Vintage. Piven, F. F., & Cloward, R.

A. (1971). *Regulating the poor: The functions of public welfare*. New York: Vintage. Ryan, W. (1971). *Blaming the victim*. New York: Vintage. Sennett, R., & Cobb, J. (1972). *The hidden injuries of class*. New York: Vintage Books. Veblen, T. (1899/1918). *The theory of the leisure class: an economic study of institutions*. New York: The Modern Library. Warner, W. L. (1960). *Social class in America: A manual of procedure for the measurement of social status*. New York: Harper Torchbooks.

36. Tables 11, and 45 (1990). *Statistical abstract of the United States: 1990*. Washington DC: Bureau of the Census.

37. Table 84 (1990). *Statistical abstract of the United States: 1990*. Washington DC: Bureau of the Census. There are other large minority groups, but, for the sake of simplicity, we use "minorities" to refer to African-Americans and Latinos.

38. We use the term "Anglos" as it is popularly used in the Western and Southwestern United States, to identify Americans of non-Hispanic, European descent.

Appendix A

The Information Society without Capitalism

Can the information society develop without capitalism? Certainly the history of the American experience argues against such a possibility. But since each nation develops within its own historical context, the American case can only point to a direction. It is no template. If we wish to understand the range of possibilities, then there is value in considering a very different social system—one dominated by central planning. If it seems odd to consider the significance of central planning at a time when State Communism has collapsed, keep in mind that though the balance has shifted central planning continues to play a role in most of the world's countries. The experience of the former Soviet Union offers insights into a course of development different from that experienced by the United States, especially since industrialization took place there without the motor of capitalism.[1]

First, there are the similarities.[2] For all practical purposes the people of the former Soviet empire enjoy universal literacy, an important accomplishment since literacy constitutes the foundation skill for all production and distribution of information and establishes a necessary condition for the rise of an information society. Moreover, the rate of college educated adults among the population stands at 12.5% (1987), and compares favorably with 20% in the U.S. (1986).[3] With these conditions alone, some of the former Soviet republics have the potential for a broadly based information society.

But there are major disparities. In terms of point-to-point interconnectedness, the Soviets achieved 110 telephones per 1,000 population in 1986, placing them in the same vicinity with Panama (104), and Uruguay (128). By contrast, penetration of telephones per 1,000 population stood at 654 in Canada (1984), 555 in Japan (1985), and 789 in the U.S. (1981) in the same period. Since most telephones in the former Soviet republics are located in the workplace and lack enhanced capabilities, the potential for interconnecting individuals lags seriously behind Western information societies. Interconnectedness via television broadcasting depicts a slightly different picture. In 1986, the Soviets reckoned 299 TV receivers in use per 1,000 population placing them within the range of most European countries, but behind Japan (580) and the U.S. (798).[4] However, encouraged first by Glasnost and now by the independence of the individual republics, it seems likely that many, if not all, of the republics to move rapidly toward the creation of a mass television audience akin to those existing in Western information societies.[5] Nevertheless, the telephone bottleneck will have to be overcome if an interconnected society is to emerge. Similarly, the distribution of computers, a measure of the productive capacity of an information society, trails far behind the West. By one estimate, the Soviets counted less than 25 computers per 100,000 population in 1980, whereas, the Americans tallied approximately 275, and the Swiss 450.[6]

It is reasonable to ask whether any of the republics possess an information workforce with sufficient skills to exploit the advantages of investments in information technologies. At least until the separate national economies make the transition from centralized planning to market driven allocation, a large portion of the labor force will continue to work in the central bureaucracy and hold information occupations. However, estimating its size and dimensions proves difficult since the bureaucracy contains workers from all sectors of the economy. Still, it seems likely that, in most republics, a large information work-force exists and the experience of information work is familiar. When added to the new emphasis on computer literacy in education, claims of a new labor force prepared to meet the needs of modern information industries do not seem farfetched, especially in those republics that are industrially advanced.

Yet if the new Russia, or any of the other republics, hope to construct an information economy, then they must organize themselves around information technologies. And, they need an information infrastructure to bear the load of the distribution of information for economic and social purposes. The drawback is that information functions have traditionally been located in the bureaucracy, which is itself an information technology. However, bureaucrats tend to horde information because control of information brings power. For example, personal computers, which open access to information, mean a decrease in control over information. Thus, an instrument capable of opening up the economies of the new republics stands within a tradition that opposes openness. It is a dilemma. To move forward, the bureaucrats must overcome their fear of information in the hands of citizens. So, unlike the United States where the desire for profit has driven much informatization, in Russia the motivating force stems from a different institution. Even in the era of Perestroika, the large government bureaucracy allocated information goods and services.

There is also a necessity for the idea of information. For the bureaucracies to modernize and for information technology to make sense, the idea of information must diffuse as a cultural fact throughout the former Soviet empire, just as it did in Western information societies. People at all levels must "understand" information as a thing. But if tradition is followed, the new leaders will seek to fashion information economies from the top down; whereas, in the West, the idea of information developed in the course of daily life.

Communism and industrialism produced the basis for a different kind of information society, one in which a central bureaucracy sustained the low growth of the information economy, the profile of the information work-force, and the distribution of information technologies. Whether that kind of information society can make the transition to an information economy driven by the market remains to be seen. But given the presence, among the population, of suitable levels of education and familiarity with information technologies, there exists greater potential than for many market oriented developing nations.

For the moment, talk across the republics is of casting off the Communist yoke and embracing open market capitalism, though private entrepreneurs are met, just as often, with ambivalence. Information markets are likely to grow, even if the obvious political value of controlling information resources will temper unconditional faith in the market. Undoubtedly, some of the republics will make the transition earlier and in better shape; but all will carry with them the shadow of Soviet culture and its wariness of open communication and easily available information.

Notes

1. Industrialization spread during the 1890s from Russia's coal, cotton, and pig iron centers. But the present economy takes its shape from Stalin's 5-year plans of the late 1920s and 1930s. Rostow, W. W. (1978). *The world economy: History & prospect.* Austin, TX: University of Texas Press, Ch. 34 (pp. 426–437).
2. A clear statistical picture of the old Soviet Union is hard to come by; as a result, the following inferences rely on scanty data.
3. *Statistical abstract of the United States: 1988* Washington DC: Bureau of the Census. Pollard, A. P. (1990). Education level of population 1939–1987. In A. P. Pollard (Ed.), *USSR facts and figures annual* (pp. 371–383). Academic International Press.
4. Figures for Japan and the U.S. are for 1985. (1988). *World statistics in brief* (Department of International Economic and Social Affairs Statistical Office Statistical Papers—Series V, No. 12 ed.). New York: United Nations Publication.
5. Mickiewicz, E. (1988). *Split signals.* New York: Oxford Press (pp. 3–30).
6. Any calculation of the numbers of computers in use in the USSR contains a large error margin. For example, Dizard and Swensrud estimate a total of 100,000 computers in use during the middle 1980s. Dizard, W. P., & Swensrud, S. B. (1987). *Gorbachev's information revolution: Controlling Glasnost in a new electronic age.* Boulder, CO: Westview Press, p. 35. But if so, this indicates an extraordinary drop from Katz' 1988 estimate of nearly 6 million for 1980, which doesn't seem likely. Katz, R. L. (1988). *The information society.* New York: Praeger, p. 99.

Appendix B

The Electronic Cottage and Walden Pond

Beyond release from physical constraints, information and communication technologies also facilitate psychological escape, and in so doing may help us to recapture a lost world by preserving an old myth. In American culture, pastoralism, the vision of living a simple rural life, forms a loose ideal for many urban dwellers. As Leo Marx observed in his analysis of technology and the pastoral ideal in America,

> It is widely diffused in our culture, insinuating itself into many kinds of behavior. An obvious example is the current "flight from the city." An inchoate longing for a more "natural" environment enters into the contemptuous attitude that many Americans adopt toward urban life [with the result that we neglect our cities and desert them for the suburbs].[1] [his brackets and quotes]

Actually, it is an old vision—one that is as intertwined with the industrial revolution as is the information society itself. As early as the founding of the republic, Thomas Jefferson's desire for a nation of yeomen farmers, to serve as the bulwark of democracy, embodied the pastoral ideal by viewing country as superior to city.[2] In fact, however, by the middle decades of the 19th century, Jefferson's America was dying, so that an individual seeking protection from the contamination of industrial civilization could only flee, as Thoreau did to Walden pond.

> Every morning was a cheerful invitation to make my life of equal simplicity, and I may say innocence, with Nature herself.... I went to the woods because I wished to live deliberately, to front only the essential facts of life, and to see if I could not learn what it had to teach, and not, when I came to die, discover that I had not lived.[3]

Thoreau's declaration of the moral superiority of the bucolic has continued to find a response in generation after generation. But unlike Thoreau, his followers have attempted to take part of the city to the country.

The information society's version can be found in the electronic cottage. In theory, the availability of phone links and personal computers offers unprecedented interconnectedness, allowing information workers to exploit the tradeoff between telecommunications and transportation. A workstation in the home permits an individual to remain productive at a distance from the office. As Toffler describes it, "Put the computer in people's homes and they no longer need to huddle. Third Wave white-collar work, like Third Wave manufacturing, will not require 100% of the workforce to be concentrated in the workshop."[4] By escaping that coercion, the electronic cottage dweller can flee pollution, crime, and congestion—even living beyond the suburbs—while still staying connected to an industrial income. The promise of the electronic cottage embraces industrial society with its technologies and forms of income; but, at the same time, it seeks to reverse one hundred years of gravitation to the industrial metropole. In other words, to Toffler and others like him, information technology retrieves Walden Pond. But unlike Thoreau, electronic cottage dwellers pursue the pastoral past by pushing into the electronic future.

Does interconnectedness finally realize the pastoral ideal? Clearly, the lure of Walden pond lingers. Yet Thoreau went to Walden having rejected both the benefits and costs of industrial civilization—or so he claimed, while electronic cottage dwellers seek to avoid only the costs. They wish to live on Walden pond, but make a living on Wall Street. There is a sharp irony here, because in its original form the pastoral ideal viewed technology as mortal threat. Now, at the end of the 20th century, rural still remains superior to urban, but retreating to nature does not mean forsaking the benefits of industrial civilization. In its reworked form, the pastoral ideal of today is pseudo-urban rather than rural. Moreover, technology looms as both problem and solution. The attraction of the electronic cottage lies in its merger of a rural setting with continued high urban income and urban comfort. What electronic cottage dwellers really seek is freedom from nature's constraints *and* from industrial society's constraints. They are unlike Thoreau, who rejected the constraints of industrial society by accepting the constraints of nature.

Notes

1. Marx, L. (1967). *The machine in the garden: Technology and the pastoral ideal in America.* New York: Oxford University Press, p. 5.
2. Jefferson was emphatic in his view and wrote of it on several occasions. To Jay, 1785, "Cultivators of the earth are the most valuable citizens." To Hogendorp, 1785, "Were I to indulge my own theory, I would wish them—Americans—to practice neither commerce nor navigation, but to stand, with respect to Europe, precisely on the footing of China. We should thus avoid wars, and all our citizens would be husbandmen." Notes on Virginia, Query 19, "Those who labor in the earth are the chosen people of God.... Generally speaking, the proportion which the aggregate of the other classes bears in any State to that of its husbandmen, is the proportion of its unsound to its healthy parts, and is a good enough barometer whereby to measure its degree of corruption." To Madison, 1787, "When we get piled upon one another in large cities, as in Europe, we shall become corrupt as in Europe, and go to eating one another as they do." To de Meunier, 1786, "An industrious farmer occupies a more dignified place in the scale of things...than

a lazy lounger, valuing himself on his family, too proud to work, and drawing out a miserable existence by eating on that surplus of other men's labor, which is the sacred fund of the helpless poor." To H. G. Spafford, 1814, "I fear nothing for our liberty from the assaults of force; but I have seen and felt much, and fear more from English books, English prejudices, English manners, and the apes, the dupes, and designs among our professional crafts. When I look around me for security against these seductions, I find it in the widespread of our agricultural citizens, in their unsophisticated minds, their independence and their power, if called on, to crush the Humists of our cities, and to maintain the principles which severed us from England." Padover, S. K. (Ed.). (1946). *Thomas Jefferson on democracy*. New York: New American Library, pp. 68, 69, 69–70, 70, 79–80, 85.

3. Thoreau, H. D. (1854/1942), pp. 64, 66.
4. Toffler, A. (1980). *The third wave*. New York: William Morrow, p. 199.

Appendix C

The Putting-Out System in the Information Age

Denise and Clara—not their real names—worked in the microelectronics industry in the 1970s and 1980s.[1] Denise arrived at Stanford University with her husband, a student, and encountered difficulty finding employment. Through contacts in her apartment complex, she met a microchip distributor, himself a student at Stanford, who would supply her with unsorted microchips in return for sorting. He offered to pay by the piece. Clara, a mother of two in southern California, found herself abandoned by her husband and in need of work that she could perform at home while spending time with her children. She responded to an ad in a local Orange County advertiser.

Microchip sorting meant receiving a large box of miscellaneous chips from the distributor, separating them according to type, and returning them in individual containers along with damaged chips. Upon his return, the distributor picked up the containers, paid by the chip, and left off another batch. The microchip distributor functioned as an individual entrepreneur. He bought excess chips, divided them among his home workers, and then resold the sorted chips to independent microchip vendors. Denise started working according to self-imposed regular hours but soon began to use every available moment, in order to increase her income. Clara expected to sort and interact with her children. The two activities interfered, however, and she did most of the sorting after the children were asleep.

About the time the routine became familiar, both began to feel pressure from the distributors to increase production. Denise's distributor encouraged her to recruit others, so she did. For a short time she sorted with an acquaintance recently arrived at Stanford until the newcomer found another job. In the evenings, Denise's husband contributed to the sorting. Clara taught her children to sort. They now spent evenings around the kitchen table separating microchips. Clara worried that her children stayed up too late and neglected their schoolwork, but she felt they needed the extra income. Both women reported feeling as though every moment spent away from sorting deprived them of income they could not afford to lose. Consequently, they lived under chronic pressure and sought escape from microchip sorting.[2] Because of the

237

mutually supportive nature of the Stanford student community, Denise located another job. After seven months of sorting, she joined a Silicon Valley firm as an administrative assistant. Clara, with children at home, continued for two years. But she never felt economically secure, especially after her distributor cut the piece rate during the 1982–83 recession. When her local church established a daycare center, she looked for work more actively and found a better paying job as a packer in a small factory producing electronic components for military aircraft. What is of interest to an analysis of the information society is that Denise and Clara worked within a production arrangement older than the industrial revolution. Known as the putting-out system to historians of the pre-industrial era, it consisted of merchant-distributors providing raw wool to peasant spinners and weavers who spun the raw wool into yarn and wove it into cloth. The work took place in peasants' cottages and the distributor paid by the piece.[3] Commonly observed in 17th century Scotland, the system also appeared in other parts of Europe. The putting-out system stands at the transition from the seamless year-round activities of peasant farmers to the segmented routines of factory laborers.[4] In County Donegal, Ireland, on the periphery of industrial Europe, the cottage looms can still be heard today.

Certainly, the putting-out system in Silicon Valley and Orange County makes a minuscule economic impact, just as the weavers of County Donegal produce a tiny percent of Europe's wool cloth. The continued existence of the putting-out system indicates that the arrival of the world's most advanced information economy does not eradicate archaic forms of production; but, instead, makes room for niches outside of the mainstream. Though Denise and Clara lived in the full bloom of the information society in Silicon Valley and Southern California, they did not benefit from its high tech fruits. Instead, they found themselves working in circumstances akin to 17th century peasants.

Notes

1. These two cases are taken from 12 unpublished interviews, 7 conducted in the San Francisco Bay area in the 1970s, and 5 conducted in Orange County, California, in the 1980s.
2. Five individuals interviewed did not report this effect.
3. Heilbroner, R. L., & Singer, A. (1984). *The economic transformation of America: 1600 to the present* (2nd ed.). New York: Harcourt Brace Jovanovich (pp. 19–20).
4. Kriedte, P., Medick, H., & Schlumbohn, J. (1981). *Industrialization before industrialization: Rural industry in the genesis of capitalism* (Schempp, Beate, Trans.) (pp. 101–107, 136–139). Cambridge, UK: Cambridge University Press. Smith, A. (1776/1902). *An inquiry into the nature and causes of the wealth of nations.* New York: American Home Library, p. 191.

Appendix D

An Information Professional at Work at Home

A growing number of Americans must balance the therapeutic value of one's media environment against productivity. For in a movement counter to that of the last 150 years, the home is once again a place of work.

What emerged during the 19th century was the detachment of work from home.[1] Craftsmen who preserved the legacy of preindustrial times by integrating work with home lost ground to the forces of industrial organization. To leave the village meant entering the manufacturing city where work and home separated. But today, the fuzzy boundaries between information work and home reopen some possibilities for merging the two, because fuzzy boundaries offer opportunities to integrate the activities of work and home in ways not possible in the early industrial period. In fact, the segmentation of work and home also established the home as a place of escape, thereby laying the foundation for the creation of a media environment. But because media environments lead to the potential for receiving many messages, individuals may also opt to recreate work and home within the same space. The results sometimes differ from the image of the home organized around the radio, the TV set, and the VCR.

Seated at a desk flanked by telephones and computer equipment, Noble Gunn looks out on the reddening foliage of central New Jersey.[2] Five ceiling length bookshelves stand black with editions of the *Federal Tax Reporter* and the *State Tax Reporter*. Textbooks from his business school days at Baruch College, stacks of folders and computer discs intermix with the *Reporters*. An IBM PC sits on the left of the desk, connected to a PS 2 network unit. A modem, 160 megabyte hard disc, letter-quality printer, photocopier, fax machine, postage meter, scales, typewriter, calculators, adding machines, and four full-size filing cabinets fill in the 11 x 18 foot room. Six telephone lines and several telephones provide answering tapes, call forwarding, call waiting, call relay, and connect his PC to larger computers at his office in Manhattan. Outside the door sprawls his spacious apartment, where he lives with his wife Juliette and their one year old son. He is at work.

At age 40, he has worked as an accountant for 16 years, and is now Managing Tax Director and sole stockholder of Gunn & Associates. He set up the home office within two years of going into business for himself. But unlike many small businesses that grow out of home activities, his grew out of the main office in Manhattan. His midtown office provides a window to the public, a place to center his business and meet clients.

To achieve such flexibility required him to invest roughly $50,000 in his home office, plus make a commitment to pay monthly service charges of around $2,500. In fact, the real story of Gunn's success lies in his organization of human and capital resources, not just technology. When asked, he refers to his work space as his study. He does not think of it as an office, but rather as a refuge from the urgencies of the business. He initially set it up in order to gain freedom from the office and still keep up with the flow of tax work. He soon learned that the new arrangement allows him to concentrate on the strategic issues of managing the firm and attracting new clients. However, over time, he has redefined his goals and now sees the home office as a means for establishing a level of quality in his life. He enjoys missing the daily commute to New York City, as well as the extra time he has to spend with his family. But he measures his greatest gains in flexibility. By taking control of time, he exercises control over his activities and feels he gets the most out of life.

Here is the crux of matter for Gunn. He stresses that for him, his working arrangement provides the means to realize the activities that matter in life. Having worked for two of the largest accounting firms, he now feels more relaxed and in touch with the seasons. Nonetheless, flexibility applies to work as well as quality of life. He also values the home office because he can get to work right away and maximize his work time, thereby making effective use of total time available. His responses to questions indicate that he spends considerable time thinking about the efficiency of his system.

Before Gunn created his "study," portions of the home office resided in several rooms including the living room. He found it hard to avoid bumping into Juliette. Friends did not always believe that he was working when they dropped by to visit. Once he relocated into one space, the social and work spheres within the home became easier to manage. Yet though it was the need to explain his working situation to friends that compelled him to articulate the differences between work and leisure, he quickly admits the ease with which he gravitates toward work when he is home. The path of least resistance allows work activities to monopolize his attention. "Distractions are constant," concedes Gunn. But he further admits that he loves his work and lets himself get wrapped up in it. One suspects that he is especially vulnerable because he runs his own business. In fact, though he concentrates his work resources into one space, the role that information plays for him and his wife is evident; the living room, which is spaciously furnished in a modern style, accommodates sophisticated video and audio equipment, while a telephone can be found in every room; magazines and newspapers lie within reach of nearly every sitting space. Even so, he complains of the intrusion of the fax machine.

"I am not working when I am at leisure," he reveals, acknowledging a preoccupation with work unless he physically takes himself out of that mode by defining an activity as leisure. He loves music and uses it as a way of exiling work related thoughts. Thus, when he works at home he maintains silence. Over the last few years, concerts have become a popular leisure activity because of the music and the isolation they afford. Similarly, he holds a private pilot's license and flies with his wife as a way of isolating himself from the distractions of phone and fax machine. The Gunns take short vacations, mostly to the Caribbean, for the same reasons, and, ironically, he sometimes drives into Manhattan—one hour away—for the solitude of the drive. Yet not all leisure isolates him. He pores over the daily newspaper and clips business related articles for later attention. In addition, he reads a wide range of magazines, and pays attention to radio and TV news. These activities, a kind of pseudo leisure involving the consumption of information, easily overlap the boundary between leisure and work. He habitually checks the fax machine and the printer, responding immediately when something comes up. Upon reflection, Gunn sees his lifestyle as the template for things to come. "This has got to be the way of the future," he muses. "But you must plan it as carefully as you plan your career. Otherwise, the scales can tip very quickly." Indeed, his office has penetrated his home, in a significant way. He experiences pseudo leisure by consuming information, and it is here that one observes a blurring of the boundaries between work and leisure in the home. True leisure, as he defines it, requires him to leave the apartment. Thus, while leisure affords him isolation from work, he must pursue it in the public sphere.

In the 1990s, Mr. Gunn represents an extreme case of work at home. The hard and soft technologies of information allows him to trade communication for distance. From his study, he holds the main office at bay while he transmits decisions and directions to Manhattan. Yet to maintain his isolation he must handle information from the main office at all hours. It seems that for professionals like Gunn, work defines life in the information society. But for all that, he represents an exceptionally successful example of what the information society has to offer, and in some ways personifies Williams' scenario of the future. Still, the issue of work versus leisure remains unresolved, and as he points out, "the scales can tip very quickly."

Less than 1% of all workers can claim a working environment similar to that of Mr. Gunn's.[3] Nevertheless, his case indicates that fuzzy boundaries can exist between work and non work. As professionals exploit information technologies in order to create individualistic work-home settings, these fuzzy boundaries seem likely to become permanent features of the information society. Previously, social commentators looked to leisure as the opposite of work assuming, like Gunn, that individuals not at work must be at leisure. But, as Gunn's case illustrates, leisure as a concept poses problems. Aside from activities specifically identified as leisure, individuals spend many non work hours in activities that do not easily fit the concept, since time spent away from work does not always constitute leisure in the sense of recuperation.[4]

Nevertheless, while there can be little doubt that millions of Americans continue to experience the segmented reality of work, home, and leisure, especially in those occupations organized along industrial lines—whether they be information occupations or not—Gunn's example points to a different reality. That leisure exists for Gunn is clear. But it comes enveloped in a flow of work and non work activities more seamless than those experienced by the stereotypic factory worker. For him and others like him, it is more appropriate to assume that when they are not at leisure they must be at work. Work forms the salient feature of Gunn's world. In fact, the fuzzy boundaries seen in his case do not result from equal forces contesting. The boundaries between work and home are fuzzy because the activities of work permeate the home. That the merger of the two spheres is increasingly attainable through the exploitation of information technologies poses another question.

Does Gunn herald the arrival of a new class? Ever since Bell postulated the centrality of theoretical knowledge attended by new information technologies as hallmarks of post-industrial society, supporters of his theory have predicted the emergence of a new class as the basis for a technocracy of the information age. Bell himself suggests a technical and professional class drawn together by their monopoly over new knowledge and manipulation of information technologies.[5] Gunn certainly qualifies as a member of this professional "class" by virtue of his position as an information professional, and the function of his profession in facilitating the system of corporate bureaucracy that typifies industrial capitalism in the 20th century. In addition, his use of information technologies and services distinguishes him from traditional professionals. Yet, Gunn gives no evidence of a class consciousness identifying the interests of his "class" in opposition to the interests of other classes. If anything, his professional identity dominates and links him to the interests of his clients. Like other professionals, he is tied to their interests and the roles they play. So, to the extent that Gunn typifies other information professionals, he, like they, is tied into the existing American power structure without exerting influence as a distinct group.

Nor does his use of computers and telecommunications services set him apart as a member of a class identified by information technology. Gunn employs no esoteric technology; every device in his offices can be purchased from any well equipped computer store, and his communications needs are readily met by all of the phone companies. Thus, although his particular application of information technologies places him apart from most other individuals, the technologies themselves cannot be considered as a badge of class identification because they are available in the general marketplace.

However, his organization of a home-work environment does place demands on the economy with consequences for the distribution of power. That is, for anyone interested in achieving a productive relationship with a distant office while still performing complex information work at home, some variation on Gunn's organization of technology must be put in place. As his brand of information work becomes more common, those who emulate it will construct home-work environments along similar lines, and demand the same technologies and services. Therefore, a pattern of demand for computer based devices and telecommunications services will emerge as these new information professionals grow in number. The industries favored will be those which produce microelectronic devices, software, and telecommunications services; along with them will come the distribution of resources and labor relations typical of those industries. The kinds of information work experienced by individuals in those industries will be reinforced with all of the plusses and minuses described in chapter 3. So, in a subtle way, the growth of a group of tele-professionals who center work both in the office and at home will establish a common relationship to society's productive and distributive processes by virtue of their existence and use of technology. In other words, as tele-professionals become a significant force in society, the demands created by their needs will enforce forces of production typical of those industries which serve them.[6] For this to occur, no new class consciousness will be necessary.

What is clear is that the realities of work heavily influence the realities of home, causing concepts such as home, non-work, and leisure to take on new meanings. As tele-professionals and their individualistic work-home environments increase in numbers, values associated with their circumstances will influence American culture—much as the factory work ethic colored views of society through the early and middle decades of the 20th century. Fuzzy boundaries will become the established pattern of public and private life, while the older fixed boundaries will retreat toward the periphery.

Notes

1. To be sure, we oversimplify. Even after the great rush of industrialization, work continued in the home; and, for many women, especially, distinctions between work and home do not reflect their reality, even today. We maintain these distinctions in this chapter, in order to draw attention to the consequences of some kinds of information work.
2. Interview conducted November 1990.
3. There is no way to tell how many information professionals perform "telework" as does Gunn. One percent is a guess. Others estimate that by the middle of the 1990s as much as half of the white collar work force could be involved in telework. But this does not seem likely. See Kraut, R. E. (1987). Predicting the Use of Technology: The Case of Telework. In R. E. Kraut (Ed.), *Technology and the transformation of white-collar work* (pp. 113–133). Hillsdale, NJ: Lawrence Erlbaum Associates. Olson, M. H. (1987). Telework: Practical experience and future prospects. In R. E. Kraut (Eds.), *Technology and the transformation of white-collar work* (pp. 135–152). Hillsdale, NJ: Lawrence Erlbaum Associates.

4. For a broad treatment of leisure see: Bellah, R. N., Madsen, R., Sullivan, W. M., Swidler, A., & Tipton, S. M. (1985). *Habits of the heart: Individualism and commitment in American life.* Berkeley, CA: University of California. Berger, B. M. (1963). The sociology of leisure: Some suggestions. In E. O. Smigel (Ed.), *Work and leisure: A contemporary social problem* (pp. 21-40). New Haven, CN: College and University Press. Berk, R. A., & Berk, S. F. (1979). *Labor and leisure at home: Content and organization of the household day.* Beverly Hills, CA: Sage. Cummings, D. W., & Herum, J. (Ed.). (1974). *Tempo: Life, work and leisure.* Boston, MA: Houghton Mifflin. Fromm, E. (1955). *The sane society.* New York: Holt, Rinehart and Winston. Kubey, R., & Csikszentmihalyi, M. (1990). *Television and the quality of life: How viewing shapes everyday experiences.* Hillsdale, NJ: Lawrence Erlbaum. Lasch, C. (1979). *The culture of narcissism: American life in an age of diminishing expectations.* New York: W. W. Norton. Parker, S. (1971). *The future of work and leisure.* New York: Praeger. Postman, N. (1985). *Amusing ourselves to death: Public discourse in the age of show business.* New York: Penguin. Pronovost, G. (1988). The social meanings of leisure. *International Sociology, 3*(1), 89-102. van den Haag, E. (1962). Of happiness and despair we have no measure. In E. Josephson & M. Josephson (Eds.), *Man alone: Alienation in modern society* (pp. 180-199). New York: Dell. Veblen, T. (1899/ 1918). *The theory of the leisure class: An economic study of institutions.* New York: The Modern Library.
5. Bell, D. (1976) p. xvi.
6. Harkness, R. C., & Staudel, J. T. (1982). Telecommunications alternatives to transportation. In H. F. Didsbury Jr. (Ed.), *Communications and the future: Prospects, promises, and problems* (pp. 229-233). Bethesda, MD: World Future Society. Hiltz, S. R., & Turoff, M. (1978). *The network nation: Human communication via computer.* Reeding, MA: Addison-Wesley. Olson, M. H. (1987). Remote office work: Changing work patterns in space and time. In *Technology and the transformation of white-collar work,* . Bell Communications Research, New Brunswick, NJ. Olson, M. H. (1987). Telework: Practical experience and future prospects. In R. E. Kraut (Eds.), *Technology and the transformation of white-collar work* (pp. 135-152). Hillsdale, NJ: Lawrence Erlbaum Associates.

Appendix E

Shareware

The acknowledgments window in John Lim's computer program "Møire Screensaver" reads, "This is a shareware program. If you like it, please send $10.00 to: ..." Mr. Lim's program darkens the screen after a specified period of inactivity and projects abstract shapes to remind the user that the computer is still on, thus preventing damage to the monitor from burned in characters. By all accounts his invention is widely valued. Similarly, Loftus Becker Jr. distributes his program "Keyboard", an application for altering the character keys, on the basis of voluntary contributions from those who use it. Unlike Lim, Becker does not even suggest an amount to be paid. While this may strike one as a bizarre way of doing business, programs like Lim's and Becker's, known as shareware in software circles, represent approximately 13% of the number of programs offered through nontraditional channels.[1]

But what a strange market this is. In effect, the seller says, "Here is my product. If you like it pay. If you don't want to pay me, then keep it anyway."[2] To the economically minded, this message jars because it appears to be full of contradictions. If shareware is a commodity, then the seller and buyer should meet to exchange software for money. But if shareware is a public resource, then the citizen should receive it at no direct cost. Some program authors distribute their creations freely as part of the public domain and include a caveat against resale. Yet neither shareware nor public domain software constitute a free good, since information does not inherently occur in super abundance—although once created, its distribution becomes hard to control. Nor is it either a public good, since the government is not the provider. Therefore, we use the term "public resource" as the closest descriptor of a system for distributing information where the user is not charged directly for the cost of producing the product, but incurs only the cost of transportation.

Shareware vendors clearly violate the conventions of the marketplace by intentionally presenting their products as both commodities and public resources. They can do so by exploiting the unique replicability of information. That is, unlike markets for material commodities, information contains no implied zero sum relationship between supply and demand. Loftus Becker retains his "keyboard" program even as he sells it or gives it away. Further-

245

more, by distributing information as both commodity and public resource, shareware authors seek diverse returns from their investment.

For example, an unknown designer will have a hard time finding a commercial publisher. Also, publishers expect a reasonable return for marketing a program, so they seek widespread consumer acceptance for their products. But a program like "Keyboard" will not draw a large following, so by "sharing" it, Becker creates an alternative market. Secondly, any shareware author seeking a reputation must publish programs. By distributing through public domain/shareware services, like the Berkeley Macintosh Users Group or EDUCORP, authors—especially unknown authors—bypass the constraints of commercial publishers and reach users who have interests in specialty programs. Therefore, the software author gains a reputation based on the quality of his or her creations.

Finally, shareware—and public domain—programs offer an opportunity for the designer to receive criticism for a product under revision. "Beta" versions circulate among users, some of whom provide feedback to the designer. In fact, numerous commercially successful programs started out as shareware beta versions. Thus, the shareware author overcomes the obstacles of publishing, reaches an audience niche, tests the program with a feedback loop, and earns income from those who care to pay. By all accounts, however, not many care to pay, many authors reporting a return rate as low as 5%.

Since the policy agenda of the last decade adopted an either/or posture—by asking if information should be distributed through the market or provided freely—shareware seems out of sync with the rhetoric of the times. But clearly shareware's success depends *both* on distribution within the market and on distribution outside of the market. In the process, it poses a completely new and interesting policy question. Should policy makers intentionally establish quasi-markets for information? Admittedly, shareware does pose a problem for traditional sellers who see information's ease of replicability as the source of lost profits. Their efforts to control distribution range from passing new copyright laws to encoding "locks" or "worms" in the program. But no legal or programmed solution can overcome the natural essence of information that shareware exploits.

In fact, shareware is only a problem to those who see the market as the sole distribution mechanism in the information society. So those who sell purely commoditized information must constantly struggle against its ease of replicability, shareware vendors benefit from this same attribute. In fact, the software industry would not have grown so dramatically without the stimulus of shareware. The shareware market presents an alternative that bears consideration. Granted, it is no replacement for the orthodox marketplace. But it does represent a relationship between producer and consumer that seems novel in the information society. As the information economy matures, the quasi-markets of the shareware kind are likely to take on important functions.

Notes

1. This estimate is based on a content analysis of the 1989 BMUG Inc. catalogue.
2. Not all shareware vendors take this laissez-faire approach. Some caution the consumer against using the program without paying.

Appendix F

Demassification and Interactive Networks

After a century of observation, the accumulated evidence indicates that there is a relation between the mass media, a mass audience, mass marketing, and mass culture. The economies of scale of spreading television programming production costs over the largest possible audience are closely related not only to the economic advantages of marketing goods and services on a national scale but also to the medium's homogenizing effects on the audience. Since the introduction of radio, the economics of mass production and mass marketing have not changed. The law of diminishing returns, however, has long since come to act to limit the extension of the television audience as a mass market. Where the audience was once conceived of as an undifferentiated mass, it is now seen as composed of characteristics that concentrate subaudiences into recognizable segments, e.g., "young unmarrieds," "home owners," "urban professionals," "affluent teenagers," etc.; i.e., what once appeared as a single lump now looks like a mosaic.[1] Admittedly, large groups can still be found at the core of the audience; but out at the periphery, there are groups for whom the least common denominator of entertainment and information is not attractive and for whom the mass marketing message is not persuasive.[2] From this perspective, the media targeted at discrete audience segments is not so much an example of "demassification" but an extension of mass marketing by other means. However, the law of diminishing returns applies here, too. The cost of identifying clusters of the television audience whose separate needs and tastes can be targeted, and of producing content and marketing strategies to serve those needs and tastes, quickly exceeds the marginal revenues available through increased sales. As the number of potentially profitable market segments has increased, the upstream channel—market research—has remained inadequate due both to its high cost and its stochastic nature. Current market research provides only generalizations about what audience segments want or what is persuasive to them. It provides snapshots and is poor at predicting trends. Also, its costs are so high in proportion to the quality of the research findings that mass audience segmentation and media targeting become inefficient at a very early stage.

But new computer-based technologies are changing all of that. For example, an interactive network could well modify this calculation of efficiency. It can provide a fully capable upstream channel, through which each individual member of the television audience can conduct an on-line dialogue about the current profile of his or her changing needs and tastes. That profile can now be specific with regard to demographics, psychographics, and consumption patterns. Interactivity—that is, the ability of an interactive network to carry this upstream information as a result of viewing choices, or as explicit responses to requests for information—stands to rewrite the rules of the game with unforeseen consequences.

Notes

1. Dickson, P. R., & Ginter, J. L. (1987). Market segmentation, product differentiation, and marketing strategy. *Journal of Marketing, 51*(April), 1–10. Wind, Y. (1978). Issues and advances in segmentation research. *Journal of Marketing Research, 5*(August), 317–335.
2. The paradigm that encouraged the view of markets as segments took hold in business theory during the 1960s. Since then, its successful application has raised it to the level of orthodoxy. What is of interest, in terms of the diffusion and reinterpretation of ideas in society, is that the rhetoric of diversity which has generated such controversy on college campuses of the '90s, takes much of its perspective from the same paradigmatic view that inspired market segmentation theory.

Appendix G

Historical Patterns in the Development of Information Technologies

From the perspective of the timeline, the very long view elicits some noteworthy patterns.

1. Until the 6th century B.C., all efforts focused on inventing systems of writing, counting, or representing time and space. Their profound significance is evident when one considers the break with tradition required by such levels of abstraction as the map and the calendar. Early farmers considered counting the seasons of such great importance that calendars—oral or written—were invented in every agricultural society, representing the first direct application of mathematics. The Sumerians stand out as developers of a sophisticated writing system, and as inventors of the library and library catalog. In terms of information technology, they were the first to experience the necessity of information permanence, and the first to invent a social institution devoted to storing and retrieving information. Such inventions imply the complexity of their civilization. Technological solutions to the problems of writing, counting, and time formed the basis for all subsequent developments of information technologies.

2. Throughout history, consistent efforts aimed at extending the advantages of writing can be observed. While the pace of technological invention seems slow from the position of the 20th century, nearly every century contains a contribution to written communication.

3. Capitalism and the industrial revolution spawned intense development of all information technologies. Industrial organization incorporated earlier knowledge systems such as science, while capitalism offered rewards—not always accruing to the actual originator—for inventing new devices and improving on existing ones. Though antecedents can be detected as early as the 16th century, momentum intensified at the turn of the 19th century and continues at a rapid pace.

4. The second half of the 20th century has witnessed a series of inventions which defy easy categorization. They consist of a convergence of functions, a synthesis of symbol manipulation, and the simultaneous extension of the eye and the ear. The ease with which a complex technology, e.g., televisioncan be

combined with other complex technologies, e.g., the calculator and the telephone, in order to produce technologies of even greater complexity, e.g., computer networks or cable television, illustrates how recent information technologies operate more as components of universal machines, than as free standing developments.

5. The overarching lesson of the history of information technologies can be found in the persistence with which humans have struggled to sharpen vision, improve hearing, communicate over distances, record time, expand memory, speed up calculations, and expand knowledge.

Notes

1. This estimate is based on a content analysis of the 1989 BMUG Inc. catalogue.
2. Not all shareware vendors take this laissez-faire approach. Some caution the consumer against using the program without paying.

Appendix H

When Television Came to West Houston Street

My mother bought the first TV set on our block and, in the spring of 1953, introduced this new technology into our neighborhood just west of the Missouri Pacific railroad station in San Antonio, Texas. I was five years old; and, when it arrived, I encountered the first television related change in my life.

Before television, the sofa and chairs of the living room faced each other. But when the set arrived, my mother declared that, in order to provide everyone with a direct view of the screen, the living room must be rearranged. So, in the flurry of excitement surrounding the arrival of the set, the men pitched in and shuffled the furniture. The new arrangement meant that I could no longer curl into my favorite stuffed chair by the front window because the television set now stood in its place. The whole family now sat aimed at the TV set; and, almost immediately, we settled into a new evening ritual, clustered around a box whose light was visible halfway down the block. Before long, neighbors appeared on the porch hoping for an invitation to see the new apparatus. I noticed that the family at the other end of the block changed their evening habit from sitting on their front porch to strolling past our window. Soon our living room became a salon of prominent status; and, my mother, its mistress, basked in her new role and presided with great style.

Although I did not know it at the time, my mother had invented a new use for a machine whose purpose seemed obvious and intrinsic to the journalists and academics commenting on its potential. I suspect that the utility of acquired status ranked low on any contemporary list of television predictions, if such a use even appeared. My mother's social aspirations were the driving force behind the transformation of our family's role in the neighborhood, and so she used her domestic power in the household to exploit the new technology for her own goals. In retrospect, I doubt that my mother saw television as directly changing her life, nor ever considered herself a passive bystander . But I lost my favorite reading spot by the window and for most of my childhood I confused cause and effect by blaming the television set.—JRS

Appendix I

Information and Communication Technologies[1]

The purpose of this timeline is to illustrate the growth of information technology as a complex interplay between conceptual and material invention, and then to place this growth within a chronological framework. In creating this timeline, we seek to meet three goals:

First, we identify the order of appearance of material information technologies such as the clock, the telescope, and the book. Second, we include a selected chronology of conceptual and social technologies which created the knowledge foundation for material invention. The phonetic alphabet, decimal counting, the library at Nineveh, and the University of Paris are examples in this class of innovations. Third, the interplay of functions is traced through a scheme of symbol notations, in order to demonstrate the alphabetical and mathematical bases, as well as the aural and visual utilities of information technologies.[2] In addition, the symbol scheme illustrates how specific information technologies are built upon previous innovations, by synthesizing the features of earlier technologies. The computer, which can be visual or aural, and can manipulate mathematical or alphabetical symbols, demonstrates the convergence of previous print and electronic innovations. By establishing the interplay of functions it is possible to identify patterns of convergence that have punctuated the course of technological change.

Historical events are presented in three axial columns: conceptual and institutional developments; information acquisition and storage devices; and, information processing and transmission devices.[3]

Conceptual and/or Institutional Developments: Conceptual developments include fundamental theories, principles, ideas, and techniques underlying the development of information technologies. Institutional developments include libraries, schools, universities, and observatories, i.e., social structures through which conceptual developments are disseminated.

Information Acquisition and/or Storage Devices: Information acquisition devices assist human information processing by directly expanding the capacities of the eye and the ear. Storage devices aid in the manipulation of information by recording, copying, logging, and/or preserving symbols, for the primary purpose of allowing access or retrieval at a later time.

Information Processing and/or Transmission Devices: Information processing devices aid in the manipulation of information by performing distinct operations, modifications, or conversions of symbols. Transmission devices communicate, transport, or distribute symbols across space.

In addition, some technologies cross over category boundaries, especially in the 20th century. They are marked by an asterisk (*). Note that not all entries in the timeline are technologies. Those entries lacking a symbol notation do not qualify as a technology.

The scheme of circles and squares denotes the functions of symbol manipulation or sensory extension. A combination of figures demonstrates how technologies build on previous discoveries by synthesizing basic features of two or more devices, e.g., the computer.

○ *Alphabet Technologies*: manipulate symbols to form words according to a phonology and/or morphology of language, having both syntactical and semantic dimensions.

● *Mathematical Technologies*: manipulate symbols for the purpose of counting, or for clarifying relationships between phenomena through quantification.

◒ refers to a combination of alphabetical and mathematical technologies.

☐ *Audio Technologies*: extend the sense of hearing.

■ *Optical/Visual Technologies*: extend the sense of seeing.

▤ refers to a combination of audio and optical/visual technologies.

Various forms of convergence are illustrated by the following combinations:

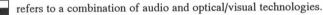 .

By overlaying the dimensions of symbol manipulation and sensory extension on the columns, the time-line identifies the periods of convergence that have punctuated the course of technological change. **

Notes

1. A version of this timeline appeared as "A Time-line of Information Technology" Schement, J. R., & Stout, D. A. J. (1990). In B. D. Ruben & L. A. Lievrouw (Eds.), *Information and Behavior, 3* (pp. 395–424). New Brunswick, NJ: Transaction. We thank Daniel Stout for his contribution to the compilation of the timeline.
2. "Alphabet" and "alphabetical" are used in their broad sense to indicate symbol systems for the representation of language, thus including syllabic, pictographic and morphemic systems as well as "alphabetic" in the narrow sense of phonemic systems.
3. B.C./A.D. notation is used because it is commonly accepted.

Time-Line

	Conceptual &/or Institutional Developments	Information Acquisition &/or Storage Devices	Information Manipulation &/or Transmission Devices
Pre-Tenth Century B.C.	■ Cave paintings introduce symbolic representation [c. 20,000 B.C.]		
		■● Egyptian calender [5,000 - 4,000 B.C.]	
		■ Pictographs on clay tablets [c. 3,500 B.C.]	
		■● Jewish calender [4,000 - 3,5000 B.C.]	
	● Egyptian number system [3,500 - 3,000 B.C.]		
	◗ Egyptian hieroglyphics as symbol system [c. 3,000 B.C.]		
	● Numerical system in Sumeria [3,000 - 2,500 B.C.]	■ Metal mirrors in Egypt [3,000 - 2,500 B.C.]	
	● Concept of 365-day year in Eqypt [3,000 - 2,500 B.C.]		
	● System of solar-lunar year in China [2,500 - 2,000 B.C.]	■ Papyrus used by Egyptians [2,500 - 2,000 B.C.]	

	Conceptual &/or Institutional Developments	Information Acquisition &/or Storage Devices	Information Manipulation &/or Transmission Devices
Pre-Tenth Century B.C.	● Decimal system used in Crete [2,000 - 1,500 B.C.] ○ Alphabet in use among Semitic people [c. 1,800 B.C.]	■ Map of Babylon [2,500 - 2,000 B.C.] ■ ○ Catalogs of written clay tablets [2,000 B.C.] □ Hearing aid or "ear trumpet" [c. 1,600 B.C.]	
Tenth Century B.C.			● Water-filled cube to measure time, weight [1,000 - 900 B.C.]
Ninth Century B.C.			
Eighth Century B.C.	○ Phonetic alphabet in use among Greeks [c. 700 B.C.]	■ ● Calenders in Babylon [800 - 700 B.C.]	
Seventh Century B.C.	■ ○ Library at Nineveh [700 - 600 B.C.]		
Sixth Century B.C.	● Length of Roman lunar year has 10 months [c. 500 B.C.]		■ ● Sundial in China [600 - 500 B.C.] ■ Regular courier service in Persia [c. 500 B.C.] Cyrus

	Conceptual &/or Institutional Developments	Information Acquisition &/or Storage Devices	Information Manipulation &/or Transmission Devices
Sixth Century B.C.	● Length of lunar month determined [c. 500 B.C.]		
Fifth Century B.C.			■ Carrier pigeons in Greece [c. 425 B.C.]
Fourth Century B.C.	● East-west line introduced as map division [320 B.C.] ■ ○ Library at Alexendria [307 B.C.] Ptolemy Soter		
Third Century B.C.	● Leap year in Egyptian calendar [c. 240 B.C.] ● Chinese weights and measures standardized [c. 220 B.C.]	■ Parchment produced in Pergamum [c. 250 B.C.]	■ ● Sophisticated sundial used in Rome [c. 263 B.C.]

	Conceptual &/or Institutional Developments	Information Acquisition &/or Storage Devices	Information Manipulation &/or Transmission Devices
Second Century B.C.	● Dividing lines of inhabited world measured [c. 194 B.C.] Eratosthenes	■ World globe [c. 140 B.C.] Crates of Mallus	■● Clepsydra water clock in Rome [c. 159 B.C.]
	College of Technology at Alexandria [c. 105 B.C.] Heron		
First Century B.C.	○ Shorthand invented [c. 63 B.C.] Mareus Tullius Tiro		■ Handwritten news sheet in Rome [59 B.C.]
			■● Julian calender adopted with leap year [c. 45 B.C.]
First Century			
Second Century	■● Systematic map drawing [c. 170] Ptolemy	■ Paper invented [105] China	
Third Century		■◒ Early compass in China [c. 270]	

	Conceptual &/or Institutional Developments	Information Acquisition &/or Storage Devices	Information Manipulation &/or Transmission Devices
▪▪			
Fourth Century			■● Jewish calender reformed [338]
Fifth Century			■ Block printing in Asia [450]
Sixth Century	● Method of dating by years of the Christian Era [c. 525] Exiguus		● Abacus [c. 500] Eurasia
Seventh Century	● Decimal Counting in India [c. 600] ● Modern numerals introduced with zero and place value [c. 680]		■○ Book printing [c. 600] China
Eighth Century	● B.C.-A.D. Notation [c. 730] Venerable Bede Arts and sciences studied [c. 750] Han Lin Academy China	■ Paper making introduced to Arabs from China [751]	■○ Printed newspaper in Peking [c. 750]

	Conceptual &/or Institutional Developments	Information Acquisition &/or Storage Devices	Information Manipulation &/or Transmission Devices
Eighth Century	● "Arabic" numerals introduced to Baghdad from India [c. 760]		■ Pictorial book printing in Japan [c. 765]
Ninth Century	● Algebra [810] Muhammed ibn Musa Formal study of astronomy [813] Baghdad Library founded at St. Gallen [816] Gosbert Cyrillic alphabet invented [c. 863] Cyrus and Methodius	■● Arabs perfect astrolabe [c. 850]	■ Calibrated candles as time recorders in England [870]
Tenth Century	● Arithmetic notation brought to Europe by Arabs [c. 975]	■ Paper manufactured in Cairo [c. 900]	■ Regular postal service [c. 942] Caliph's empire ■● Water clock [c. 950]

	Conceptual &/or Institutional Developments	Information Acquisition &/or Storage Devices	Information Manipulation &/or Transmission Devices
Eleventh Century	Decimal System [1080] Azachel	■ Real lenses [1050] Alhazen Astrolabes introduced to Europe [1050]	■ Movable type [1041 - 1049] Pisheng
Twelvth Century	● University of Paris founded [1150] forerunner of modern university "Geography" [1154] Mohammed al-Idrisi	■ Paper manufactured [c. 1150] Arabic Spain ■◒ Magnetic compass mentioned in English literature [1195]	■ Use of woodcuts for capital letters [1147] Monastery at Engleberg
Thirteenth Century	● Introduction of Arabic Numerals to Europe [1202] "liber abaci" Fibonacci Treatise on Lenses [1270] Vitello	■◒ Pivoted magnetic compass [1269] Petrus Peregrinus ■ Compound lenses [1270] Bacon	

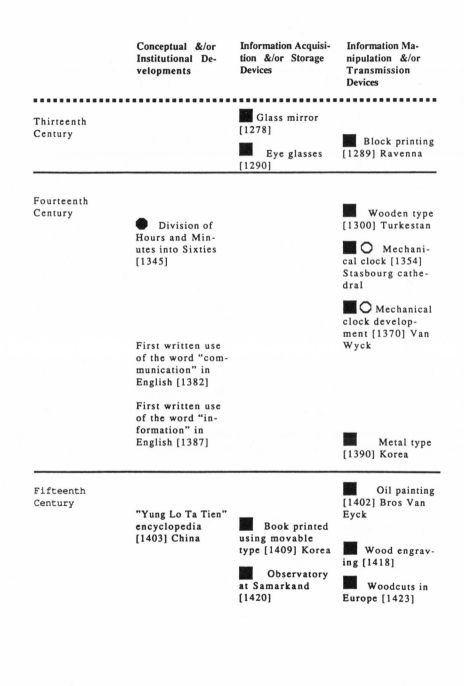

	Conceptual &/or Institutional Developments	Information Acquisition &/or Storage Devices	Information Manipulation &/or Transmission Devices
Thirteenth Century		■ Glass mirror [1278] ■ Eye glasses [1290]	■ Block printing [1289] Ravenna
Fourteenth Century	● Division of Hours and Minutes into Sixties [1345] First written use of the word "communication" in English [1382] First written use of the word "information" in English [1387]		■ Wooden type [1300] Turkestan ■ ○ Mechanical clock [1354] Stasbourg cathedral ■ ○ Mechanical clock development [1370] Van Wyck ■ Metal type [1390] Korea
Fifteenth Century	"Yung Lo Ta Tien" encyclopedia [1403] China	■ Book printed using movable type [1409] Korea ■ Observatory at Samarkand [1420]	■ Oil painting [1402] Bros Van Eyck ■ Wood engraving [1418] ■ Woodcuts in Europe [1423]

	Conceptual &/or Institutional Developments	Information Acquisition &/or Storage Devices	Information Manipulation &/or Transmission Devices
Fifteenth Century	◓ Scientific Cartography [1436] Banco Laws of Perspective [1440] Alberti ● Foundations of Trigonometry [1470] Muller ◒ Ship's Log [1472-1519] Profession of Book Publisher established [1492]		■ Modern printing [1440 - 1460] Gutenberg and Schoeffer ■ Copper plate engraving [1446]
		42-line "Mazarin" bible at Mainz [1453 - 1455] Gutenberg and Fust	■ Metal plates used in printing [1453]
		■ Observatory in Nürnberg [1472] Bernard Walther ■● Terrestrial globe constructed [1492] Behaim	■ Copper etching [1483] Wenceslaus von Olnutz
Sixteenth Century			■○ Regular postal service between Vienna and Brussels [c. 1500] ■● Portable watch with iron main-spring [1500]

Conceptual &/or Institutional Developments	Information Acquisition &/or Storage Devices	Information Manipulation &/or Transmission Devices

Sixteenth
Century

■● Intricate cathedral clocks developed [c. 1500 - 1650]

■ Multicolored woodcut [1508]

■ Eye glasses for shortsightedness [1518]

● Reinvention of taxi meter for coaches [1528]

Theory suggesting longitude can be computed from differences in time [1530] Regnier Gemma Frisius

Manual of production of paints and inks [1533]

■ Astronomical map [1539] Alesandro Piccolomini

■ First map of Flanders [1540] Gerardus Mercator

"Index Librorum Prohibitorum [1543] Pope Paul III

"Cosmographia Universalis" [1544] Sebastian Münster

	Conceptual &/or Institutional Developments	Information Acquisition &/or Storage Devices	Information Manipulation &/or Transmission Devices
Sixteenth Century	● Elaboration of algebraic symbols [1544] Stifel		
	"Biblioteca Universalis" [1549] Konrad von Gesner		
		■ Camera with lense and stop for diaphragm [1558] Daniello Barbaro	
	Academia Scerotorum Naturae at Naples [1560] The first scientific society		■ Lead pencil [1565] Gesner
	● Use of triangulation system in surveying [1581-1626] Willebrord snell van Roijen		■● Gregorian calender revision [1582]
	● Decimal system [1585] Simon Stevin	■ Compound microscope [1590] Jansen	
		■ Revolving theater stage [1597]	
Seventeenth Century	Treatise on terrestrial magnetism and electricity [1600] Gilbert		

	Conceptual &/or Institutional Developments	Information Acquisition &/or Storage Devices	Information Manipulation &/or Transmission Devices

Seventeenth Century

Academia dei lincei at Rome [1603]

First law of motion [1609] Galileo

■ Telescope [1608] Lippersheim

● Discovery of logarithms [1614] John Napier

● First logarithm table [1617] Henry Briggs

● Infinitesimal calculus [1636] Fermat

■ Periscope [1637] Hevel, Danzig

■ Fountain pen [1636] Schwenter

Calculation of focuses on all forms of lenses [1647]

● Barometer [1643] Torricelli

● Calculating machine [1650] Pascal

● Law of probability [1654] Pascal

□● Pendulum clock [1657] Huygens

● Law of probability tied to insurance [1660] Jan de Witt

■ Mirror-telescope [1666] Newton

■ Paris observatory [1667]

Conceptual &/or Institutional Developments	Information Acquisition &/or Storage Devices	Information Manipulation &/or Transmission Devices

Seventeenth Century

■ Speaking tube [1671] Morland

● First determination of speed of light [1675] Roemer

■ Greenwich observatory [1675]

● Differential calculus [1680] Liebnitz

Newton's "Principia" [1687]

Eighteenth Century

■● Physicians' pulse watch with second hand [1707] Floger

■ Stereotype [1710] Van der Mey and Müller

● Mercury thermometer [1714] Fahrenheit

■○ Typewriter [1714] Henry Mill

■ Three color printing from copper plate [1719] Le Blond

■ Stereotype [1727] Ged

■ Light images with silver nitrate [1727] Schulze

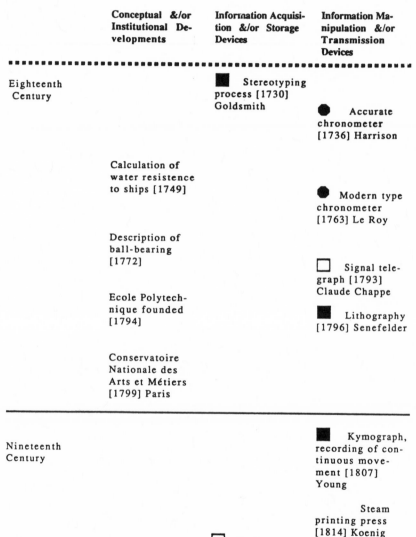

	Conceptual &/or Institutional Developments	Information Acquisition &/or Storage Devices	Information Manipulation &/or Transmission Devices
			● Calculating machines [1823 - 1843] Babbage
			■ Chromo-lithography [1827] Zahn
Nineteenth Century	Ohm's law [1830] determining flow of electricity through a con ductor, G. S. Ohm	■ Paper matrix stereotype [1829] Genoux	
	Laws of Electrolysis [1833]		□ Magnetic telegraph [1833] Gauss and Weber
	● Application of statistical method to social phenomena [1835]		□ Needle telegraph [1837] Wheatstone
			□ Electromagnetic telegraph [1837] Morse
		■ Daguerrotype [1839] Daguerre and Niepce	■ Electrotype [1839] Jacobi
			■ Callotype [1839] Talbot
	Electromagnetism [1840] conversion of mechanical energy to electrical energy, Faraday	■ Microphotography [1840] Donne	
		■ Paper positives in photography [1841] Talbot	
	● Spectrum analysis [1843] Miller		■○ Typewriter [1843] Thurber

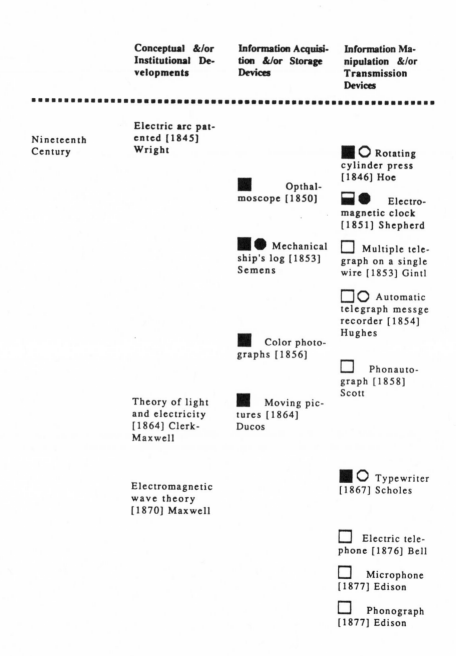

	Conceptual &/or Institutional Developments	Information Acquisition &/or Storage Devices	Information Manipulation &/or Transmission Devices
Nineteenth Century	Electric arc patented [1845] Wright		■ ○ Rotating cylinder press [1846] Hoe
		■ Opthalmoscope [1850]	■ ● Electromagnetic clock [1851] Shepherd
		■ ● Mechanical ship's log [1853] Semens	□ Multiple telegraph on a single wire [1853] Gintl
			□ ○ Automatic telegraph messge recorder [1854] Hughes
		■ Color photographs [1856]	□ Phonautograph [1858] Scott
	Theory of light and electricity [1864] Clerk-Maxwell	■ Moving pictures [1864] Ducos	
	Electromagnetic wave theory [1870] Maxwell		■ ○ Typewriter [1867] Scholes
			□ Electric telephone [1876] Bell
			□ Microphone [1877] Edison
			□ Phonograph [1877] Edison

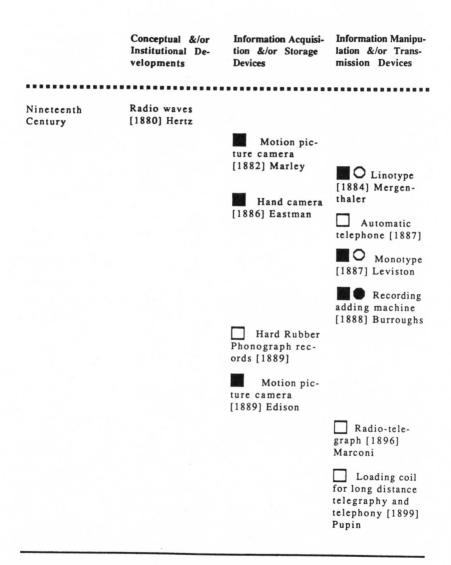

Conceptual &/or Institutional Developments	Information Acquisition &/or Storage Devices	Information Manipulation &/or Transmission Devices
Nineteenth Century	Radio waves [1880] Hertz	
	■ Motion picture camera [1882] Marley	
		■ ○ Linotype [1884] Mergenthaler
	■ Hand camera [1886] Eastman	
		□ Automatic telephone [1887]
		■ ○ Monotype [1887] Leviston
		■ ● Recording adding machine [1888] Burroughs
	□ Hard Rubber Phonograph records [1889]	
	■ Motion picture camera [1889] Edison	
		□ Radio-telegraph [1896] Marconi
		□ Loading coil for long distance telegraphy and telephony [1899] Pupin

	Conceptual &/or Institutional Developments	Information Acquisition &/or Storage Devices	Information Manipulation &/or Transmission Devices
▪▪			
Twentieth Century	Quantum theory [1900] Planck		☐ Transmission of human speech via radio waves [1900] Fessenden
		▪ Ultramicroscope [1903] Zsigmondy	☐ Radio-telephone [1903]
		▪● Electrocardiograph [1903] Einthoven	☐ Thermionic tube used to send radio waves [1904]
	Theory of relativity [1905] Einstein		
		▪ Three-color screen photography [1907] Lumiere	
		▪ Television-photograph [1907]	
		▪● Gyrocompass [1910] Sperry	
		▪ Reflecting telescope [1917]	Vacuum tube [1912] de Forest
		▪ Space photography in discovery of asteroids [1920]	
			▪● Self-winding wristwatch [1922] Harwood

Conceptual &/or Institutional Developments	Information Acquisition &/or Storage Devices	Information Manipulation &/or Transmission Devices

Twentieth
Century

◨ Sound-motion pictures [1923] de Forest

■ Iconoscope [1924] Zworkin

■ Television transmission of recognizable human images [1925] Baird

□ Electrola [1926]

■ Color motion picture demonstrated [1928] Eastman

■ Color television [1928] Baird

■ Coma-free mirror telescope [1930]

■ Radar [1935] Watson

□ Frequency modulation [1939] Armstrong

■ Electron microscope demonstrated [1940] Radio Corporation of America

■● "Electronic brain", automatic computer in U.S. [1942]

Idea of communications satellite proposed [1945] Clarke

Conceptual &/or Institutional Developments	Information Acquisition &/or Storage Devices	Information Manipulation &/or Transmission Devices

Twentieth
Century

■● Electronic digital computer [1946] University of Pennsylvania

Transistor [1947 Bell laboratory

Mathematical Theory of Communication [1948] Shannon, Weaver

☐ Long-playing record [1948] Goldmark

■ Port radar system [1948]

■ Cable television [1950]

■ Optical scanners developed [1954]

■ Ultra high frequency radio waves generated [1955] MIT

■ Ion microscope [1956] Müller

☐ Transatlantic cable telephone [1956]

■ Visual telephone [1956] Bell Labs

☐ Stereophonic recordings in common use [1958]

■● "Second generation" computers [1958]*

Conceptual &/or Institutional Developments	Information Acquisition &/or Storage Devices	Information Manipulation &/or Transmission Devices

■■■

Twentieth
Century

Information Acquisition &/or Storage Devices:

■   Weather satellite transmitting cloud cover images [1960]

■   150-inch reflecting telescope [1970]

■   Video cassette recorder [1975]

Information Manipulation &/or Transmission Devices:

■   Radio-reflector satellite [1960]

□   Experimental communications satellite [1960] NASA

■   TIROS I weather satellite transmitting Television images [1960]

■●   "Third generation" computers using integrated circuits [1965]*

Microprocessor or semi-conductor chip [1971]

■●   Experimental coast-to-coast computer network in U.S. [1972]

■   Cable TV integrated with TV satellite transmissions [1975]

■   Fiber optics [1975]

■○   Teletext in Britain [1976]

Conceptual &/or Institutional Developments	Information Acquisition &/or Storage Devices	Information Manipulation &/or Transmission Devices
■■		
Twentieth Century		■ ○ QUBE interactive cable television in U.S. [1977]
		☐ Cellular telephone [1977] AT&T
		■ ○ Videotext [1979] British Telephone Authority
		▤ ◕ 16K microcomputer [1980]
		▤ ◕ 256K microcomputer [1986]

* = Also used for information storage.

** For other examples of timelines see Grun, B. (1946/1979). *The timetables of history*. New York: Simon and Schuster. Mumford, L. (1934/1962). *Technics and civilization*. New York: Harcourt, Brace, and World. Grun's timeline has gained wide distribution in recent years, but Mumford's is one of the earliest attempts to assemble a comprehensive list of technological inventions. Of interest is Mumford's inclusion of material information technologies, which constitute 20% of his total. In addition, he incorporates social information technologies such as processes, treatises, and applications. Taken together, they amount to 74% of all inventions in his list. Yet he never recognized the common theme of information.

Name Index

Subject Index